DOWN TO EARTH
Studies in Christianity and Culture

DOWN TO EARTH
Studies in Christianity and Culture

THE PAPERS OF
THE LAUSANNE CONSULTATION
ON GOSPEL AND CULTURE

---

edited by

Robert T. Coote *and* John Stott

WILLIAM B. EERDMANS PUBLISHING COMPANY
GRAND RAPIDS, MICHIGAN

Copyright © 1980
Lausanne Committee for World Evangelization
Box 21225, Nairobi, Kenya
Box 1100, Wheaton, Illinois 60187 U.S.A.

This American edition published 1980 through special arrangement with
the Lausanne Committee for World Evangelization by Wm. B. Eerdmans Publishing Co., Grand Rapids, Michigan 49503

Library of Congress Cataloging in Publication Data

Main entry under title:

Down to earth.

  Abridgment of book published in 1979 under title:
Gospel and culture.
1. Christianity and culture—Congresses.
I. Stott, John R. W. II. Coote, Robert T., 1932-
II. Gospel and culture.
BR115.C8G67   1980   261   80-128
ISBN   0-8028-1827-7

In encouraging the publication and study of this volume, the Lausanne
Committee for World Evangelization does not necessarily endorse every
viewpoint expressed in it.

Contents

III. CULTURE, CHURCHES, AND ETHICS

Foreword

"CULTURE" HAS BEEN ON THE AGENDA OF communication theorists for a very long time. And recent well-known books like Richard Niebuhr's *Christ and Culture* (1952) and Eugene Nida's *Customs and Cultures* (1954), *Message and Mission* (1960), and *Religion Across Cultures* (1968) have introduced the topic to a wider public. Yet only, I suspect, as a result of the Lausanne Congress on World Evangelization in 1974 has the evangelical constituency as a whole come to acknowledge the central importance of culture for the effective communication of the Gospel. At Lausanne René Padilla startled his listeners by describing some missionaries as exporters of a "culture Christianity" rather than of the authentic Gospel. Paragraph 10 of the Lausanne Covenant is entitled "Evangelism and Culture." No responsible messenger of the Gospel can ignore the subject any longer.

"Gospel and Culture" is not a topic of purely academic interest. On the contrary, it is the burning practical concern of every missionary, every preacher, every Christian witness. For it is literally impossible to evangelize in a cultural vacuum. Nobody can reduce the biblical Gospel to a few culture-free axioms which are universally intelligible. This is because the mind-set of all human beings has been formed by the culture in which they have been brought up. Their presuppositions, their value systems, the ways in which they think, and the degree of their receptivity or resistance to new ideas, are all largely determined by their cultural inheritance and are filters through which they listen and evaluate.

The overriding reason why we should take other people's cultures seriously is that God has taken ours seriously. God is the supreme communicator. And his Word has come to us in an extremely particularized form. Whether spoken or written, it was addressed to particular people in particular cultures using the particular thought-forms, syntax, and vocabulary with which they were familiar. Then when God's Word actually "became flesh," the "flesh" he became was that of a first-century, male, Palestinian Jew. Thus both Inspiration and Incarnation—two fundamental evangelical truths—are models of sensitive cross-cultural communication, and summon us to follow suit.

To Christian obedience we add Christian strategy. Church growth statistics in large areas of the Third World are thrilling to read. Yet the great mass movements into the church have, generally speaking, involved people of broadly "animistic" background. By comparison very few of those who have inherited one of the major "culture-religions"—Hindus, Buddhists, Jews, Moslems and Marxists—have been won to Christ. As a historical example I mention Adoniram Judson of Burma. When he died in 1850, after thirty-seven years of devoted and sacrificial labor, during which he returned home to the United States only once, he left about seven thousand converts from the animistic Karens, but a mere one hundred Burman converts from Buddhism. Why was this? What are the reasons for people's resistance to the Gospel? How are we to explain the pitifully small "dent" which has been made, for instance, on the 600 million Hindus of India or the 700 million Moslems of the Islamic block? Although different answers are given to these questions, they are all basically cultural. The major challenge to the worldwide Christian mission today is whether we are willing to pay the cost of following in the footsteps of our incarnate Lord in order to contextualize the Gospel. Our failure of communication is a failure of contextualization.

The problem facing every cross-cultural messenger of the Gospel can be simply stated. It is this: "How can I, who was born and brought up in one culture, take truth out of the Bible which was addressed to people in a second culture, and communicate it to people who belong to a third culture, without either falsifying the message or rendering it unintelligible?" It is this interaction between three cultures which constitutes the exciting challenge of cross-cultural communication. And then, when the message has been understood and received by the hearers, further questions arise. How should they relate to their own culture in their conversion, in their ethical lifestyle, and in their church life?

Culture in revelation and in hermeneutics (i.e., in the writing and the reading of the Bible), in evangelism and in conversion, in ethics and in churches: these were the six aspects of "Gospel and Culture" which brought thirty-three of us to Willowbank in Bermuda in January 1978, under Lausanne auspices, for six strenuous days of thought and debate. Our Consultation was not lacking in cultural drama. The theologians and the anthropologists, having different starting points, did not always reach the same destination. Africans and Asians had to complain of Euro- American dominance, while an uninhibited Latin American brother protested in uninhibited Latin American style against the oppressive behavior of the Anglo-Saxon moderator who sought to impose on the proceedings a Westminster parliamentary model, and who now penitently confesses the error of his ways!

At the end of our Consultation the *Willowbank Report* was issued and may be found on page 308. This book contains an abridgement of the seventeen papers submitted to the Consultation. Each individual author has approved the final text of his contribution. But the delicate editorial task was performed with conscientious skill by Robert Coote. To him, to Peter Savage who coordinated the Consultation so efficiently, and to their agency Partnership in Mission which made their services available, we express our heartfelt thanks. In addition, we acknowledge with great appreciation the many hours of editorial assistance and manuscript preparation by Peter and Rebecca Johnston and Susan Trenwith. Partnership in Mission has also shouldered the work of preparing the full, unexpurgated text of the Consultation papers for publication by the William Carey Library, Pasadena, California.

In issuing this material, we are far from claiming that we have produced a definitive treatment of the topic. Readers will observe the modest note struck by several contributors. "The results of our research are necessarily tentative" and "our viewpoint . . . may be defective," writes Ananda Kumar of India. "This is only an initial stumbling effort by one man," says Charles Taber, which is "subject to correction by the whole Body of Christ." With these humble sentiments all the contributors would agree. Much more work remains to be done—in culture and communication theory, in interdisciplinary methodology, in multi-cultural exchange, and not least in specific case studies. One forum for fur-

ther debate, launched by Partnership in Mission as a result of the
Willowbank Consultation, is the quarterly dialogue-journal *Gospel
in Context,* edited by Charles Taber.

We need to pray for one another that out of our further
thinking, talking, debating, and writing may come some constructive contributions towards the evangelization of the world for
which and into which, on the first Christmas day, the Lord of glory
came.

London, Christmas 1978   JOHN STOTT

1. Religion and Culture
—A Historical Introduction

by Stephen C. Neill

STEPHEN NEILL, *for many years missionary and bishop of the Anglican Communion in South India and East Africa, is the author of* A History of Christian Mission, Jesus Through Many Eyes, Salvation Tomorrow, *and other volumes. He is at present resident scholar at Wycliffe Hall, Oxford, and is writing a history of Christianity in India.*

THROUGHOUT HUMAN HISTORY, RELIGION and culture have been inextricably connected. There has never yet been a great religion which did not find its expression in a great culture. There has never yet been a great culture which did not have deep roots in a religion. (Will Marxism prove to be the exception?)

We can speak of religion and culture as separate entities, but in actual living they are very closely entwined. The influence of religion can be clearly seen in three central areas of human experience which are generally regarded as cultural rather than as specifically religious: (1) language, (2) social custom, and (3) art.

THE INFLUENCE OF RELIGION ON CULTURE

The influence of religion in all these three areas can be seen more clearly in Islam than in most other religious systems. Islam claims that in the Koran a revelation has been given not only for the spiritual and liturgical aspects of human life, but for the social, the political, the economic, and the personal as well.

So Islam has consecrated one language as the language of worship and of religious expression. The prescribed prayers must be said in Arabic and not in any other language. The Koran cannot be translated into any other language, since the language is an essential part of the revelation. In the early days of Islam a serious attempt was made to eliminate every other language and to make Arabic the sole medium of communication. The success attained by Islam, though not complete, is very remarkable. In Egypt, Greek totally disappeared, and Coptic was reduced to serve as the liturgical language of a minority. In North Africa no other language is spoken, until we come to the Tuareg and other independent peoples of the Sahara.

Social custom tends to be uniform throughout the Islamic world. Male circumcision, though not actually required by the Koran, is accepted everywhere as obligatory. Both men and women are expected to observe a great many prescriptions with regard to dress, nomenclature, sanitary habits, and so forth, which have in one way or another become part of the Islamic tradition.

The strict prohibition of any representation of the human form, though comprehensively disregarded by the Moguls in India, has laid its heavy hand in most areas on the development of Islamic art. Architecture and calligraphy have been the two forms of art in which the Islamic world has excelled.

This Islamic totalitarianism is not a thing of the past; it is possible to observe it in operation in any part of the world in which Islamic propoganda is intense and has the support of the ruling powers. In Sabah, for example, it is the declared policy of the government to make Malay, the language of the Muslim minority, the sole official language in the hope that the non-Muslim languages, Chinese and English, will be relegated to the areas of purely private discourse. Any Chinese who accepts Islam is expected at the same time to adopt a Muslim name, to accept the use of

Islamic dress, and to conform to many of the social usages demanded by the Islamic tradition.

Hinduism can be seen operating in a rather similar fashion. As Hinduism spreads among the hill peoples of non-Aryan origin, these peoples are absorbed into the caste system, which is wholly alien to them. More freedom for caste-variation is permitted than would be the case under absorption into the world of Islam, but with government policy making Hindi the national language, the old tribal languages are reduced to a status of inferiority, and it seems probable that some, at least, will disappear.

Thus, Islam and Hinduism demonstrate that the introduction of a new religion, or new religious principles, inevitably involves far-reaching cultural and social changes with the destruction of much of the older culture.

THE GOSPEL AS DESTROYER,
PRESERVER, AND CREATOR OF CULTURE

This is as true of Christianity as of any other religious faith. Jesus came as Savior, but he also came as destroyer. Loyal as he was to his Jewish inheritance, he was critical as well as faithful. In a single pungent saying, he abolished the distinction between clean and unclean meats—it is what comes forth from a man that defiles him and not what enters into him from outside. His teaching has made a clean sweep of the entire ritual and ceremonial law of the Jews. Circumcision, central in the Old Jewish law, is now nothing in the world. Christians may have their children circumcised, if they wish to do so, but this has nothing to do with the new covenant in Christ; it adds nothing to the perfect salvation given through him. Likewise, the old law of sacrifices has been completely abrogated. The Epistle to the Hebrews tells us why: when the one perfect sacrifice has been offered, there is no place for any further ritual sacrifice.

The radical character of what Jesus had done was not immediately evident even to believers. The first great controversy in the infant church related to the status of Gentile believers in the church. The progress of the debate is clearly seen in the contrast between the Epistle to the Galatians and that to the Romans. In Galatians, circumcision is a burning issue; the whole nature of salvation is at stake. When Romans is written, it has become no more than a question relating to the peaceful co-existence of different groups within the church. There must always be a place for differing customs and for mutual concessions. If Jews and Gentiles are to meet at the Lord's table, Gentiles must have respect for the age-long traditions of Judaism, even if they regard them as no more than prejudices of the Jews, and must not insist on their own way of doing things.

Similar problems arise today. Some missionaries in India have become vegetarians out of respect for the traditions of the high-caste Hindu. Others eat neither beef nor pork, because of the intense repugnance felt by Hindus and Muslims for parts of European practice.

Some religions have been modified by the Christian impact; others have died out—a subject to which perhaps inadequate study has been directed. For example, we should remember that there were rivals to Christianity in the early days of the church. It seemed at one time that Gnosticism, or the special form of it called Manicheanism, might win the world. But nowhere in the world today are there either Gnostics or Manicheans (though there are still strange survivals of both in remote corners of the world and in the underground of the great religions). The dualism of matter and spirit which they offered has not commended itself to the minds of men in later ages. The mystery religions, of which Mithraism was one, did not have a very long career. They could not in reality provide that which they promised—assurance of immortality and inner transformation. They were undone by their lack of factual content, and a serious and consistent theology. The church triumphed because it offered the reality, where these others gave only the shadow.

The fate of the ancient Greek and Roman gods was rather different. No one today worships Zeus or Hera or Apollo, not so much because they were not entirely edifying figures as because they represented a world outlook which, in the days of Paul and John, was already passing away. These were the gods of city-states, to be worshiped as a matter of civic duty by the citizens of those states. With the immense extension of the Roman empire and Greek culture, there was no particular purpose that they could serve. The Greek cities which stretched from Marseilles to the

Hindu Kush found a certain unity in the quasi-religious teaching of the later Stoicism with its noble idea of the universal city of man. The Roman empire was held together by the cult of the emperor, a political form of religion with little spiritual content. Neither of these had staying power. Man yearned for something other than these substitutes. Philosophy was too cold a mistress. One could not really worship the Roman emperor. Men found in the warmth of the Gospel what they could not find in the old ways.

Despite its function as a destroyer, the Gospel was also a preserver. It is easy to find fault with the synthesis resulting from the Constantinian fusion of church and state, but it should not be forgotten that for eight centuries the eastern empire was the bulwark of the West against Islam, and saved Europe until Europe was strong enough to save itself. When at last it fell, it passed on to the West many of the treasures of the ancient world, and these the western church in its turn has preserved and passed on to us, who would have been immeasurably poorer if all this had been lost.

Through all the centuries of conflict and weakness, neither branch of the church, eastern or western, forgot the vocation of the church to be universal home of all the nations, and so to be (though this was not the primary purpose of its preaching) not only the preserver of ancient cultures but the creator of new worlds of culture. Thus Byzantium reached out to Russia and laid the foundations of the great cultures of the Slavic races. Gregory the Great with prophetic insight saw that a new world must be called in to redress the balance of the old. His mission to the Angles was far more than a sentimental gesture to a people he so mistakenly associated with angels; it was also a great strategic concept.

Unlike the eastern church, which recognized a variety of liturgical use and language, Rome imposed on northern Europe a single liturgical language, and Latin became the common means of communication between all educated men from Iceland to Sicily, a factor of unity which was not lost until the end of the eighteenth century. But the vigor of the northern nations resisted total assimilation. In spite of the steady influence of the Latin of the church, in spite of conquest by Danes and Normans, the English still obstinately speak a language the basis of which is of Teutonic and not of Romance origin.

In the field of religion the story is very different. The victory of Christianity was complete. Lord Bryce once commented on our misfortune in that the Romans were not interested in the culture and religion of the peoples whom they conquered, and never set out to record systematically their ideas and usages. In consequence we know sadly little of the religion of the Britons and other Celtic peoples, except through underground survivals.

When the first renaissance dawned in the eleventh century and the great languages of modern Europe began to emerge from the dominance of Latin, they were unashamedly the expression of a great Christian culture, varied within its Christian unity, which found its creative outlet in such glorious achievements as the *Divina Comedia* of Dante Alighieri, Chaucer's *Canterbury Tales,* Lincoln Cathedral, Giotto, and the beginning of modern music. Many factors contributed to this splendid outburst of genius; the most creative factor of all was the Christian Gospel transmitted through the Christian church.

THE EARLY CHURCH AND CULTURE

We have seen, then, that the Gospel can serve as the destroyer, the preserver, and the creator of cultures. We can now turn the clock back and look more closely at the fortunes of the church in its first cultural environment, the world of Greece and Rome. The story can be summed up in a sentence—the church entered into easy relations with that culture only when the religion which underlay it had ceased to be a living force.

In the earliest days Paul found it possible to adopt an attitude of reasoned tolerance. There must be no compromise; yet for people who had realized that an idol is nothing in the world, the eating of meats offered to idols did not need to cause any unbearable scruples of conscience. Persecution was on the horizon, but the empire had not yet become the great persecuting power.

By the third century the world outside the church had become the world of the persecutors and of the evil spirits who inspired the persecutors. Tertullian the lawyer had come into the church as an adult convert, bringing with him an intimate knowledge of the world from which he had come and for which he had an almost pathological dislike. He realized that every part of that old life was linked to non-Christian ideas and non-Christian worship—and how can there be any fellowship between Christ and idols, between Jerusalem and Athens? Tertullian represents an extreme point of view, but it was without doubt shared by a great many people in his day and for a hundred years after his time.

For example, it was difficult for Christians to make use of the public baths, not so much because of the notorious immorality of the baths, but because of the regular worship of local spirits of fountains and streams there. Furthermore, a Christian could not serve as a magistrate, since in that capacity he would be required to take part in civic worship, which in good conscience, he could not do. And a Christian could not serve as a soldier, not so much because that trade might involve him in the taking of life (the early Christians were not pacifists), but because the soldier was required to worship the standards of his regiment. It is obvious that such change in religious allegiance could not but have consequences in the world of social custom and public order.

The change in attitude from a world-denying faith to one of greater openness was slow in coming. When the Alexandrians began to encourage the study of pagan literature and philosophy, they encountered strong opposition in the church. But ultimately, as the religions of Greece and Rome ceased to be living realities, the church felt free to take into itself the treasures of the ancient culture. When Christians obtained liberty to build churches, they naturally followed the best model that they knew, and the typical Christian church looked just like a Roman basilica. In the same way, the Christian scholar roamed through the broad fields of ancient literature. Augustine had been a professor of rhetoric before he became a Christian; Jerome had to blame himself for preferring Cicero to the Latin version of the Scriptures. It is fairly easy to discover what the Fathers had read. Virgil was, of course, the favorite of those who spoke Latin, and was treated almost as though he had been a Christian poet. The Greeks were thoroughly familiar with Homer, whom every Greek schoolboy knew almost by heart. They read Plato, especially the *Timaeus,* because of their interest in the doctrine of creation. The later Stoicism was still an influence. Plotinus was known but exercised less influence than might have been expected. But in every one of the Christian writers of the third and fourth centuries, Scripture was supreme, and the scriptural reference was constant.

Some of the Greek Fathers wrote Greek with considerable elegance; in Augustine patristic Latin rose to magnificence. But the ancient culture was never more than a tool for the elucidation of Scripture and for the expression of biblical truth. Nowhere was there any suggestion that the ancient culture could in any way serve as an independent source of revelation. The Fathers may not always have been successful in doing what they set out to do, but there can be no doubt as to their aim. The Bible was always text; other writings were never anything more than commentary.

How did ordinary Christians settle down to live in the midst of a non-Christian culture from which they could not entirely segregate themselves? To some extent they did separate themselves from the world around them, but it was not possible to go and live on a desert island. Some measure of adaptation and discrimination was necessary.

The Christians found it necessary to distinguish between those things which must immediately and totally be forbidden, those which were undesirable and—it was hoped—would gradually die out, and those which were merely cultural, representing no more than differences of habit and tradition. For instance, the Romans, like the highlanders in Scotland, regarded the wearing of breeches as a barbarous habit, but if Christians of barbarous origin wished in such matters to follow the customs of their ancestors, there was no need to forbid them to do so.

It is self-evident that if a religion is to win credit as a potentially universal religion, it must show itself capable of adaptation to a great variety of situations. It is equally evident that no other religion so far can compare with Christianity in its capacity for just this kind of adaptability. Christians do not always realize how fortunate they are in that Jesus Christ gave us so few specific or precise commandments, and that those which he did give are not time or situation conditioned.

This becomes plain at once if a comparison is made between Christianity and Islam. In that religion, for example, the rules governing the fast of Ramadan are quite clearly laid down. These rules can be observed without excessive difficulty in Arabia, but if Ramadan happens to fall in June or July, they cannot be observed north of the Arctic circle because there the sun never sets at all. Even in a less extreme situation, sincere and devout Muslims are asking whether the fast can be observed in accordance with the traditional rules under the conditions of work demanded in an industrial society. For the Christian such problems do not exist; we are less tied to locality and to exact regulations.

There are, however, limits to adaptability. Christians, now as then, have to ask whether there are certain customs and social usages which are wholly incompatible with the Christian Gospel, and whether there are others which may be tolerated for a time or for any foreseeable future. On many issues there may be differences of opinion among Christians; in certain areas there is likely to be near unanimity of judgment.

SOME CUSTOMS WHICH CANNOT BE TOLERATED

Christians of all persuasions would probably agree that the following practices must be given up by all those who wish to call themselves Christians:

1. Idolatry, that is, the observance of customs and ceremonies, including those associated with birth, marriage, and death, which imply the existence and claims of deities other than the one true God, to whom alone worship and adoration may be paid.

2. Witchcraft and sorcery in their evil forms, in which alien powers of darkness are called in to injure human beings.

3. Female infanticide, defended by some people as the best means of preventing the increase of population beyond the capacity of the land to support it, but condemned by Christians because of the Christian doctrine of the sacredness of all life.

4. Twin-murder, especially when it is supposed that one of the twins is the child of an evil spirit.

5. Cannibalism, as involving disrespect to the person of another human being even where murder is not involved.

6. Head-hunting; although this is so central in the life of some people that its abolition causes grave disruption of the entire social structure.

7. Private vengeance and the blood feud, as practiced among many peoples of Arabia until recent times, and perhaps even at the present time.

8. Physical mutilation as a legal penalty, as recently reintroduced in Pakistan in accordance with Islamic law.

9. Cattle-raiding; this comes hard on the Masai, who believe that at the creation God gave all the cattle to the Masai, and that cattle-raiding is simply the recovery of stolen property.

10. Ritual prostitution, as familiar to Paul in Ephesus and Corinth and in many other cities of the Levant, and as widely practiced in India until recent times, and even perhaps at the present time in certain places.

There would, I think, be general agreement that the abandonment of such practices must be required as a condition for baptism.[1]

SOME CUSTOMS WHICH CAN TEMPORARILY BE TOLERATED

There is a second class of customs which may be impossible to abolish immediately, though Christians must desire that these customs should in time disappear. We may give the following as examples:

1. Slavery, which is permitted by Islamic law, and is still practiced in some Islamic countries. The British put down the slave-trade, but in Tanzania, wisely, did not abolish the status of slave until 1922. The situation may be more complex than is imagined by those who have not studied the subject closely. Before 1862, in an American state where the emancipation of slaves was forbidden by law, a man might find himself a slave-owner by inheritance.

2. The caste system. A system which condemns eighty million people, with religious sanctions, to a status of permanent

---

[1]Professor John Mbiti has pointed out parallels to many of these in western society; but in no case are such customs enforced in the West by religious sanctions.

social and economic inferiority, is clearly contrary to the law of God and the principles of Christ. The church could do no more than point to the evils of the system and to work quietly for its disappearance. The independent government of India has legally abolished untouchability without touching the religious claims on which the system is based. More generally, the demand that Christians should totally cut themselves off from all caste connections has not proved workable. If put into effect, it would have meant simply that the Christian church would have become a new caste among the many; this is what happened to the Thomas Christians in Kerala, and resulted in their ceasing to be a witnessing and expanding community. And where a mass movement takes place, the new community is bound to reflect a good many of the features of the old.

3. Tribalism. This cannot but be modified by incorporation into the wider fellowship of the church. But it is still a great power in many parts of the world, not excluding Europe and North America. Whether it can be allowed to survive in any form within the church is one of the major problems faced by the churches today.

4. Polygamy. Every polygamous marriage means that one young man will not be able to marry at the normal age. The presence of a large number of marriageable but unmarried young men produces very grave social disruption. Almost all Christians agree that this form of the family must disappear; not all are agreed as to the rate and manner of its disappearance.

Frequently problems arise in connection with marriage rules and regulations. The traditions of the Christian churches are based on Jewish and Roman views of family life, but these are not applicable everywhere. For example, in the West marriage between cousins, though not encouraged, is not prohibited; but in India marriage between cousins in the male line is absolutely forbidden. Marriage between uncle and niece is generally disallowed by the Christian tradition, but in some castes in India marriage of a man with his elder sister's daughter is almost obligatory. This is open to grave objections, not only on the ground of propinquity of blood but also because of the usual disparity in age.

SOME CUSTOMS TO WHICH OBJECTIONS NEED NOT BE TAKEN

Outside such areas in which Christian principle may be involved, there is a vast range of customs which differ, but of which it is impossible to say categorically that one is in all circumstances better than another.

In India in almost all churches men and women sit separately on opposite sides of the church. Westerners prefer the custom of members of the same family sitting together. In India it is the custom for men and women to eat separately. A few missionaries tried to change the custom; the vast majority felt that this was a matter which must be left to the Indian Christians themselves to decide. Today in some westernized families the custom of men and women eating together has been adopted, but it cannot be said that the change has become general. In India for any man to touch any woman in public is still in many areas a grave social impropriety. (In East Africa, when young women students came up to me with outstretched hand expecting to shake hands, I experienced a frisson of horror, and had to remind myself that I must not expect to behave in Africa as I had been accustomed to behave in India.)

In Kerala men when bathing will remove all their clothing under the water; no Tamil is likely ever to do such a thing. Westerners use both hands in eating. In India the strict rule is that the right hand only is used for eating and the left for drinking. The Chinese eat with chopsticks, and regard with distaste the Indian habit of eating with the right hand.

It is possible to go on endlessly. There seems no particular reason why such customs should be changed, or the customs of one community be imposed upon another. The important thing is that when Christians move from one cultural area to another, they should try to understand and respect the customs of those among whom they have come to live.

A good many changes are likely to take place simply on the grounds of convenience. A great many men in India now have their hair cut short (''the Christian crop'' in local parlance) and wear trousers for no reason other than that they find the European way of doing things more convenient than the old. When two communities live in close proximity, many changes and exchanges are to be expected. No objection can be taken, provided that reasonable attention is paid to ideas of decency and to the expectations of each of the communities concerned.

WHERE DOES IT ALL END?

We must come back, however, to the world of principle. All that has been said in this article may be related to a single principle which can be expressed in a single brief phrase: Christ is the Lord of all life. Everything in the life of the individual, of the family, of the church, of the community, must constantly be referred back to him for judgment. No culture, no civilization, no ordering of society, is sacrosanct since all are imperfect. Christ through the Holy Spirit is the continual critic of all churches and all societies, demanding sometimes that what had seemed good should be thrown away, at other times that what had once seemed menacing as undermining the stability of society should be accepted as good and right.

Immense changes have been recorded in historic times. Western society was remarkably slow to realize that slavery is an abomination, wholly incompatible with the doctrine of Christian freedom. But the lesson, once learned, seems to have been learned for good; it is unlikely that it will ever be forgotten. Even a century ago there was strong opposition in India to the education of girls; the missionaries had literally to bribe the parents into sending their daughters to school. Since independence arrived thirty years ago, women have served as cabinet ministers, as governors of provinces, and finally as prime minister.

The list of changes is endless; a whole book could be written about them. The lesson is simply that societies are much less static than is often supposed, that cultures are living and growing things in a perpetual process of change. A special responsibility rests on Christians to be sensitive to the movement of history, to discern the signs of the times, to distinguish between that which is of real advantage and that which has a merely deceptive attractiveness, to ensure that the will of God becomes the criterion of change, and that the whole life of man is conformed to the likeness of Christ and renewed according to the pattern which God himself has revealed to us in the life of the Lord Jesus Christ.

Part

I. *Culture*
and the Bible

2. *Culture and the New Testament*

by I. Howard Marshall

I. HOWARD MARSHALL *is reader in New Testament Exegesis at the University of Aberdeen. He is author of* The Gospel of Luke: A Commentary on the Greek Text, I Believe in the Historical Jesus, *and other volumes.*

JESUS CHRIST WAS BORN "IN THE FULNESS OF time," into a world that had been shaped by a vast cultural revolution. The revolution began under Alexander the Great, whose policy was to spread the Greek way of life throughout his domains, from the Adriatic in the West to India in the East, from Macedonia in the North to Egypt in the South.

The Hellenistic way of life, as it has come to be called, was characterized by the use of the Greek language as a universal means of communication, the spread of trade, the setting up of a Greek type of political system (seen especially in the growth of cities each with self-government), and along with this the spread of Greek thinking, literature, and art.

In some cases the advancing waves of Hellenism led to the stifling of native ways of life, but more often it produced a mixture of the old and the new, so that, while the Greek element was always obvious, the local manifestations could vary considerably.

Palestine, the land of the Incarnation, was affected no less than the rest. Jesus, the apostles, and the early church came on the scene soon after Rome had taken up the cultural torch. We can hardly fathom the riches of the Gospel they proclaimed without appreciating something of the cultural mix which characterized their time and place. It is thus fitting that in approaching the relationship between ''Gospel and Culture'' we should pay attention to ''Culture and the New Testament.''

WHAT IS CULTURE?

To begin with, we must define what we mean by ''culture.'' We are hampered by at least two factors. First, the observer of culture is in fact a prisoner of his own culture and therefore unable to obtain total objectivity. Secondly, the source material, in this case the New Testament, does not directly or explicitly deal with the concept of culture. (The Christian moralist has a similar problem when he tries to assemble the biblical teaching relevant to the problem of abortion, when in fact that particular problem was simply not present to the consciousness of biblical writers.)

1. *Culture refers to the whole activity of man in his ability to control and utilize the environment.* When we go back in time to a comparatively simple state of affairs and distinguish between, say, ''Stone Age culture'' and ''Iron Age culture,'' we are referring to two total types of human response to the environment. As the historian attempts to describe the whole life of the people of these particular ages, he finds that these ''cultures'' are distinguished by different levels of technical knowledge and skill that dictated the way of life of the peoples. Iron age people discovered ways of dealing with natural resources that enabled them to do various things that were not possible in the Stone Age, things which would be regarded as constituting progress in the control of the environment and an advance in the resulting standard of living.

2. *Culture describes those powers of man which go beyond the mere ability to survive and which are concerned with the production of things or activities which are aesthetically pleasing.* A stone age artisan might make a rough cooking pot, adequate for its task, or a more polished and decorative one—no more adequate for its purpose of cooking but having the additional virtue of being pleasing to the eye and a delight to handle. Culture in this sense presupposes in men and

women the leisure and the ability to do things other than those required for mere survival.

3. *Culture is a set of values.* The Greeks valued the dramatic and plastic arts (sculpture, etc.), and they passed on these values to the Romans who in turn gave them a place in their own life. However, the Vandals did not value such things and as a result did not practice them. There was in each case a set of values recognized, whether consciously or unconsciously, by the community and upheld by some kind of philosophical or religious ideology which gave status to those values. Thus a culture represents a definite attitude to human life, and is characterized by the adoption of a set of values.

4. *Culture is a social phenomenon.* In the extreme case, one may make a beautiful object simply because it brings pleasure to oneself. But ordinarily speaking, such objects are made for the benefit of people at large, and the standards by which they are evaluated are those of the group as a whole. A cultured person is one who is recognized as such by other people. It follows, too, that the standard of culture in a given group is not necessarily the standard of each individual but is a characteristic of the society as a whole.

5. *Culture is characterized by a specific way of thinking.* One thinks of the standards of fair play associated in England with cricket, such that certain types of conduct in ordinary life could be condemned by the comment "that's not cricket," whereas one would not say "that's not football." Here we have a set of ethical values somehow associated with a particular sport in a way that is not found in some other sports. This difference in ways of thinking may be regarded as cultural and goes down to the roots of human behavior.

6. *Culture may consist of various separable parts.* We tend to talk of "western culture" as if it were an integrated whole, each part fitting logically and coherently into one grand system. But we should remind ourselves that different individuals or groups will be affected by the culture of their society to varying extents, and that its various elements will have grown up piecemeal and do not necessarily stand in organic relationship to one another.

Thus, in summary, the word "culture" can refer variously to the particular ways in which people learn to control their environment, to develop intellectual and aesthetic values and expressions of them, and to produce an ideology which upholds these values. Culture is a social phenomenon, and can have various, separable parts. Culture means a way of thinking, an approach to life in the world.

With this definition of culture in mind, we are ready to consider the cultural environment in which the New Testament writings were created.

CULTURAL DYNAMICS IN PALESTINE

The world of the New Testament was a world in which different cultures or ways of life were in contact with one another, leading to assimilation between them as well as to sharp collisions. The most significant case is Palestine itself.

The traditional picture of Palestinian Judaism has been one of a small group of Jews who were intensely loyal to the Jewish law and whose leaders, such as Nehemiah, adhered to a policy of rigid segregation so that they might keep their religion pure from defilement with paganism.

However, recent research has shown that Palestinian Judaism may have been more influenced by Hellenism than this simplified picture suggests. Martin Hengel, for instance, in his survey of the character of Palestinian Judaism in the third and second centuries B.C. (*Judaism and Hellenism,* London, 1974), shows that throughout this period Hellenistic influences had a very deep effect on the thought and life of the Jews.

Prior to the Maccabean revolt, the upper classes, including the priestly hierarchy, cooperated with the Seleucid rulers by accepting a Hellenistic "democratic" constitution and also by promoting Greek education, literature, and forms of sport. True, efforts to speed up the process of Hellenization led to armed revolt and eventual defeat; but even so, the leaders of the traditionalist revolt eventually became infected themselves by the Hellenistic life-style.

This is not surprising when we stop to consider the numerous sources of Hellenistic influence in Palestine. Greek was used as a language and many orthodox Jews bore Greek names. There was considerable foreign trade and movement of foreign troops;

methods of warfare were Hellenistic. There was also a very large non-Jewish population in Palestine, to such an extent that the Jews were a minority in their own land. Our familiar Bible maps are often seriously misleading in that they only print the Jewish towns actually named in the New Testament and ignore the many Gentile towns that were scattered up and down the land.

We also find Jews writing works in the Greek language and expressing themselves in Greek styles of work. And what they wrote shows the influence of Greek literature and ideas. An extreme case is that of Philo. This man was a Jew, brother of the Roman governor of Palestine, living the life of a rich man, and spending his life in the cultured occupation of a philosopher producing a remarkable eclectic system in which Plato, the Stoics, and Moses were joined to one another. Philo wrote throughout in Greek and was unable to read the Pentateuch in Hebrew. He remained a loyal Jew, but he well illustrates the syncretistic character of the age in which ideas of all kinds were being thrown together.

Thus, it is important to bear in mind that the cultural relationships of Christianity were part of a broader process of cultural assimilation in Palestine which was still going on in the first century, and which also provides a background against which we can assess the nature of what was going on in the early church.

LANGUAGE AND THOUGHT-FORMS

This brief overview of the historical-cultural background of Palestinian Judaism should help us as we consider the effects of culture on the Gospel. Two influential cultural factors were (1) the language, and (2) the thought-forms in which the Gospel was expressed.

To begin with, the New Testament is written in the Greek of the time, rather than in any special ''language of the Holy Ghost'' (as once was suggested!). Moreover, the decisive words and concepts which were used, both in the teaching of Jesus and in the preaching and teaching of the early Christians, were drawn from the Old Testament. We can, therefore, say that the Gospel is expressed in the language and thought-forms of a particular culture (or group of cultures), and that the form in which we have it is tied to this particular culture.

This raises a crucial question. Since the New Testament *is* tied to a particular culture, what effect does this have on the application of New Testament principles in other cultural contexts? Two examples of attempts to deal with this problem may be noted.

1. In his controversial book *Man as Male and Female* (Grand Rapids, 1975) P. K. Jewett raises the problem of the effect of culture on the New Testament teachings regarding male/female relationships. He argues that the central teaching of the Bible regards man and woman as equals with complementary functions. The problem is that there are passages in which the subordination of woman to man is also taught, culminating in the command that women should not be allowed to teach men, since this would question male authority.

Faced by these two streams of thought, Jewett in effect suggests that the latter represents the thinking of Paul as conditioned by a Jewish environment in which the inferiority of women was accepted, and that we ought to regard this line of thought as a hangover from the past and not be governed by it. In other words, we should distinguish between the attitude of Paul the apostle of Christian liberty and the attitude of Paul the Jewish rabbi—and we should be governed by the former, not the latter.

This is a good example of how the presentation of the Gospel may be associated with a particular outlook characteristic of a certain culture, and the question is whether we are entitled to break the association.

Conservative scholarship has traditionally maintained that we should adhere to Paul's principles, but the method of carrying them out in a changed cultural situation may be different from what it was in the first century and so we may feel at liberty to do today what Paul specifically forbade. Thus a veil no longer has whatever significance it had in the first century, and to make a woman today wear a garment which is not in common use is no longer significant but rather ludicrous. In the same way, it can be argued that today a woman teaching or ministering is not regarded as a sign of insubordination in our culture, and therefore a teaching ministry by women is quite compatible with an acceptance of the principles that lay behind Paul's prohibition of this.

But, if I understand him aright, Jewett is claiming that even some of Paul's underlying principles may require amendment in the light of the total biblical revelation. It is not just a case of rejecting an imperfect implementation of a Christian principle; for Paul backs up his practice with points of principle which, in Jewett's view, are incompatible with other major biblical principles.

This raises difficulties. The cynic may be tempted to observe that the view of man and woman held by Jewett is not unlike that found in modern western culture with its emphasis on the emancipation of woman, and he may go on to wonder whether Jewett has been led to identify as central in the biblical revelation that element which is most congenial to modern western society; in other words, is Jewett simply interpreting the Bible from his own (time-bound) cultural setting and discarding what does not fit in with it? On the other hand, however, it might be said that it is precisely the development of a high view of woman in contemporary culture as a result of biblical teaching which has given Jewett the insight to recognize that some of the biblical teaching on this matter is obsolete and time-bound.

In either case, it can be argued that Jewett's approach leads to subjectivism (how shall we differentiate between biblical principles which are passé and those which are still valid?), and though there is room for subjective difference of opinion on many points of biblical interpretation, the task of exegesis is surely to move on beyond mere subjectivity. More strongly, it may be claimed that Jewett is simply replacing one cultural relativism (divinely sanctioned by inscripturation) with a new relativism in which we assess Scripture by the standards of our culture. Jewett would perhaps claim that he is assessing Scripture by Scripture, but this still leaves him open to the charge that he is establishing a canon within the canon and depriving certain passages of the New Testament of their authority.

This is perhaps not the place to attempt a more satisfying solution. The point is simply that Jewett's solution (admittedly open to criticism) illustrates very well the kind of questions and issues which are raised when one undertakes to apply biblical principles to contemporary cultural situations.

2. Another attempt to deal with the problem by separating the content of the biblical revelation from the form in which it is expressed can be seen in Rudolf Bultmann's program of demythologization. He argued that the truths of the Gospel were expressed

in the form of myths which no longer speak to modern man. He proposed that the myths expressing the truth should be stripped away, that is, demythologized to lay bare their essential message, and that this message should then be re-expressed in the "myths" of modern people. In other words, just as the biblical message must be translated out of an ancient language into a modern one, so too the ancient "mythical" form of the message must be "translated" into a corresponding modern form. Behind Bultmann's concern was not simply the fact that the ancient "myths" might be unintelligible to modern man, but also his claim that the world view which they presupposed (especially its acceptance of the supernatural) was unacceptable to modern man with his scientific outlook.

While Bultmann's desire to make the Gospel intelligible in the modern world is praiseworthy, it is regrettable that his actual performance is so unsatisfactory. He operates with a very loose and inadequate understanding of "myth"; he assigns much that should be regarded as historical (e.g., the physical resurrection of Jesus) to the category of "myth"; he fails to reckon with the fact that our modern world view with its rejection of the supernatural may need to be corrected by the biblical revelation; and in the course of his "translation" of the biblical message into modern terms, a good deal of the original content appears to get lost.

The difficulties raised by the approaches of Jewett and Bultmann indicate that there is no easy solution to the problem of separating the content of the Gospel from the cultural forms in which it has been expressed. The problem is like that of translation from one language to another; we have constantly to check the translation against the original to make sure that nothing which is vital in the original linguistic form of the message has been omitted in the new form.

One factor which may be relevant to the problem is that at certain points the original biblical revelation seems to have been capable of transcending the cultural categories available for its expression. Here I am thinking of the way in which a term like "Messiah" was available to express the significance of Jesus. But once the existing term was applied to Jesus it began to shift in meaning and was filled with a new content so that henceforth it was used in a new way. Jesus was indeed reticent about applying the term to himself precisely because the popular usage of the term (and popular usage *is* the meaning of a word) did not express what he conceived to be his own mission and destiny. As the term came into Christian usage, it took on a new meaning which corresponded to Jesus' understanding of messiahship. Thus it is possible to be creative within the bounds of a particular culture and to produce something which transcends the original cultural elements. This suggests that the essential content of the Gospel may be something that is not tied to one particular form of expression.

THE EFFECT OF CULTURE
ON THE FORM OF THE GOSPEL

A further factor which suggests that the process of "translation" of the Gospel is possible is the way in which the spread of the church led to the expression of the Gospel in new ways in order that it might be comprehensible by more people. It had to be expressed in a different language (Greek) rather than Hebrew or Aramaic. At the same time, new categories of understanding were pressed into service. Less comprehensible thought-forms from the past needed to be replaced by contemporary ones. The title "Son of Man," for instance, had no pre-history outside Jewish circles; the Greek form of the phrase was grotesque. It is not surprising, therefore, that the title totally disappeared from use outside the traditions of the teaching of Jesus. Other ways of expressing the significance of Jesus had to be found. A title such as "Lord" came into more frequent use, and while this had been used in Jewish Christianity, it probably developed in meaning through the influences of secular Greek usage, such as its use as a title of dignity by the Roman emperors. A term like "redemption," which is used in a rather vague way in early Christianity against an Old Testament background of Yahweh's deliverance of his people, assumed much more definite contours when it was understood against the background of its use in Greek society (in the manumission of slaves). These are good examples of the cultural stock of the Graeco-Roman world being put to the service of expressing the Gospel.

This process could be taken to a surprising extent, as the following two illustrations show. In Acts 17:28 Paul describes the character of God by means of two quotations: "In him we live and move and have our being,'' and ''For we are indeed his off-spring.'' Not only are these quotations from pagan poets but they also refer unequivocally to Zeus, the chief god in the Greek pantheon. And yet Paul uses them to depict the character of the Christian God. Evidently he was prepared to allow their truth, but only if Zeus was recognized as somehow depicting Yahweh; yet it is obvious that much of what pagans said about Zeus certainly could not be applied to Yahweh. Only where it was in agreement with the Old Testament and Christian revelation in Jesus was Paul prepared to take the step.

The second illustration is Paul in debate with Christian heretics such as the Gnostics who thought salvation came through knowledge. Paul was prepared to take over their vocabulary and apply it to Jesus. A possible example of this may be the term ''fulness,'' as it appears in Colossians, which may have been used by gnosticizing teachers in their own way but which Paul was quite prepared to take over and reapply to Christ.

In these various ways we can find examples of the development of the Christian Gospel through the use of categories drawn from other sources—pagan and heretical. It should not need to be said here that the truth of ideas is independent of their origin, and that to assert the Hellenistic origin of a concept rather than Old Testament origin is not to declare it false; fears that the discovery of a non-Jewish background for New Testament concepts renders their truth suspect are false, although sometimes scholars have argued in this way.

In summary, we have considered the way in which the surrounding culture conditioned the expression of the Gospel message, and seen that, although the message is necessarily expressed in the categories of particular cultures, it can break through the limits of existing cultural categories of expression, and can be re-expressed in terms of fresh cultural categories which may lead to its enrichment.

THE EFFECT OF THE GOSPEL ON CULTURE

We turn next to the question of how the Gospel can affect the surrounding culture. This is most obvious in the New Testament in the case of behavior and style of life. The followers of Jesus were pious Jews like their Master and followed a way of life typical of Palestinian Jews. It involved adherence to the Jewish law which was concerned with and legislated for every aspect of life. It can be assumed that for the most part they lived according to the law.

Yet even in the Gospels we have accounts of the critical questions that arose when Jesus and the disciples failed to observe the accepted mores. Why did they not keep the Sabbath in the prescribed manner? Why did they ignore the ritual rules of cleanliness, both in their habits of eating and in their association with sinful people? What was happening was that Jesus was criticizing the character of the surrounding culture, or the character of certain aspects of it, in the light of the principles of the religion which he taught—a religion which cut cleanly through the tedious legalism of the Pharisaic way of life.

Moreover, there were latent trends in his teaching which were to lead to further criticisms of the whole Jewish way of life. Thus, by his commendation of the centurion's faith (Matt. 8:10 ff.) he helped prepare the way for the accession of Gentiles into the church. The response of Gentiles to the Gospel raised the twin questions of whether they needed to embrace Jewish practices in order to be saved, and whether Jews could have fellowship with them other than on the terms allowed by the Jewish law. Gentiles ranked as "unclean" in contemporary Jewish understanding (though not according to the Old Testament), and circumcision and observance of the law of Moses were regarded as necessary for salvation.

It cost the early church a tremendous struggle but two essential points were recognized: (1) Gentiles did not need to be circumcised or keep the law of Moses but only to believe in Christ (with all that that involved) in order to be saved; and (2) Jew and Gentile stood on an equal footing, so that Gentiles no longer ranked as "unclean" in relation to Jews.

Two other changes in way of life developed at the same time. The first concerned worship. The temple ceased to have any significance for Christians. The same was true of synagogue worship, although—since the synagogue was more than a building for Jewish worship and acted as the focus of Jewish community life—it is likely that Christian Jews continued to associate with it so far as they were able.

The other change was that the teaching of Jesus on things clean and unclean was recognized as destroying the whole distinction between clean and unclean foods, and thereby a drastic change in Jewish eating habits must have taken place. These and other changes thus led to the development, for Christian Jews, of a quite new life-style.

The attitude of the church to pagan ways of life at first glimpse produced less spectacular changes. Outside Judaism there was a much greater range of ways of life within the general gamut of Hellenistic civilization. There were so many different religions, each with their own group of adherents, that the development of a fresh one was not particularly noteworthy, and there was nothing culturally odd about belonging to the Christian church rather than to some mystery sect. Within a pluralistic culture it is hard to produce a life-style that cuts clean against the general way of life of the culture.

But although the Gospel did not create a headlong clash with Hellenistic civilization simply because there was no one culture, it did produce a new way of life alongside the several existing ones, and it thus profoundly affected the lives of converts.

The point may be illustrated in the realm of ethics. The New Testament writers certainly inveighed against the sins of paganism and urged their readers not to continue in their old way of life with its carousing, sexual immorality, and general misbehavior. There could be a very real change of life for people who had lived immoral lives.

Still, the new moral teaching offered by Christianity did not offer a way of life so markedly different from the ideals of certain areas of Hellenistic culture. This can be seen in the example of the various "House tables" or ethical codes for different classes of society which are found in the Epistles. Some of the teaching in these is remarkably close to pagan (and also to Jewish) moral teaching. It has been Christianized, but in some cases it did not need a lot of change to accomplish this. The fact is that Stoics and Epicureans both recognized the existence of moral values, and their understanding of these values in practical terms was not all that different from the Christian understanding. I do not want to minimize the extent of the differences, especially the significant difference enshrined in the Christian new commandment of love, but the fact remains that many pagans would have recognized Christian ethics as being fairly similar in character to the ethical teaching of the best philosophers of the time.

Nevertheless, there were occasions where Christians ran up against pagan culture. We need to ask ourselves why Christians were so persecuted. D. R. A. Hare *(The Theme of Jewish Persecution of Christians in the Gospel According to St. Matthew,* Cambridge, 1967) has suggested that a society can tolerate a certain amount of deviation from its general way of life, but once people start to question or attack the symbols of cultural solidarity they go beyond the limit of toleration. So the Jews persecuted the Christians because they attacked the temple and the law of Moses. The Romans persecuted the Christians when they refused to take part in the worship of the emperor which was the formal sign of loyalty and hence a cultural solidarity. It was only when the symbols of national and imperial solidarity were challenged, and when the superior morality of Christianity, such as that prescribed in 1 Peter, touched upon uneasy pagan consciences that pagans turned to persecution.

In summary, we can see that the effect of the Gospel was to challenge sharply the life-style of Judaism as a religious and national culture, and also to challenge the life-style of Gentiles by creating a new way of life in a pluralistic pagan setting. It was impossible to be a Christian and live as one had formerly lived. The new faith led to a new way of life.

THE NEW TESTAMENT ATTITUDE
TO CULTURAL VALUES

Finally, we turn to the particular question of the relation between the Gospel and culture in the sense of aesthetic values and the things associated with them.

This is a difficult subject to probe since the New Testament is primarily a book about religion and not about the cultural life of Christians. Consequently, any information on the latter comes out incidentally and indirectly rather than explicitly.

But we can note that Jesus was evidently interested in the natural world around him and was a keen observer of the rural scene from which he drew many of his illustrations. He displayed considerable artistic power in the use of words, so that his parables and metaphorical sayings stand out for their literary power and effect. He had a positive attitude towards the world around him, so that life in the world was a joy for him.

The early Christians remained consistent with Jesus' view. The one text that is specifically devoted to this attitude is Philippians 4:8: ''Whatever is true, whatever is honorable, whatever is just, whatever is pure, whatever is lovely, whatever is gracious, if there is any excellence, if there is anything of praise, think about these things.'' Here we have a positive commendation of what is good in the world as being worthy of the attention of the Christian. The New Testament writers condemn culture only at those points where it has become contaminated by sin and no longer achieves the divinely intended purpose. It is the attitude of selfishness and lack of love which makes the enjoyment of culture sinful.

This is confirmed by one of the few texts which is self-conscious of the problem of surrounding culture. The nearest thing that the New Testament has to a word for ''culture'' is ''world'' *(kosmos)* which expresses the organized life of mankind in the created world. *Kosmos* is not simply the created universe inhabited by man; it is much more—human society itself as it inhabits the universe and stands over against God. 1 John 2:15 contains a warning not to love the world. As the verse immediately makes clear, the world in this context means the sinfulness of human society, and the Christian is not to be attracted by what is sinful, by temptations to self-aggrandizement of whatever kind. Yet God loved the world and he pronounced it ''very good.'' This means that in the last analysis the Christian's positive attitude to culture is based on the Creator's own delight in and approval of his creation (except insofar as it is tainted by sin).

We must also reckon with the question of whether the *new* creation embraces human culture. While our evangelical doctrine of salvation tends to be intensely individualistic, concerning itself with the redemption of individual persons, is there any sense in which human institutions and culture participate in the new creation?

The Book of Revelation speaks of the sinful Babylon replaced by the city of God, and ''new Jerusalem.'' Does this imply the creation of a new human culture? The language used argues for a radical break—heaven and earth flee away; new

Jerusalem descends from above. Yet we must take seriously the implication of Revelation 21:24-26, which makes a special piont of the fact that human culture—"the glory and honor of the nations"—is to be present in the city of God as part of the glorification of the Creator and Redeemer of the world.

If we neglect this positive emphasis on culture, we face two difficulties:

1. The whole human cultural enterprise seems doomed to destruction and is of no ultimate, lasting value; it is therefore doubtful whether it is worth pursuing. Evangelical eschatology typically works with a "complete break" type of future expectation in which all human history and achievement is ultimately of no significance—we brought nothing into this world and we can take nothing out of it. But although we may hold this view in theory, in practice we live otherwise—are we being sinful in "living otherwise"?

2. Culture is inextricably bound up with people; it is people who form societies, and so if the people move over into the next world, to some extent their societies and thus some aspects of their culture go with them. It can be objected that this is not so; for example, the cultural institution of marriage is abolished in heaven where they neither marry nor are given in marriage. I would, however, agree with C. F. D. Moule *(The Gospel According to Mark,* Cambridge, 1965) that this is because *all* human relationships are raised to a new level of fellowship and intimacy.

These difficulties suggest that our traditional understanding of New Testament teaching in terms of a sharp discontinuity at the "End" may be wrong, and it raises afresh the question of the possibility of the redemption of culture in the new world.

Certainly, while it is sin-denying, Christianity is not world-denying. The New Testament attitude to cultural values is a positive one. It anticipates the prominent place of "culture" (in some form) in the Kingdom to come by speaking of a city, the nations, and the great throng from every tribe and tongue. Contrary to traditional evangelical eschatology, the God revealed by the New Testament writers surely has in mind the conservation and transformation of human culture and human society in the world to come.

3. Culture and the Old Testament

by S. Ananda Kumar

S. ANANDA KUMAR *is professor of biblical studies, Karnataka Theological College, Karnataka State, South India. He heads a team involved in village evangelism.*

TODAY WE HEAR A GREAT DEAL ABOUT THE importance of culture in the propagation of the Gospel. Certainly much damage can come to the mission of the church if cultural factors are ignored. Even though "culture" is not an explicit subject of the Old and New Testaments, biblical studies have made it clear that human cultures have played a far more significant role in biblical history than we may at first be prepared to recognize. Perhaps we can learn from the Bible itself neither to overemphasize nor to underestimate the significance of culture. That culture forms an inseparable part of the content and context of the Holy Scriptures, yet at the same time stays below the surface, suggests both the value and the limitation of culture in the task of world evangelization.

Culture is the core and driving force of civilization both ancient and modern. The word "culture" comes from the Latin *colere,* meaning to cultivate. It indicates man's environment as shaped and patterned by the whole of human activity. Culture is essentially a social phenomenon and is realized in the individual through encounters with other members of society. History witnesses to the fact that religion is a chief source of culture; in the ancient world, especially, religion and culture were inseparably bound together. This is still the case today in many societies, including India.

Culture, with all its merits and limitations, has played a fundamental role in God's self-disclosure in human history. Divine revelation does not come in a vacuum. It can only come with reference to culture, that is, in relation to the religious environment, language and understanding of man; otherwise we could not understand it. It is the greatness of God's mercy that he voluntarily limits himself to the vehicles of human culture to make himself known.

Christians have accepted the Bible as a reliable record of God's dealing with mankind in history. Further, it is an inspired record, so that, in the words of J. I. Packer, "The biblical record of God's self-disclosure in redemptive history is not merely human testimony to revelation, but is itself revelation" ("Inspiration," *New Bible Dictionary*). This revelation has come to us in two stages. The first, the Old Testament, belongs to the pre-Christian period and forms the basis of the second and final stage in Christ. Our Lord, his apostles, and the early church looked upon the Old Testament as authoritative Scripture. Their testimony as to its divine inspiration witnesses to the fact that God's self-disclosure did not come in a cultural vacuum.

We can appreciate the rich cultural context of the Old Testament by looking at several examples of teaching and practice which the inspired Word enjoined upon ancient Israel. We will take one example each from the areas of doctrine, religious ritual, social institutions, and ethics.

DOCTRINE: THE CREATION ACCOUNT IN GENESIS 1

The similarities and parallels between ancient Near Eastern creation cosmogonies and the Genesis account of Creation are well known. Of course, many key differences stand out in the Genesis record; these are not difficult to explain in light of the divine purpose, as we shall see shortly. But justice cannot be done to our subject by overemphasizing the differences and ignoring the parallels. However exalted our theory of inspiration of the Holy Scriptures, we have to take account of the similarities.

The most striking parallels with the Genesis account are found in the Babylonian Creation Epic:

1. In both accounts, the world begins in a state of darkness, water, and chaos.

2. "Tehom" of Genesis 1:2 ("the deep" in the Authorized Version and "the raging ocean" in the Good News Bible) is the Babylonian "Tiamat," used like a proper name. Tiamat was the Babylonian goddess of the Great Deep, with a dragon's body.

3. God divides the primeval waters by means of the firmament (GNB has "dome" in Gen. 1:6-8). This corresponds to the episode in the fourth of the seven tablets of the Babylonian Creation Epic:

> He [Marduk, the supreme deity] split her [Tiamat] like a
>   fish . . . in two halves,
> From the one half he made and covered the heaven:
> He drew a barrier, placed sentinels,
> Commanded them not to let its water through.

4. In Genesis 1:3 light appears before the creation of the heavenly bodies. In the Babylonian Epic light, which belongs to the essence of the "upper gods," appears before the coming of Marduk, the youngest of the gods.

5. The creation of the sun, moon, and stars on the fourth day (Gen. 1:14-19) is parallel to the creation of the heavenly bodies by Marduk, recorded in the Fifth Creation Tablet.

6. Creation of the beasts of the field, wild animals, and creeping things (Gen. 1:24, 25), is also found on a fragment (but it is not certain whether it belongs to the same Creation Epic series).

7. Creation of man to inhabit the earth is mentioned: "I will make man . . . I will create man, who shall inhabit the earth." This is parallel to God's declaration in Genesis 1:26: "Let us make man in our image." The relation between man and the Creator is expressed here in the Genesis account; the same is found in the Babylonian Creation Epic: "My blood will I take, and bone will I fashion, I will make man. . . ." Such a relation is not expressed with reference to the creation of other things and animals either in Genesis or in the Babylonian Creation Epic.

8. In Genesis, God beholds all that has been created by the Word of his mouth and calls it good. With this we can compare the hymn of praise to Marduk:

> God of pure life, God of kindly breath, Lord of hearing and grace, creator of fulness, maker of abundance, God of the pure crown, raiser of the dead, . . . may one rejoice over the Lord of Gods, Marduk, cause one's land to abound, himself enjoy peace. Firm abideth His word. His command changeth not. No God hath caused the utterance of His mouth to fail.

9. Finally, the seventh day of the Sabbath of divine rest is essentially of Babylonian origin.

It should be observed that, except for the exchange in the position of the creation of the plant world and the heavenly bodies, the order followed in the Genesis account is the same as in the Babylonian Creation Epic. The parallels of content and order cannot be mere coincidence. Four responses are offered by biblical scholars:

1. The Babylonian cosmogony is just a "heathen" myth which has nothing to do with the divinely inspired record of creation. This does not seem like a very adequate answer.

2. Both accounts have a common origin. This is a possibility, but thus far there has been found no trace of a document more ancient than that of the Babylonian Creation Epic.

3. Genesis 1-11 is "aetiological prophecy," that is, a revelation about the past. This is certainly true, but it leaves unanswered the question about the similarities with the Babylonian Creation Epic.

4. The most obvious and satisfactory explanation seems to be that the Babylonian Creation Epic has more or less influenced the Genesis account. Owen C. Whitehouse seems correct in saying, "It is to Babylonia, the land of the highest and most ancient Semitic culture, we must look for the most fruitful clues to ancient Hebrew thought and life" ("Cosmogony," *Hastings Dictionary of the Bible*). Still, as J. A. Thompson points out ("Creation," *New Bible Dictionary*), the fact that Babylonian influence can be seen does not necessarily mean that the Genesis account was borrowed directly. We shall see the implications of this in a moment.

Accepting the hypothesis that the Genesis account did not totally ignore or reject the Babylonian Creation Epic, in spite of the latter's undesirable elements, the limits of its influence may be outlined as follows:

1. While there is affinity between the two, there are also differences and distance between them.

2. The Genesis account did not incorporate all the elements of the Babylonian account.

3. Some of the elements received from the Babylonian account are so modified that they can be recognized only in the background of the Genesis record.

In other words, the Babylonian account has been subjected to a thorough process of critical theological reflection, so that the biblical account is far more than a mere reproduction of the Babylonian Creation Epic. S. H. Hooke's observation is apropos:

> The point of the parallels is not . . . to emphasize the dependence of Hebrew symbolism upon Babylonian myths, but to emphasize the fact that the Hebrew writers . . . did not invent a symbolism to express the various aspects of the divine activity, but took what lay ready to their hand, the material which they had inherited as part of their early cultural contacts, and transformed it into the vocabulary of the divine speech. ("Genesis," *Peake's Commentary on the Bible*)

Now we are ready to examine the process of elimination, adaptation, and transformation by which the Genesis account distances itself from the Babylonian Creation Epic. In this process we see how divine inspiration uses culture to communicate along lines familiar to the audience, yet by virtue of new and refined content impresses upon its readers its divine authority. We begin with elements in the Babylonian account which have been virtually eliminated in the Genesis account:

1. The Genesis account rejects all polytheistic references in the Babylonian mythology. On the other hand, it begins with a solemnity ("In the beginning God . . .") which belongs to God alone and which is lacking in the Babylonian account.

2. All references to fighting between the gods and their struggle to overcome the dragon of the chaos are omitted, as incompatiible with the sovereignty and majesty of the one universal God.

3. Reference to idolatry or anything reminiscent of idolatrous practices has been totally eliminated. Thus, sun and moon, which were objects of worship both at the time of the inscription of the Babylonian tablets and at the time of the writing of the Genesis account, are deliberately called simply "the greater light" and "the lesser light" (Gen. 1:16).

4. Elements which are grotesque, unlovely, or confusing are eliminated. For example, instead of man being made out of a mixture of Marduk's blood and earth, we read the simple statement, "Let us make man in our image. . . ."

Other elements have been adapted rather than eliminated:

5. In order to dramatize that the Creator-God is the God of order and almighty power, both accounts begin with darkness and chaos. The Genesis account differs in that it is purified of the mythological details.

6. In both accounts light appears before the creation of heavenly bodies, emphasizing that the Creator-God is the God of light. Again, the mythological details mentioned in the Babylonian Creation Epic have been omitted.

7. Both accounts note that the heavenly bodies are given to rule the day and night as well as to determine the seasons; but the Genesis account is stripped of all idolatrous implications. (By way of contrast, the Babylonian version makes special reference to the moon god Nannaru.)

Finally, there are significant elements which echo the Babylonian Creation Epic but which have undergone a thorough process of transformation:

8. Tehom (Gen. 1:2a) parallels the Babylonian Tiamat, but the mythological background has been ignored. Tehom conveys a new meaning, that is, the depth of the dark sea or ocean (cf. Pss. 33:7; 104:6). The biblical term refers not to some goddess but rather to the reality of a physical feature of the sea which can be experienced even today.

9. It is possible to translate Genesis 1:2b, "a great wind swept over the deep," in which case we might have another echo of the Babylonian Creation Epic where Marduk arms himself with the winds in order to overcome Tiamat. But the biblical account clearly symbolizes the invisible operation and influence of the Almighty God. The mythological idea has given way to the noble spiritual truth of God's action in bringing chaos into order by his own power.

10. The crude mythological element of splitting Tiamat in two gives way to God dividing the primeval chaos into heaven and earth. The reader is appealed to by the reality—which he experiences daily—of sky above and earth beneath. This is retained in the Genesis account without any contamination with mythological elements.

11. That man has relation to God as well as to the world in which he lives had been brought out both in the Babylonian Epic and also in Genesis. But, as noted earlier, in the latter the mythological details of Marduk's blood being mixed with earth to create man have given way to the sublime language "Let us make man in our image, after our likeness."

One of the most striking differences in the two accounts is highlighted by H. E. Ryle:

> The narrative begins with a statement assuming the Existence of the Deity. It is not a matter of discussion, argument, or doubt. The Israelite Cosmogony differs in this respect from that of the Babylonians, Phoenicians, Egyptians, etc. The Cosmogonies of the ancients were wont to be preceded by Theogonies. The existence and nativities of the creating divinities were accounted for in mythologies which were often highly complicated, and not seldom grotesque. The Hebrew narrator, by beginning with the Creation, emphasized his entire freedom from, and exclusion of, polytheistic thought. *(The Book of Genesis,* pp. 1, 2)

Thompson states:

> The fact of inspiration preserved the writer of Genesis 1 from the language and crudities of contemporary polytheism, but the writer remained an ordinary man who used

his eyes to good advantage as he sought to describe the way in which God brought this world into being . . . for there is depth and dignity in Genesis 1 that is not to be found in the Babylonian story. (op. cit., p. 270)

Eugene H. Maly adds:

The primitive cosmology of the author's time is used to teach the creation of all things by God. The absolute power of the transcendent God is emphasized. Whereas the pagan epics depict creation as the result of a struggle between the gods and forces of chaos, the biblical account stresses the effortless activity of the one God. The imagery borrowed from these other accounts becomes material for the author's polemic against the myths; it also helps to make the picture live for his readers. (''Genesis,'' *The Jerome Biblical Commentary.*)

Our own summary is as follows: The inspired writer of Genesis 1 made use of already existing material from the non-Israelite culture of the ancient world of the Near East. But in doing so, he used great caution and care (cf. Luke 1:1-4). The divine revelation involved the elimination of polytheistic and idolatrous elements as well as of undignified, absurd, and crude mythological factors which were contrary to the sovereignty, majesty, and dignity of the Creator-God, who revealed himself in the history of Israel. As the Israelite theologians interacted with the framework and content of the pagan concepts around them, they were guided and enlightened by God, so that the whole ''contextualization'' process from beginning to end was controlled and sanctified by God himself to produce an indigenous theology relevant to Israel's situation.

In the same way other Old Testament doctrines like the Seventh-Day Sabbath, covenant, circumcision, and so forth, could be dealt with in detail, and would yield further enlightenment on the process of cultural contextualization. Such a study would correct traditional misunderstandings, deepen our knowledge of the divine inspiration of Scripture, and widen the horizon of our theological apprehension. It would enhance our ability to evaluate good and bad influences in our culture, broaden the vision of mission in its cultural context, and help us see the movement of the Spirit of God in a new light.

RELIGIOUS RITUAL: PROHIBITION RE COOKING A KID IN ITS MOTHER'S MILK

"You shall not boil a kid in its mother's milk" (Exod. 23:19; 34:26; Deut. 14:21). This prohibition has puzzled commentators for centuries. J. B. Taylor calls it "the strange Mosaic prohibition," and says it "probably referred originally to a Canaanite ritual" ("Milk," *New Bible Dictionary*). Some writers say it was given "to avoid its heathen associations," but these "associations" are not explained.

As we have seen in regard to the creation account in Genesis 1, cultural elements are not necessarily rejected simply because of their "heathen associations." Beliefs or practices rejected by Israel were always rejected on some solid theological ground. Let us look at this prohibition more closely, therefore, and see why it is that in this particular example of contextualization the inspired writer called for the complete rejection of a local practice.

In the two Exodus passages, the context deals with harvest sacrifices and festivals. In Deuteronomy 14 the prohibition appears at the end of a long passage on "clean" and "unclean" animals, and therefore some commentators have seen it as part of the Mosaic dietary code. (Modern Jewish dietary laws, forbidding the eating of meat and milk products at the same meal, are based on this injunction.)

The discovery and deciphering of the Ras Shamra Tablets in the 1930s, at the site of ancient Ugarit in northern Syria, lent weight to an explanation connected with harvest time. D. M. G. Stalker writes:

> The significance of this prohibition has now been made clear by the Ras Shamra texts [which state that] a kid was cooked in its mother's milk to procure the fertility of the fields, which were sprinkled with the substance which results. In this case, a Canaanite practice is rejected, no doubt because it savoured of magic. ("Exodus," *Peake's Commentary on the Bible*)

Another authority says it was used to "besprinkle . . . all the trees, fields, gardens, and orchards. This was done at the close of their harvests for the purpose of making trees and fields more fruitful the following year" (Cudworth, in James M. Freeman, *Man-*

ners and Customs of the Bible, Logos, p. 73). Macalister adds, ". . . the broth [was] sprinkled on the ground as a sacrifice to propitiate the harvest gods and ensure fruitfulness" ("Food," *Hastings Dictionary of the Bible*).

So the practice of boiling a young goat or sheep in its mother's milk was an idolatrous, polytheistic Canaanite fertility ritual, with strong elements of cult magic. This practice was performed by the Canaanites at their feast of harvest. The comparable event in Israel, known as the Feast of Weeks, could easily have become an occasion for assimilation of pagan influences. The ritual ordinances of Israel, including the one under discussion, were designed to preserve the distinctive character of the community of Yahweh, and to avoid assimilation with the cultic practices of Israel's neighbors. (A somewhat similar New Testament injunction might be the prohibition regarding food offered to idols: 1 Cor. 10:14-22.) Because of the idolatry and magic associated with boiling a kid in its mother's milk, the inspired Old Testament writer called for a complete rejection of this pagan practice.

SOCIAL INSTITUTIONS: KINGSHIP IN ISRAEL

The idea of kingship in Israel did not spring up spontaneously. Rather, as the Bible indicates, it arose in response to the influences of the surrounding pagan peoples (1 Sam. 8:5 ff.). The office of "king" was known among the Semitic peoples of the Middle East long before the Hebrews settled in the Promised Land, and the word for "king"—*melek*—was a common Semitic word. Though its origin is uncertain, *melek* may be connected with an Assyrian and Aramaic word meaning counsel or advice, so that it signified "counselor" or "ruler." The title is applied to the rulers of small city-states in Canaan and its neighborhood, as well as to rulers of wider territories such as Egypt, Moab, Syria, and in later times Assyria, Babylonia, and Persia.

The monarchy arose in Israel in reaction to the political power of the Philistines. In the biblical data there appear to be two versions or traditions about the origin of the monarchy (cf. 1 Sam. 8:1-22; 10:17-27; 12:1-25, with 9:1-10, 16; 11:1-15). Most commentators recognize a fusion of anti-monarchy and pro-monarchy sources in these passages. Though the two perspectives are not readily reconciled, there is something to be said for the view that the monarchy first willed by the people was later allowed and willed by God, and eventually by Samuel himself, although at the outset he was opposed.

Now let us see to what extent the monarchy in Israel was borrowed unchanged from Israel's neighbors and to what extent it developed along unique lines. The borrowed elements include the following:

1. The very term *melek.*

2. The Canaanite kings were leaders in war and sometimes led the troops to battle in person (cf. Gen. 14:1-12). This model was followed in Israel as well: for instance, Saul on Mt. Gilboa (1 Sam. 31:2) and Ahab at Ramoth Gilead (1 Kings 22:29 ff.).

3. The Canaanite kings were typically the supreme judges, to whom final appeal might be made from the findings of local elders or professional judges (cf. 1 Sam. 14:1-20; 1 Kings 3:16-28).

4. They were also the chief persons from the cultic point of view to offer sacrifice, to bless the people, and to take the lead in organizing the nation's worship (cf. 2 Sam. 6:13, 17; 24:25; 1 Kings 5-8; 8:14; 12:26-32).

5. There was the idea of sacral kingship as the diety's anointed. The king was regarded as sacrosanct (cf. 1 Sam. 24:10; 26:9; 2 Sam. 1:14, 16).

6. The office of the king was thought to be hereditary like that of the priest (cf. 1 Sam. 20:30 ff.; 1 Kings 2:15; 14:21; 15:25; 16:29).

7. The scepter was the sign of supreme authority (cf. Pss. 45:6-7; 110:2; Gen. 49:10; Esther 4:11).

8. The use of oriental courtly language, such as the extolling of the king in exaggerated felicitations and songs, and the development of a definite stock of stereotyped titles, comparisons, epithets, and styles of address. Israel, too, shared these courtly forms of address, perhaps through the medium of older traditions from Canaanite Jerusalem (cf. Ps. 110).

9. The idea of the divine sonship of the king, who is magnified as the one with whom a new era of peace and righteousness dawns and to whom the ends of the earth are assured. In this connection, see the "Royal Psalms": 2, 20, 21, 45, 72, 101, 110, and 132.

10. The application of the term *melek* to the godhead or deity.

Among the elements in the Israelite kingship which are different than those found in Canaan and surrounding areas are these:

1. The Israelite monarchy did not develop simultaneously alongside religion. By the time of Saul and David, the faith of Israel had already developed along its own original lines.

2. The monarchy was not a basic element in the faith of Israel. Yahwism, in fact, brought the monarchy a certain degree of tension and pointed beyond the monarchy for Israel's ultimate hope.

3. There is no hint whatsoever of the deification of the Israelite or Jewish monarchy.

4. The ideal in Israel set kingship apart from despotism and dictatorship, in contrast to the typical oriental monarchies. (Jezebel's action in the Naboth affair was characteristic of pagan notions of the power and privilege of the court; 1 Kings 21:5-15.) The presence and ministry of the prophets of Yahweh challenged the kings' authority whenever they misused it (e.g., Nathan's rebuke of David; 2 Samuel 12). It was never forgotten that the office was instituted for the good of the nation and that it ought to be a help and not a burden to the people. In the people's minds, law and custom superseded the kingly authority. Of course, the king, who according to ancient ideas embodied the people, was necessarily a prominent object of the gracious promises of Yahweh. Nevertheless, the Israelite religion remained stronger than the adopted forms of kingship.

The list could be extended. But the above items are enough to support our conclusion: In their religio-politico-social environment, the people of God were guided to incorporate those elements of kingship from the surrounding culture which would be beneficial to the nation, while rejecting those elements which were outside the divine framework of social righteousness and justice and contrary to human dignity and welfare.

ETHICS: POLYGAMY AND CONCUBINAGE

Assuming that monogamy is God's ideal, it is pertinent to ask why polygamy was practiced in ancient Israel and why the Old Testament fails to condemn it. The inspired writers prohibited other undesirable social practices; why not polygamy?

Polygamy and concubinage predate Israel by many centuries. Ancient codes of the Middle East seek to regulate polygamy as an established institution. In addition to polygamy and concubinage—often associated with power and wealth—there were instances of bigamy which indicate that even men of no particular prominence entered into plural marriages (e.g., Elkanah, 1 Sam. 1:2 ff.).

To understand the Old Testament attitude toward polygamy, we must take into account the social causes of the practice. These include:

1. The desire for numerous offspring could not normally be fulfilled through monogamy. This desire, which is still prevalent throughout eastern countries, was especially powerful among the Hebrews.

2. The barrenness of a wife made the family atmosphere unhappy. Abraham's case is directly ascribed to this, and among many peoples polygamy is permitted on this ground alone.

3. When there was a disproportionate number of females, they could not be married in any other way except through polygamy. In the Orient, for a young girl to remain unmarried was an insult to her as well as to her family.

4. After a war, women captives accentuated the problem of the overpopulation of women. Polygamy helped provide a solution (cf. Deut. 21:10-14).

5. Polygamy was common among wealthy and influential men, who gained prestige and honor by having plural wives, the wives being part of the display of wealth.

6. In a number of cases the wife or wives were willing to give their own slave girls to the husband as concubines. Sarah, Leah, and Rachel are examples: Genesis 16:1-4; 30:9-13. Even when they themselves had children this custom was not prohibited.

7. In ancient times people felt insecure, and their safety lay in numbers and joint-family system. This also played a part in motivating polygamy.

8. The position and importance offered by numerous alliances, as for example in the case of Solomon, was a factor in polygamy.

"Marriage is the state in which men and women can live together in sexual relationship with the approval of their social group." This definition (Wright and Thompson, "Marriage," *New Bible Dictionary*), when applied to ancient Israel, prohibits neither polygamy nor concubinage.

In truth, however, the best that can be said about polygamy is that it was legally maintained rather than successfully managed. In the Old Testament, polygamy is seen as leading to quarrels, jealousies, and family troubles, and kings are clearly warned against it. If there were such evils and sorrows in polygamy, and if monogamy is the ideal marriage relationship, why was it allowed in the Old Covenant at all?

It has been suggested that (1) God had ordained monogamy at the start but man in his sinfulness managed otherwise; (2) the Mosaic Law aimed at mitigating rather than removing evils which were inherent in the state of society in that day; and (3) God left it to man to discover by experience that his original institution of monogamy was the proper relationship. (This is borne out by the fact that by the time of the prophets, monogamy is increasingly looked upon as the ideal, with monogamous marriage presented as the symbol of union between God and his people; e.g., the book of Hosea.)

But perhaps the most satisfactory explanation is found in the distinction between imperfection and corruption. Divine inspiration, while not countenancing corruption, does make allowances for imperfection. The obvious example is in the sacrifices for sin as prescribed in the Mosaic Law. Though these were imperfect, they were allowed by God until the coming of the perfect sacrifice in

Christ. Only then was the imperfect fully exposed and consequently abandoned. Polygamy and concubinage belong to the same category of imperfection in the realm of ethics. It is in this sense that our Lord spoke of the weightier and lighter matters of the Law. For instance, he stated that the offering of sacrifices was less important than practicing mercy (Matt. 9:13; 12:7).

But it should be underlined that divine inspiration does not permit corruption, either in religion or ethics. Child-sacrifices and sacred prostitution are examples; these were absolutely forbidden in the Old Covenant, though they were common among some of Israel's neighbors. In regard to polygamy, however, providence made a concession for a time to human imperfection, which was subject to greater light at a later time. This points to the patience of God as he seeks to bring us into harmony with his will and purpose. Likewise, a proper contextualization of the Gospel will take into account the imperfection of men and women in the present state of society; yet at the same time it will absolutely forbid that which is fundamentally counterposed to the will of God in Jesus Christ.

CONCLUSION

The results of our research are necessarily tentative. Our viewpoint in one matter or another may be defective, and the evidence available to us through archaeology and historical studies may be insufficient to arrive at assured conclusions. We are grateful to know that our salvation is not affected by these limitations.

The purpose of our study has been to see how and to what extent the Spirit of God used the cultural environment of the Old Testament writers as they contributed to the inspired record. It seems clear that God did indeed speak in the context of the surrounding cultures, borrowing and adapting non-Israelite forms and concepts, in order to convey his message to his ancient people in terms that would be familiar and meaningful to them. Though thus related to the surrounding cultures, Israel's religious and social life nevertheless exhibited key differences. These are to be directly attributed to the divinely inspired ministry of Moses and the subsequent prophets and writers, through whom God disclosed his holy will and purpose for his people.

Regardless of the light we have received from extra-biblical sources which have helped us arrive at our present understanding of the Bible, we should never forget that the latter is the Word of God. It is both timely and timeless. Whether our understanding of it is correct at all points, whether the insights gained through historical and cultural studies are entirely valid or not, the Bible remains the Word of God. To speak in terms of one of our examples, Genesis 1 is the Word of God for us, not the Babylonian Creation Epic, even though the former may be appreciated best when seen against the background of the latter.

Let us never lose sight of the fact that the Bible is God's Word, especially when we are engaged in investigating extra-biblical "evidences." We may be enriched through scientific studies, but our ultimate Source is God, the Creator and Savior. At best our studies are *means,* while God is our Life and Goal. Beyond him is nothing, and in him is everything.

4. Towards a Theology of Gospel and Culture

by Bruce J. Nicholls

BRUCE J. NICHOLLS, *former director of the Theological Research and Communication Institute, New Delhi, India, is executive secretary of the Theological Commission of the World Evangelical Fellowship.*

AT THE 1974 LAUSANNE CONGRESS ON WORLD Evangelization, evangelicals began to seriously question the relationship of the Gospel to culture. Eleven years earlier, at the WCC Faith and Order Commission in Montreal, E. Kasemann raised the hermeneutical question, signaling the gathering interest in contextualization which highlights the interaction of the Gospel with receptor cultures. But perhaps the most influential of all was the publication in 1972 of the WCC Theological Education Fund report *Ministry in Context,* which took up contextualization in light of the technological revolution and the spread of secularity. Henceforth, there could be no retreat from Gospel-and-culture issues.

To understand culture involves understanding the total "design for living" of a people. It means perceiving the world view (which may be consciously or unconsciously expressed) and the religious and spiritual elements that are normally the dominant factors in any cultural framework. Culture is a way of behaving and thinking that includes value systems and social institutions (family, law, education, etc.). Because culture is the sum total of behavioral patterns learned by instruction, observation, and imitation, it is constantly changing; therefore the task of relating the Gospel to a particular culture is always a continuing one.

TWO APPROACHES TO CONTEXTUALIZED THEOLOGY

As a broad generalization we may speak of two approaches to the task of formulating a theology of Gospel and culture—"existential contextualization of the Gospel" and "dogmatic contextualization of the Gospel."

The first approach begins with culture. It seeks to develop interaction between the subjective questions of man in history and an existential understanding of the Word of God. That is, it begins with two relatives and expects to find only tentative theological formulations in a progression to a synthesis of understanding.

The second approach reflects a concern for biblical theology as a fixed and authoritative orientation point. It, too, seeks to translate and communicate the biblical message with understanding to each particular culture. But, unlike existential contextualization, it transcends the boundaries of particular cultural conceptual forms and practices and starts with a dogmatic framework rather than a cultural one.

Of course, no approach, including dogmatic contextualization, can be "objective" in the absolute sense. All attempts at theologizing are colored by the pre-understandings of the enculturized receivers of the gospel message. Luther's commentary on Galatians was influenced by his antagonism to the Pope, Barth's commentaries on Romans by his existentialism, and so forth. But the grammatico-historical exegetical method, which takes seriously the language, historical background, and purpose of the biblical writers, reduces cultural pre-understanding to a minimum. This is what makes possible a comprehension of biblical theology. The Bible's teaching on its own perspicuity assures the faithful student of this possibility, and it is on this basis that we can speak of the Scriptures as "the only infallible rule of faith and practice."

EXISTENTIAL CONTEXTUALIZATION QUESTIONED

Existential contextualization, lacking a normative theological framework of belief and practice, runs the risk of syncretism and universalism. If the biblical account of the Gospel is not accepted as normative, then culture tends to become semi-absolutized. This, I suggest, is what is happening in many emerging Third World theologies. It is accentuated by the search for national identity and by an over-reaction to western paternalistic Christianity.

S. Wesley Ariarajah, in "Towards a Theology of Dialogue" (*Ecumenical Review,* Jan. 1977) illustrates the point. In reaction to the "teutonic captivity" of theology, he argues that all theology is "story telling," and adds, "Anyone who approaches another with an *a priori* assumption that his story is 'the only true story' kills the dialogue before it begins." The implication appears to be that the Judeo-Christian "Creation-Fall-Redemption" story is no more valid than the Hindu or Buddhist story.

Most attempts to contextualize theology in India have tended to follow the path of relativizing the Gospel and absolutizing one or the other of the Hindu conceptual frameworks. For example, Brahmabandhav Upadhyaya (1861-1907) attempted to indigenize Christian theology in terms of Shankara's *advaitic* philosophy of non-dualism. He interpreted the trinity in terms of *Brahman* (the Absolute or Pure Being) as *sat chit ananda* (being, intelligence, and bliss). His use of these impersonal categories resulted in his natural theology progressively weakening biblical concepts. More recently other Roman Catholic scholars such as Raymond Panikkar, author of *The Unknown Christ of Hinduism,* have given new credence to Upadhyaya's ideas.

A. J. Appasamy provides another example. His use of the concept of *bhakti* (which he translated as "love"), based on the modified non-dualism of Ramanuja, led to a reduction of the Gospel, as for example in his treatment of the Johannine "I and my Father are one," which he limited to a moral union of love and obedience. Still another example is P. Chenchiah's (1886-1959) use of the philosophy of Shri Aurobindo and of the emergent evolution of Bergson. He found no place in his Aryan cultural framework for atonement or conversion or for the church. He left us with an Arian Christ and a truncated Gospel.

Existential contextualization also generally denies on philosophical grounds that God's self-revelation could be in any sense verbal and propositional. Many spokespersons limit revelation to man's reflection on and interpretation of God's acts in history. In place of an objective Word of God, they look to the immediate guidance of the Holy Spirit. For example, Lesslie Newbigin comments:

> Revelation is not the communication of a body of timeless truth which one has only to receive in order to know the whole mind of God. Revelation is rather the disclosure of the direction in which God is leading the world and his family. The stuff of the Bible is promise and fulfillment. . . . The work of the Spirit . . . is to lead the church to see all things . . . in their relation to Christ as head of all men and all things. He will lead the church into the fulness of truth as it is in Jesus, . . . (*The Good Shepherd,* Madras 1974, pp. 123 ff.)

I fear that it is this kind of fusion between the work of the Holy Spirit inspiring the biblical writers and the Holy Spirit illuminating the believing receivers that accounts for the open-endedness of existential contextualization.

Of course, all attempts at theologizing are culturally conditioned. In addition to Asian theologies we may think of Thomistic theology, Calvinistic theology, liberation theology, African theology, and so forth. The question is, on what basis are these attempts to be evaluated? I suggest that there is only one basis, namely, biblical theology.

PRINCIPLES OF DOGMATIC CONTEXTUALIZATION

Grammatico-historical exegesis involves a "distancing" between the reader and the biblical text which provides maximum objectivity in dogmatic contextualization. But "distancing" by itself is no guarantee against distortion. There also must be a determination on the part of the theologizers to place themselves "under" the authority of the Scriptures. But more than this, there must be a reliance on the Holy Spirit. As the Lausanne Covenant states, "He [the Holy Spirit] illumines the minds of God's people in every culture to perceive the truth freshly through their own eyes and thus discloses to the whole church ever more of the many-colored wisdom of God." Evangelicals standing within the tradition of Anselm's *credo ut intelligam* ("I believe so that I may understand"), believe that it is the Holy Spirit that enables them, through the Scriptures, to know the mind of God.

Form and content are key considerations in any contextualization of the Gospel. On the pre-understanding that the Bible is the inspired Word of God, we must ask, can the biblical form of the Gospel be changed without changing the content? For example, can we drop a term like "father" (referring to God) if we are dealing with a culture that does not relate well to the positive biblical content of that word? Or is this, and other biblical cultural forms, essential to the meaning of the Gospel?

To begin with, it must be affirmed that God was not at the mercy of human culture. On the contrary, God the Holy Spirit overshadowed the cultural forms through which he revealed his Word in such a manner that these forms conveyed what he intended. That is, the inspiration of the sacred text went *beyond* what is involved in contemporary contextualization efforts; it was more than a mere process of elimination and adaptation of pagan cultural forms. In his sovereignty God chose a Hebraic cultural form and transformed it over the centuries for his purpose, with the result that there is a supra-cultural character to his self-revelation. Although it might be argued that he could have chosen an Indian or Chinese cultural form, I suggest that, in that event, the nature of these cultures would have been different from what we know them to be today.

In other words, there is a uniqueness about biblical theology, so that only with qualification are we able to say that the way biblical writers used their cultural forms serves as a model for our own contextualizing of theology.

The biblical use of "father," in analogy of divine relationships and of God's relationship to man, is an example of a cultural form that is not dispensable. Granted the term carries different conceptual content in patriarchal, matriarchal, and Marxist cultures, and therefore the biblical form will need to be used with cultural sensitivity. But I am unable to accept the plea of those who say, for example, that the term is upsetting to Africans and should not be used in the African context. This fails to appreciate the unique value of the cultural form and God's sovereign choice of it to reveal his attributes to us.

Thus, there are "conceptual" forms found in Scripture which are ontologically essential to the message. On the other hand, there are other biblical forms, which might be called "symbolic," for which we are free to find substitutes if the originals are outside the experience of the receiving culture. Examples include "white as snow," and "small as a mustard seed." The process of contextualization will seek alternative forms in such cases, whereas with ontologically essential forms the receiving people will need to be introduced to and taught the content of the biblical forms.

This raises the question as to whether the "dynamic equivalence" principle, commonly employed in Bible translation work, is applicable in the task of contextualizing theology. A word of caution is in order here, lest we forget that cultures are not neutral. They are generally oriented to one or another religious world view which may be alien to the biblical world view, with the result that acceptable cultural forms may be lacking for communicating key biblical concepts. In the several Hindu cultures, for example, where are the indigenous forms that "have the same impact" as the original biblical concepts of creation, incarnation, resurrection of the body, substitutionary atonement, or grace? When the receptor cultures lack "dynamic equivalence" forms, it is essential that a "formal correspondence" form be explained and taught. Used properly, the "dynamic equivalence" approach aids communication, but the danger is that it may lead into the trap of cultural containment. Many contemporary cultural forms need to be judged rather than fulfilled. In the final analysis, the concept of the Trinity, or of Christ as the "lamb of God," can be conveyed to a Muslim or a Buddhist only by the Holy Spirit.

Sometimes it is possible for the Christian communicator to use a pagan cultural form and give it a new meaning which corresponds with biblical thought. Paul did this when he took *metamorphosis* ("transformation") out of its Hellenistic structure and set it in a Christological framework. On the other hand, Paul sometimes employed a word found in both Hellenistic and Jewish cultures and used it in the Hebrew sense when there were differences in its meaning. An example is *mysterion,* which in its Hellenistic setting belonged to a cultic practice in which worshipers received a secret initiation in order to be identified with the deity and the cosmic forces represented by it. Paul, however, used *mysterion* in the Jewish sense of a special revelation by God about his plan for the future (quite a contrast with the Hellenistic notion that to disclose a secret was to forfeit the power of the mystical identity!). Paul's carefulness is in contrast with those contextualized theologies which attempt to retain alien conceptual forms at the expense of the biblical revelation. To do so is to open the door to syncretism.

BIBLICAL FOUNDATIONS TOWARD A THEOLOGY OF GOSPEL AND CULTURE

The fundamental foundation of a theology of the Gospel and culture is the doctrine of God as the Creator-Savior. This can be viewed in two aspects: man's solidarity in Adam and man's solidarity in Christ.

Solidarity in Adam

The high point of the divine creation is man made in God's image. Three observations follow: (a) there is a relational continuity between man and God; (b) there is a relational discontinuity due to the Fall; and (c) there is a divine mystery between the sovereignty of God and the freedom of man in culture. We will consider each of these in turn.

1. The relational continuity between man and God: Man was created in the image of God (Gen. 1:26, 5:1, 9:6; 1 Cor. 11:7). The early church and the Eastern Orthodox churches have stressed the ontic or essential content of this image, usually in terms of reason, freedom, and personality. The Reformers and evangelical theologians have generally stressed that the image is primarily relational in terms of knowledge, love, righteousness, and holiness (Eph. 4:24; Col. 3:10).

There are a number of universal elements in this relational continuity which provide a positive basis for contextualization as the fulfillment of culture:

a. The obedient worship of the Creator. The chief end of man individually and corporately is to worship God and enjoy Him forever. All religious cultures have some concept of the Supreme Being in either personal or impersonal forms.

b. The choice of moral values. All cultures have a sense of justice based on an understanding of moral law and human responsibility. Conscience is either good or bad, depending on man's response to the ever-present call of the living God and the dictates of his moral law.

c. The power of rational communication. Man is able to formulate rational concepts and to communicate them to others. He has the capacity to distinguish truth from falsehood. He understands the law of contradiction as the chief law of logic. Thus, in every world view there is a basic logical coherence.

d. The gift of creativity. The Creator has given to mankind the capacity to create aesthetically pleasing forms of sculpture, art, music, and poetry, to engage in philosophical reflection, and through scientific knowledge to have dominion over creation itself. The ability to create and enjoy beauty and order in form and design is derived from the Creator himself.

e. The corporate basis of society. God created man, male and female, with the family as the basic relational unit of society (Gen. 2:18-24). Marriage and the family belong to the creation order and may be enjoyed by peoples of all cultures. God created man for the wider society of community and ordained the structures of government and property ownership for order and human well-being.

2. Relational discontinuity due to the Fall. If the foregoing elements of man's relation to God were the whole story, a theology of the Gospel and culture would be self-evident. The tragedy is that man not only seeks God but also rebels against him and selfishly demands his autonomy, creating tensions in human society that demand the judgment of God on culture. Therefore, we must speak of our discontinuity as well as our continuity in Adam.

The account of the Fall in Genesis 3 and man's oppression of man in Genesis 4 (along with the theological interpretation in Romans 1 and 2) offers an up-to-date microcosm of man in society. There is no part of man's constitution that is not corrupted by the Fall, and consequently no element of culture that does not abuse the *imago Dei.* The end is death (Gen. 2:17, 3:4, 14-17). Culture is never neutral, it is always a strange complex of truth and error, beauty and ugliness, good and evil, seeking God and rebelling against him. Elements in this relational discontinuity that evidence God's judgment on culture include:

a. The rebellion against the obedient worship of the Creator. Idolatry is the practice whereby man closes the gap between the Creator and the creature, creates deity in his own image or the image of the created world, and through the mystique of magical identity with creation placates or controls his man-made gods. Idolatry is the fundamental sin of man and of society (Rom. 1:18-32).

b. The abuse of the moral law. Justification by the law—as in first century Judaism or contemporary nominal Christianity—is in reality the abuse of the law. In Hindu culture, the principle of *Karma* is divorced from the law-giver and becomes an absolute principle and tyrannical master to which even the gods are subject. Forgiveness is thus impossible and any idea of substitutionary atonement absurd. Properly understood, the moral law would lead neither to self-righteousness nor to despairing resignation.

c. The perversion of man's rationality in communication. Man rationalizes his desires and experiences, and life ends in meaninglessness, silence, and despair. This is true both of the Hindu *advaitic* philosophy of non-dualism and of western existentialism and logical positivism. Francis Schaeffer in *The God Who Is There* has ably demonstrated this line of despair through philosophy to art to music and to the new theology.

d. The misuse of the gift of creativity. Man creates that which is ugly and cruel, wantonly despoils creation, and through the abuse of scientific knowledge hastens his self-destruction and that of the whole created world.

e. The fragmentation of the corporate basis of society. Man abuses sex and marriage and subverts institutions for his self-aggrandizement, creating disorder in the family and lawlessness in society. In the assertion of his autonomy man perpetuates acts of aggression and cruelty.

3. The divine mystery between the sovereignty of God and the freedom of man in culture: The living God is not a deistic God who stands indifferent before the arrogance of man in his rebellion. He is the sovereign God who loves the whole world and calls all men to himself in repentance and faith. He leaves no one without a knowledge of himself. Because of God's general revelation to mankind, sin is always sin against better knowledge; all are "without excuse" (Rom. 1:20). It is only the goodness of God that keeps man from self-destruction and from the total disintegration of society.

A clear distinction between general revelation and special revelation is necessary to develop an adequate theology of the Gospel and culture. Without a general revelation man would have no knowledge of God as Creator. Without special revelation he is ineffective and powerless to obey the moral law and find salvation. For example, although there are forms of propitiation and expiation in the earliest Hindu *Rig Vedas,* the Hindu sacrificial system offers neither hope nor power of salvation.

If the distinction between God's general revelation and special revelation is lost, salvation is generally reduced to the level of mystical identification of the creature with the Creator or to agnosticism. Theology becomes anthropology. Further, it leads to a confusion between salvation in Christ and God's sovereign action in history, as in liberation theology in which salvation history becomes the salvation of history, and "New China" theology (in which Chairman Mao is not merely "my servant" alongside Nebuchadnezzar and Cyrus but becomes "a savior" of his people and of the world).

Solidarity in Christ

The transformation of our solidarity in Adam into solidarity in Christ (Rom. 5:12-19) is the Christian hope for a new society and a new culture. Christ is the New Man, the beginning of a new humanity. In Christ, the image of God in man is restored, and in the lordship of Christ the Kingdom of God becomes visible. The Church, as the new community of the people of God, is the mystical body of Christ; when his lordship is explicitly acknowledged, it becomes the visible expression of Christ's reign. The vertical dimension of personal salvation in Christ is invalidated if it does not result in a renewal of horizontal relationship with one's neighbor, for as James argues, "faith without works is dead" (James 2:17, 20, 26). Therefore, while the Church is distinct from the world as a new called-out community, it cannot be separated from involvement in the world, but must always be light and salt to all men.

The Church's function in the world is to be God's agent to

plant new churches, to expand the boundaries of the Kingdom, and to demonstrate the reality of the new society. It is to be a model for the world to see, a covenant community pointing to the millennial reign of Christ and to the new heaven and the new earth in which righteousness dwells. Where the people of God are truly the realm of God's reign, they will progressively manifest a new life-style, bringing existing cultures into conformity with the image of Christ. While we cannot at present speak of a Christian culture (for the sinner is never wholly sanctified in this life and society never perfected), yet we must be bold to work towards new cultures which anticipate God's plan for society under the lordship of the resurrected Christ. The life-style of the universal Church ought to be a model for Christ-centered cultures which are both universal in their expression and at the same time rooted in the historical cultural situations of each particular people.

But God's involvement with the world extends beyond the Church. His sovereign action as the Creator-Savior extends to all men, for the creation mandate is for all men. God is at work in China today as he was in ancient Nineveh or Babylon. He restrains the evil actions of men, demonic principalities and powers, institutionalized social and political evils, and prepares communities to receive the Gospel. At the Cross these powers were dethroned, but their final destruction awaits the return of Christ. Therefore the Church has political, economic, and social responsibilities under the hand of God. It ought to be the conscience of society, the inspiration for human justice, and a testimony to the love of God for all men. Thus, the Church in India, small and weak as it is, is the ultimate hope of a better "design for living" for the whole of Indian society.

THE PROPHETIC PRINCIPLE
IN CULTURAL TRANSFORMATION

The ministry of the prophet of the Lord in biblical times is the key to understanding the role of the Gospel in contemporary cultures. The prophetic principle is the opposite of the accommodating syncretistic principle which seeks to harmonize man in society with the forces of nature and the spirit world.

The prophetic principle runs throughout biblical history,

separating Israel into "my people" and "not my people" (Exod. 3:7, 6:7). Israel was "not my people" in times when they were overconfident of their distinctive kingship and nationhood. When they were victorious over their enemies and in full possession of their land, they also tended to compromise their faith with elements from the surrounding pagan cultures of Canaan and Assyria, assimilating pagan religious ideas and customs and entering into mixed marriages.

Israel was "my people" when they were conscious that Yahweh was their King and lived by their covenant promises in obedience to the Law. In times of national weakness and vulnerability to external oppression, they tended to be more conscious of their calling to suffering servanthood and the intrusion of pagan influences upon their faith was minimal. At such times the prophet's "thus saith the Lord" restrained the conditioning influence of pagan culture and disciplined the people in obedience to the Word of God.

True dogmatic contextualization is always reforming; it is the opposite of a pan-en-theism which is man's natural tendency to synthesize creation and redemption. The prophets called for reformation of belief, worship and fidelity to the Law, including an appeal for social and economic justice. The prophetic voice was one of promise and fulfillment, of judgment and hope. By contrast, present-day "existential contextualization" efforts often lack the eschatological note of the return of Christ, the resurrection of all from the dead, the final judgment, and the promise of a new earth and a new heaven.

It is only a church that is sure of its calling as a covenant community of faith and that is obedient as God's servant for mission and world evangelization that will be able to adapt and transform the symbolic forms of other cultures, giving them new meaning so that they become the bearers of the Word of God. Such a church need not fear syncretism or loss of evangelistic motivation through involvement in society. The free exercise of the prophetic word of the Lord will be its sure basis for faithful dogmatic contextualization. The prophetic principle brings about cultural transformation in four ways:

a. The prophet calls for a de-culturalization within the believing community of the accretions to biblical faith. In the patriarchal period we see how Abraham and his descendants were progressively de-cultural-ized from their Mesopotamian culture as nomads in the promised land, during captivity in Egypt and in the wilderness journeyings. Much of Israel's subsequent history is written from the point of view of the call for the destruction of the Baalization of Yahweh-worship. The Exile was another period of de-culturalization in which the covenant community was purified of idolatrous influences. Jesus Christ, himself, was a severe critic of the Judaism of his day.

In western culture the Gospel is distorted by accommodation to Platonic and Aristotelian philosophy, by humanistic Enlighten-ment influences, and by egalitarian and Marxist ideologies. In Asia and Africa, contextualization of the believing community must include the de-culturalization not only of these western accre-tions but also of indigenous concepts that are contrary to the Word of God.

b. The prophet of the Lord also judges and condemns the wider com-munity in regard to those elements of culture that are contrary to the Word of God. Idolatry, pagan sexual morals, and corrupt political and eco-nomic practices come under the judgment of the prophets from Moses to John the Baptist. Similarly, in the contextualization of the Gospel in Indian cultures the prophet of the Lord will condemn such evils as idolatry, tantric philosophies of ritualistic sex, caste distinctions, unjust dowries, and so forth.

c. The prophet of the Lord is God's agent to recreate and transform cultural elements that are consistent with God's revelation and which may be adapted and utilized in the service of the Kingdom. The Gospel fulfills as well as destroys. For example, the adaptation of "meditation" in worship and the transforming of the Hindu "extended family" are Indian cultural forms that find a new level of fulfillment in the Gospel. Similarly, there are elements of Islamic culture and wor-ship that are "convertible."

d. The Gospel brings with it new elements in culture. For example, many Third World cultures lack anything like the biblical mes-sianic hope. This has to be supplied as new teaching. Some Asian cultures interpret sin only in terms of "shame." The biblical con-cept of guilt, atonement, and forgiveness are new elements which the Gospel brings to these situations. Similarly, the biblical experi-ence of the grace of God is distinctive because it flows from a unique Cross. The hope of the resurrection, as distinct from the common Asian view of immortality, is another example with profound implications for one's attitudes to the body.

Only as we assert the proper place of ''Thus saith the Lord,'' in the spirit of dogmatic contextualization, can we be true to the normative Word of God and effective in communicating the Good News to those who live in darkness.

5. Hermeneutics and Culture
—A Theological Perspective

by C. René Padilla

C. RENÉ PADILLA *is director of Ediciones Cereteza, Buenos Aires, Argentina, associated with the International Fellowship of Evangelical Students. He is editor of* The New Face of Evangelicalism, *an international symposium on the Lausanne Covenant.*

THE WORD OF GOD WAS GIVEN TO BRING THE lives of God's people into conformity with the will of God. Between the written Word and its appropriation by believers lies the process of interpretation, or hermeneutics. For each of us, the process of arriving at the meaning of Scripture is not only highly shaped by who we are as individuals but also by various social forces, patterns, and ideals of our particular culture and our particular historical situation. ("Culture" is used in this paper in a comprehensive way to include, not only technical skills, life-style, attitudes, and values of a people, but also their thought patterns, cognitive processes, and ways of learning, all of which ultimately express a religious commitment.)

One of the most common approaches to interpretation is what may be called the "intuitive" approach. An example is found in a letter written a century ago by J. Hudson Taylor, founder of the China Inland Mission. In it he reveals his "spiritual secret," based on Jesus' words according to John 7:37: "If any man thirst, let him come unto me and drink." Here is how Taylor read and applied this text:

> What, can Jesus meet my need? Yes, and more than meet it. . . . He not only promises me drink to alleviate my thirst. . . . "From within him shall flow rivers"—rivers like the mighty Yangtze, ever deep, ever full. In times of drought brooks may fail, often do, canals may be pumped dry, often are, but the Yangtze never. Always a mighty stream, always flowing deep and irresistible!

In this commentary Taylor is not particularly concerned to explore the original setting of the text (the Festival of Booths in first-century Jerusalem) or to ask how the original listeners or readers understood it. Nor does he pause to ask what influences in his own contemporary setting are likely to influence his reading. Instead, he joins the many Christians who assume that as long as the Bible is available in their own language, they have direct access to the meaning of the ancient text. This approach, with its emphasis on immediate personal application, is found in many of the older commentaries and in contemporary popular preaching and devotional literature.

In contrast with this is the "scientific" approach, which employs the tools of literary criticism, historical and anthropological studies, linguistics, and so forth. It is adopted by a large majority of biblical scholars, and by educated Christians interested in serious Bible study (as contrasted with mere Bible reading). It appreciates the need for understanding the original context, but it may be weak on personal application (especially as practiced by scholars).

A serious problem of both methods is that they tend to be naive about the way contemporary social, economic, and political factors and other cultural forces affect the interpretive process.

A third approach is the "contextual" approach. To the strengths of the intuitive and scientific methods the contextual approach adds an appreciation of the role of today's world in conditioning the way contemporary readers are likely to "hear" and understand the text.

The Word of God originated in a particular historical context—the Hebrew and Graeco-Roman world. Indeed, the Word can be understood and appropriated only as it becomes "flesh" in a specific historical situation with all its particular cultural forms. The challenge of hermeneutics is to transpose the message from its original historical context into the context of present day readers so as to produce the same kind of impact on their lives as it did on the original hearers or readers.

Thus, hermeneutics and the historical situation are strongly linked. Without a sufficient awareness of the historical factors, the faith of the hearers of the Gospel will tend to degenerate into a "culture-Christianity" which serves unredeemed cultural forces rather than the living God. The confusion of the Gospel with "culture-Christianity" has been frequent in western-based missionary work and is one of the greatest problems affecting the worldwide church today. The solution can come only through a recognition of the role that the historical context plays in both the understanding and communication of the biblical message.

TRADITIONAL HERMENEUTICS

In the process of developing a sound contextual hermeneutic, the strengths and weaknesses of the more traditional approaches must be appreciated.

The unspoken assumption of the intuitive model is that the situation of the contemporary reader largely coincides with the situation represented by the original text. The process of interpretation is thought to be rather straightforward and direct (diagram 1).

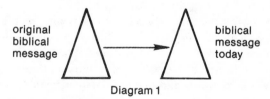

original
biblical
message

biblical
message
today

Diagram 1

This approach brings out three elements essential to sound biblical hermeneutics. First, it clearly assumes that Scripture is meant for common people and is not the domain of trained theologians only. (Was it not the rediscovery of this truth that led the sixteenth-century Reformers to translate and circulate the Bible in the vernacular?) Second, it highlights the role of the Holy Spirit in illuminating the meaning of the Scripture for the believers. Third, it emphasizes that the purpose of Scripture is not merely to lead readers to an intellectual apprehension of truth but to elicit a conscious submission to the Word of God speaking in Scripture. These elements are of particular importance at a time when, as Robert J. Blaikie protests, "Only as meditated through the scholarly priesthood of 'Biblical Critics' can ordinary people receive the truth of God's Word from the Bible!" *(Secular Christianity and the God Who Acts,* Hodder and Stoughton, p. 27).

On the other hand, the intuitive approach can easily lead to allegorizations in which the original meaning of the text is lost. Someone has said that allegory is the son of piety. The fantastic interpretations by such reputable theologians as Origen and Augustine, Luther and Calvin, are more or less sophisticated illustrations of a piety-inspired approach to the Bible. The question to be posed to this approach is whether the appropriation of the biblical message is possible without doing violence to the text.

The scientific approach also has its merits and defects. Anyone with even a superficial understanding of the role of history in shaping the biblical revelation will appreciate the importance of linguistic and historical studies for the interpretation of Scripture. The raw material of theology is not abstract, timeless concepts which may be simply lifted out of Scripture, but rather a message relative to historical events, a message whose narration and interpretation are colored by the Semitic and Graeco-Roman cultures of the biblical authors. One of the basic tasks of interpretation, therefore, is the construction of a bridge between the modern readers or hearers and the biblical authors by means of the historical method. Thus the *Sitz im Leben* ("life situation") of the biblical authors can be reconstructed, and the interpreters, by means of grammatico-historical exegesis, can extract those normative (though not exhaustive) and universal elements which the ancient text conveys. These elements may then be applied to the modern readers or hearers (though, among scholars, this latter aspect of the task is generally thought to fall outside the field of biblical scholarship and is left to preachers and devotional writers). This view of the interpretive process is represented in diagram 2.

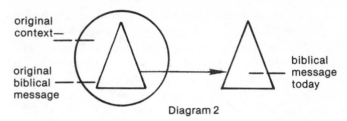

Diagram 2

This approach throws into relief the historical nature of biblical revelation. In a way, it widens the gulf between the Bible and modern readers or hearers. In so doing, however, it witnesses to the fact that the Word of God today has to do with the Word of God which *was* spoken in ancient times by the prophets and apostles. Unless modern interpreters allow the text to speak out of its original situation, they have no basis for claiming that their message is continuous with the message recorded in Scripture.

The problem with the scientific approach is, first, that it assumes that the hermeneutical task can be limited to defining the original meaning of the text, leaving to others its present application. Second, it assumes that the interpreters can achieve an "objectivity" which is neither possible nor desirable. It is not possible, because contemporary interpreters are stamped with the imprint of their particular time and place as surely as is the ancient text, and therefore they inevitably come to the text with historically conditioned presuppositions that color their exegesis. It is not desirable, because the Bible can only be properly understood as it is read with a *participatory involvement* which allows it to speak into one's own situation. Ultimately, if the text written in the past does not strike home in the present it has not been understood.

THE CONTEXTUAL APPROACH
AND THE HERMENEUTICAL CIRCLE

How can the chasm between the past and the present be bridged? An answer is found in the contextual approach, which combines insights derived from classical hermeneutics with insights derived from the modern hermeneutical debate.

In the contextual approach both the context of the ancient text and the context of the modern reader are given due weight (diagram 3).

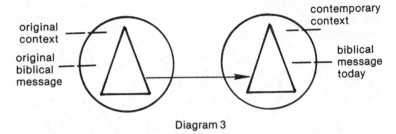

Diagram 3

The diagram emphasizes the importance of culture to the biblical message in both its original and contemporary forms. That is, there is no such thing as a biblical message detached from a particular cultural context.

However, contrary to the diagram, the interpretive process is not a simple one-way process. For whenever interpreters approach a particular biblical text they can do so only from their own perspective. This gives rise to a complex, dynamic two-way interpretive process depicted as a "hermeneutical circle," in which interpreters and text are mutually engaged. The dynamic interplay will be seen more clearly if we first examine the four elements of the circle: (1) the interpreters' historical situation; (2) the interpreters' world-and-life view; (3) Scripture; and (4) theology.

1. The interpreters' historical situation. Interpreters do not live in a vacuum. They live in concrete historical situations, in particular cultures. From their cultures they derive not only their language but also patterns of thought and conduct, methods of learning, emotional reactions, values, interests, and goals. If God's Word is to reach them, it must do so in terms of their own culture or not at all.

This is clear from the Incarnation itself. God did not reveal himself by shouting from heaven but by speaking from within a concrete human situation: he became present as a man among men, in Jesus, a first-century Jew! This unmistakably demonstrates God's intention to make his Word known from within a concrete human situation. Because of the very nature of God's Word, we can only know this Word as a message contextualized in a particular situation.

Yet our contemporary understanding of the biblical message is always relative to our situation or culture. There is no guarantee that it will completely coincide with the message in its original context. No culture as a whole reflects the purpose of God; in all cultures there are elements which conspire against the understanding of God's Word. In more technical language, it may be said that the interpreters' "pre-understanding" tends to prevent their interpretation from being a true reflection of the biblical message. If this is recognized, it follows that every interpretation is subject to correction and refinement; there is always a need for safeguards against syncretism, that is, cultural distortions of the Word of God. Syncretism occurs whenever there is accommodation of the Gospel to premises or values prevalent in the culture which are incongruent with the biblical message.

On the other hand, every culture possesses positive elements, favorable to the understanding of the Gospel. This makes possible a certain approach to Scripture which brings to light aspects of the message which in other cultures remain less visible or even hidden. The same cultural differences that hinder intercultural communication turn out to be an asset to the understanding of the many-sided wisdom of God; they serve as channels to aspects of God's Word which can be best seen from within a particular context.

Eugene Rubingh illustrates this in his article "The African Shape of the Gospel" (*His* Magazine, October 1972, pp. 9 ff.), showing that the "primal vision" characteristic of African culture places the African in a privileged position to understand that "each is part of all, and the Kingdom embraces every facet, every moment, every act."

The historical situation also contributes to the interpretive process by posing questions which demand scriptural answers. It is with these culturally rooted questions that theology has to deal. In many ways, it is this inquiry, together with the scriptural answers, that is the crucial element in the contextual approach.

Thus, the hermeneutical task requires an understanding of the current concrete situation as much as an understanding of Scripture. No transposition of the biblical message is possible unless the interpreters are familiar with the frame of reference within which the message is to become meaningful. There is, therefore, a place for auxiliary sciences such as sociology and anthropology which can enable interpreters to define more precisely the horizons of their situation, even as linguistic, textual, and historical studies can help them in their comprehension of the text and its original context. The deeper and richer their understandings of the contemporary situation, the deeper and richer will be the questions they ask of the Bible and the answers they find in it.

2. *The interpreters' world-and-life view.* We have already pointed out that interpreters approach Scripture from their particular perspectives. They have their own world-and-life view, their own way of apprehending reality, in a great measure derived from their historical situations. This imposes certain limits but also enables them to see reality as a coherent whole. Whether or not they are conscious of it, this world-and-life view, which is religiously determined, lies behind all their activities and colors their understanding of reality in a definite way. As Peter Berger has put it, ''Every 'definition of the situation' implies specific theoretical presuppositions, a frame of reference, in the last resort a view of reality'' (*Pyramids of Sacrifice,* Doubleday, p. 30). We can extend this observation to biblical hermeneutics and say that every interpretation of the text implies a world-and-life view.

Western theology generally has been unaware of the extent to which it is affected by the materialistic and mechanistic world-and-life view. It is only natural, for instance, that those who accept the modern ''scientific'' view—which assumes a closed universe where everything can be explained on the basis of natural causes—will have difficulty taking the Bible at face value whenever it points to a spirit-world or to miracles. Western theology, therefore, greatly needs the corrective provided by Scripture in its emphasis on a personal Creator who acts purposefully in and through history; on creation as totally dependent upon God; on man as the ''image of God,'' affected by sin and redemption. Such elements are the substance of the biblical world-and-life view apart from which there can be no proper understanding either of reality or of Scripture. It may well be that what prevents westerners from entering in to the ''strange world of the Bible'' is not its obsolete world-and-life view but their own secularistic and unwarranted assumption with regard to the powers of reason!

3. *Scripture.* Hermeneutics has to do with a dialogue between Scripture and the contemporary historical context. Its purpose is to transpose the bibilical message from its original context into a

particular twentieth-century situation. Its basic assumption is that the God who spoke in the past and whose Word was recorded in the Bible continues to speak today to all mankind in Scripture.

Although the illumination of the Spirit is indispensable in the interpretive process, from one point of view the Bible must be read "like any other book." This means that the interpreters have to take seriously that they face an ancient text with its own historical horizons. Their task is to let the text speak, whether they agree with it or not, and this demands that they understand what the text meant in its original situation. In James Smart's words,

> All interpretation must have as its first step the hearing of the text with exactly the shade of meaning that it had when it was first spoken or written. First the words must be allowed to have the distinctive meaning that their author placed upon them, being read within the context of his other words. Then each word has to be studied in the context of the time in order to determine . . . what meaning it would have for those to whom it was addressed. . . . The religious, cultural and social background is of the greatest importance in penetrating through the words to the mind of the author. . . . The omission of any of these disciplines is a sign of lack of respect not only for the text and its author but also for the subject matter with which it deals. (*The Interpretation of Scripture,* SCM, p. 33)

It has been argued, however, that the approach described in this quotation, known as the grammatico-historical approach, is itself typically western and consequently not binding upon non-western cultures. After all, it is said, a particular hermeneutic is itself dependent upon presuppositions which are culturally determined; it must not be regarded as having universal validity.

What are we to say to this?

First, no interpreters, regardless of their culture, are free to make the text say whatever they want it to say. Their task is to let the text speak for itself, and to that end they inevitably have to engage with the horizons of the text via literary context, grammar, history, and so on.

Second, western theology has not been characterized by a consistent use of the grammatico-historical approach in order to let the Bible speak. Rather a dogmatic approach has been the dominating factor, by which competing theological systems have muted Scripture. Abstract conceptualization patterned on Greek philosophy have gone hand in hand with allegorizations and typologies. Even sophisticated theologians, losing sight of the historical nature of revelation, have produced capricious literary or homiletical exercises. A case in point is Karl Barth's "Christological" interpretation of Genesis 2 (*Dogmatics* III, 1, pp. 367 ff.).

Third, some point to the New Testament use of the Old as legitimizing intuitive approaches and minimizing the importance of the grammatico-historical approach. But it can hardly be claimed that the New Testament writers were not interested in the literal meaning of Old Testament Scripture. Though important questions about the New Testament's use of the Old remain to be answered, there is little basis for the idea that the New Testament specializes in highly imaginative exegesis, similar to that of rabbinic Judaism. Even in Paul's case, despite his rabbinic training, there is such restraint in the use of allegory, for instance, that it can hardly pass unnoticed. As James Smart has put it, "The removal of all instances of allegory from his [Paul's] writings would not change the structure of his theology. This surely is the decisive test" (*Interpretation,* p. 30).

The effort to let Scripture speak without imposing upon it a ready-made interpretation is a hermeneutical task binding upon all interpreters, whatever their culture. This does not mean, of course, that total objectivity is possible. But unless objectivity is set as a goal, the whole interpretive process is condemned to failure from the start.

Objectivity, however, must not be confused with neutrality. To read the Bible "like any other book" is not only to take seriously the literary and historical aspects of Scripture but also to read it from the perspective of faith. That is, since any book should be read in the light of the purpose for which it was written, and since the Bible was written that God may speak in and through it, it follows that the Bible should be read with an attitude of openness to God's Word, with a view to conscientious response. The understanding and appropriation of the biblical message are two aspects of an indivisible whole—the *comprehension* of the Word of God.

4. Theology. From several perspectives, it is evident that culture plays a decisive role in the formulation of theology, theology being the outcome of interpretation. First, to be true to the incarnational principle it must take root in a particular situation. Second, if the Word of God is to be more than an abstraction, theology must break into the raw material of life in the historical context. It must respond to the critical questions raised in each particular time and place. Only thus can the Word be experienced concretely, in all its dimensions, and employed as the criterion by which all cultural values and practices are evaluated. Third, if the Word of God is to receive an intelligent response when it is proclaimed, it must be effectively communicated, and that means finding authentic points of contact between the message and the concrete situation. If the proclamation is to be more than an invitation to mere intellectual assent, it must include the contextualization of the Word as one of its essential marks. Otherwise, it will produce spurious conversions or negative response which reflect not so much a rejection of the Word as faulty communication.

Of course, the hermeneutical task is not limited to dealing with the questions raised within the historical context; it must also communicate the questions that the Word of God poses to the situation. Only when the whole situation is placed under the Word of judgment and grace is the interpretive process complete.

Given these considerations, it is clear that theology cannot be reduced to the repetition of doctrinal formulations borrowed from other latitudes. To be valid and appropriate, it must reflect the merging of the horizons of the historical situation and the horizons of the text. It will be relevant to the extent that it is expressed in symbols and thought forms which are part of the culture to which it is addressed, and to the extent that it responds to the questions and concerns which are raised in that context. It will be faithful to the Word of God to the extent that it is based on Scripture and demonstrates the Spirit-given power to accomplish God's purpose. The same Spirit who inspired Scripture in the past is active today to make it God's personal Word in a concrete historical situation.

Daniel von Allmen has suggested that the pages of the New Testament itself bear witness to this process, as the early Christians, dispersed by persecution from Palestine, "undertook the work of evangelism and tackled the Greeks on their own ground. It was they who, on the one hand, began to adapt into Greek the tradition that gave birth to the Gospels, and who, on the other hand, preached the good news for the first time in Greek" ("The Birth of Theology," *International Review of Mission,* January 1975). They did not consciously set out to "do theology," but simply to transcribe the Gospel faithfully into pagan contexts. Following this initial effort came the word of the poets—Greek-speaking Christians who gave expression to the faith received, not in a systematically worked theology, but by singing the work which God had done for them. According to von Allmen, here is the origin of a number of hymns quoted by the New Testament writers, particularly the one in Philippians 2:6-11. After the poets, came the theologians with the twofold function of insuring that the new ways of expressing the faith corresponded to apostolic doctrine and showing that all theological statements must be set in relation to the heart of the Christian faith, that is, the universal lordship of Jesus Christ.

In other words, the driving force in the contextualization of the Gospel in apostolic times was the primitive church's obedience to God's call to mission. What is needed today, says von Allmen, is missionaries like the Hellenists, who "did not set out with a theological intention," and poets like the authors of the hymns quoted in the New Testament, who "were not deliberately looking for an original expression of their faith," and theologians like Paul, who did not set out to "do theology." Concludes von Allmen, "The only object of research which is allowed, and indeed commended, is the kingdom of God in Jesus Christ (cf. Matt. 6:33). And theology, with all the other things, will be added unto us."

I would only add the observation that neither the proclamation of the Gospel nor the worship of God is possible without "theology," however unsystematic and implicit it may be. In other words, the Hellenistic missionaries and poets were *also theologians*—certainly not dogmaticians, but proclaimers and singers of a living theology through which they expressed the Word of God in a new cultural context. With this qualification, von Allmen's conclusion stands—the way in which Christianity was Hellenized in the first century sets the pattern for producing contextualized theology today.

DYNAMICS OF THE HERMENEUTICAL CIRCLE

The aim of the interpretive process is the transformation of the people of God within their concrete situation. To show adequately the way in which this is accomplished through the interaction of the elements of the hermeneutical circle would require a motion picture rather than a static drawing. In general, a change in the situation of the interpreters (including their culture) brings about a change in their comprehension of Scripture, while a change in their comprehension of Scripture in turn reverberates in their situation. Thus, the contextual approach to the interpretation of Scripture involves a dialogue between the historical situation and Scripture, a dialogue in which the interpreters approach Scripture with a particular perspective (their world-and-life view) and approach their situation with a particular comprehension of the Word of God (their theology), as indicated in diagram 4.

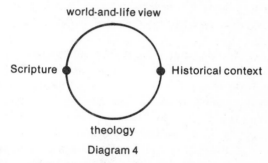

Diagram 4

We begin the hermeneutical process by analyzing our situation, listening to the questions raised within it. Then we come to Scripture asking, "What does God say through Scripture regarding this particular problem?" The way we formulate our questions will depend, of course, on our world-and-life view; that is, the historical situation can only approach Scripture through the current world-and-life view of the interpreters. Lack of a good understanding of the real issues involved in living in a particular situation will be reflected in inadequate or misdirected questions, and this will hinder our understanding of the relevance of the biblical message to that situation. Scripture does not readily answer questions which are not posed to it! Asking the wrong or peripheral questions will result in a theology focused on questions no one is asking, while the issues that urgently need biblical direction are ignored.

On the other hand, the better our understanding of the real issues in our context, the better will be the questions which we address to Scripture. This makes possible new readings of Scripture in which the implications of its message for our situation will be more fully uncovered. If it is true that Scripture illuminates life, it is also true that life illuminates Scripture.

As the answers of Scripture come to light, the initial questions which arose in our concrete situation may have to be reformulated to reflect the biblical perspective more adequately. The content of theology, therefore, includes not only answers to specific questions raised by the situation but also questions which the text itself poses to the situation. (Thus, the grammatico-historical approach to Scripture—in which every effort is made to let Scripture speak for itself—is seen to be the logical consequence of the view in which Scripture is regarded as authoritative for faith and practice.)

The deeper and richer our comprehension of the biblical text, the deeper and richer will be our understanding of the historical context (including the issues that yet have to be faced) and of the meaning of Christian obedience in that particular context. The possiblity is thus open for changes in our world-and-life view and consequently for a more adequate understanding and appropriation of the biblical message. For the biblical text, approached from a more congenial world-and-life view, and addressed with deeper and richer questions, will be found to speak more plainly and fully. Our theology, in turn, will be more relevant and responsive to the burning issues which we have to face in the receptor culture.

Hermeneutics may thus be conceived as having a spiral structure in which, under the guidance of the Holy Spirit, a richer and deeper understanding of the Bible leads to a greater understanding of the receptor culture, and a deeper and richer understanding of the receptor culture leads to a greater comprehension of the biblical message from within the receptor culture. As interpreters, we are involved in a continuous mutual engagement between the horizons of the text and the horizons of our culture. Neither our understanding of the text nor our understanding of our concrete situation is adequate unless both constantly interact and are mutually corrected. As that is done, we progressively approach Scripture with the right questions from the right perspective, and our theology is in turn more biblical and more relevant to the situation. We go from the receptor culture through our (increasingly biblical) world-and-life view to Scripture, and from Scripture through our (increasingly relevant) theology to the receptor culture, always striving for a merging of our own horizons with those of Scripture.

THE CONTEXTUALIZATION OF THE GOSPEL

The present situation of the church in many parts of the world provides plenty of evidence to show that all too often the attempt has been made to evangelize without seriously facing the hermeneutical task. Western missionaries have often assumed that their task is simply to extract the message directly from the biblical text and to transmit it to hearers in the "mission field" with no consideration of the role of culture in the whole interpretive process. This follows a simplistic pattern which does not fit reality (diagram 5).

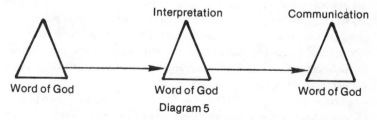

Diagram 5

This simplistic approach to evangelism has frequently gone hand in hand with a western version of Christianity which combines biblical elements with elements of Greek philosophy and of the European-American heritage and places an unbalanced emphasis on the numerical growth of the church. As a result, in many parts of the world Christianity is regarded as an ethnic religion— the white man's religion. The Gospel has a foreign sound, or no sound at all, in relation to many of the dreams and anxieties, problems and questions, values and customs of people. The Word of God is reduced to a message that touches life only on a tangent.

When this problem is fully appreciated, one can hardly disagree with Wibert R. Shenk's affirmation, that "in spite of some surface signs of success, the modern missionary movement has failed at a profound level until today. The church which is the product of this historic movement suffers seriously from spiritual and intellectual rootlessness" ("Theology and the Missionary Task," *Missiology,* July 1973).

It would be easy to illustrate the theological dependence of the younger churches on the older churches, which is as real and as damaging as the economic dependence that characterizes the "underdeveloped" countries! Suffice it to mention that an amazing quantity of Christian literature published in these countries consists of translations from English (ranging from "eschatology-fiction" to "how-to-enjoy-sex" manuals) and that in a number of theological institutions the curriculum is a xeroxed copy of the curriculum used at similar institutions in the United States.

The urgent need everywhere is for a new reading of the Gospel *from within* each particular historical situation, under the guidance of the Holy Spirit. The contextualization of the Gospel will not consist of an adaptation of an existing theology to a particular culture. It will not be aided by a benevolent missionary paternalism intended to help the "native" to select cultural elements which may be regarded as positive. It can only be the result of a new, open-ended reading of Scripture with a hermeneutic in which Gospel and culture become mutually engaged in a dialogue whose purpose is to place the church under the lordship of Jesus Christ in its historical situation.

It is only as the Word of God becomes "flesh" in the people of God that the Gospel takes shape within culture. According to God's purpose, the Gospel is never to be merely a message in words but a message incarnate in his church and, through it, in culture. The contextualization of the Gospel demands the contextualization of the church, which is God's instrument of the manifestation of Christ's presence among the nations of the earth.

6. Hermeneutics and Culture
—An Anthropological Perspective

by Charles R. Taber

CHARLES R. TABER *has worked in Central and West Africa, first as a missionary and later as a United Bible Societies translation consultant. He is editor of the missiological journal* Gospel in Context, *and former editor of* Practical Anthropology, *a pioneer missions journal of applied anthropology.*

THE QUESTION I WISH TO ADDRESS IS EASY to state, but hard to answer. It is simply this: given the Scriptures, how does one go about discovering what they mean?

Notice that this question will not go away no matter what view one holds about inspiration. Even if we believed—what few if any Christians believe—that the Bible was dictated to the writers word for word by the Holy Spirit, and even if we had the original biblical writings in our hands, we would still be faced with texts in three very human languages: Hebrew, Aramaic, and Greek. They would still be texts composed of sections, paragraphs, sentences, clauses, phrases, and words put together according to the rules of those three languages. They would still be texts written originally to people whose cultural, social, and historical contexts were very different from ours. We would still, therefore, be faced with the question of finding from those texts what God wants *us* to know and feel and be and do.

Unfortunately, the whole history of Christian interpretation of the Bible shows that there is no such thing as guaranteed, infallible passage of information from the Bible to human minds. If there were, Christians equally competent and honest and committed would come to identical interpretations; but as we can clearly see, they do not. For reasons which seemed good to God, and which we are therefore bound to accept, he did not choose, when he gave us the Holy Spirit to help us understand the Bible, to bypass normal human approaches to interpreting messages, but to use them. And these approaches are conditioned, colored, and limited by our human finiteness, our human sinfulness, and our human cultural, social, and historical contexts.

It is my purpose, then, to explore some of the principal aspects of the processes by which people interpret messages, and to see how these can apply to our own efforts to understand and obey the Scriptures.

A MODEL OF INTERPRETATION AND COMMUNICATION

This paper is based on a model from communication science, enriched with concepts from anthropology and linguistics. According to this model, a speaker or writer (called a Source, or S) formulates a message (M), which a hearer or reader (called a Receptor, or R) interprets. S and R may consist of one person each, or of many. Some messages are spoken, as were those of most of the Old Testament prophets and the earliest Christian witnesses; and some are written texts, which is what we have today from the original witnesses.

Every message contains both explicit information and implicit information. Explicit information is spelled out in the words and sentences of the M. Implicit information is not spelled out because S relies on R to supply it. This implicit information is necessary for the understanding of the M, and if R does not or cannot supply it, he will misunderstand M.

Any information which S and R share can potentially be left implicit; in fact, leaving information implicit is an important factor in the feeling of "we-ness" which exists between an S and an R who are close, and also a means of making M obscure to outsiders. If S makes information explicit which should be left implicit, R may well feel that S is pushing him away or questioning his intelligence. (Think of how impatiently we say "I know" when someone belabors the obvious.)

In terms of the Bible, many of the difficulties we have in interpreting II Corinthians are caused by the fact that Paul left so much implicit which the original readers knew but which we do not. This example clearly underlines the difference between implicit information, which is necessary for understanding, and omitted information, which is not. If implicit information is lost, M is mutilated.

BASIC DEFINITIONS AND CONCEPTS

With this foundation laid, we can now explore the topic of hermeneutics which is the discipline that guides our efforts at interpreting texts. We may begin by discussing several key terms and concepts.

1. *Interpretation* is the process by which R assigns a meaning to M. Notice that I have purposely said "*a* meaning," leaving M indefinite, since it often happens that the meaning R assigns is not the one intended by S.

2. *Meaning* is a most difficult and complicated concept. It involves in a very inclusive way all that R thinks M intends him to do.

To begin with, he may see that if he believes the information contained in M, he will need to add to or to change some of his previous beliefs. If this involves only the addition of facts to his knowledge, R may accept it without difficulty. But if R thinks M will require him to change his whole world view, he may well have second thoughts or even reject M. Or, if his existing world view seems to him to be no longer satisfactory, he may accept the new one offered in M.

R, on the other hand, may see in M a challenge to his ordinary patterns of behavior; if he accepts M, he will have to conduct himself differently. Again, if the change is merely a matter of superficial social custom, he may or may not accept it readily, depending on what advantage he sees in the proposed change. But if M seems to require a radical shift in his ethical framework, it will take a much deeper motive to lead him to accept it.

Finally, R may see that if he accepts M, it will demand of him a total shift of his life commitment and allegiance; or, as Paul put it, a turning to God from idols (1 Thess. 1:9). In fact, this radical redirecting of one's whole life is the central purpose of the Gospel of Jesus Christ; it is only when people have been transformed that the Gospel has reached its goal. The other two kinds of responses mentioned above—adding information and changing behavior—are important, but only as they relate to this one. Just to cram people's heads with facts is not in itself helpful; and changing a set of behavior patterns is in itself just legalism.

Another way of looking at *meaning* is to distinguish between the use of a word simply *to point to* something (which I call *reference*) and the use of a word *to say something about it* (which I call *signification*). For example, "Jimmy Carter" and "the President of the United States" have, right now, the same reference; that is, they both point to the same human being. But one label is a proper name which has no signification (except that "Jimmy" is a male name), while the other has a very full signification, since it relates to and contrasts with the significations of other words like "dictator," "king," "prime minister," and so on. Both reference and signification must be kept straight if we are to understand the Bible. When the apostles said that Jesus was the Messiah (Christ in Greek), it was crucial that their hearers realize (a) what the concept Messiah or Christ signified, and (b) that it was applicable to a particular human being from Nazareth named Jesus.

That aspect of meaning which I have called signification can be rigorously analyzed by means of certain linguistic techniques which have been developed in the last few decades (see Taber 1976; Nida 1975a, 1975b).

3. In interpreting M, R obviously makes use of his full knowledge of the meanings of the words and sentences he finds there. It is at this level that good lexicons and grammars of the biblical languages can help us. But R makes use of a great deal more than his knowledge of the language, and it is to this that we now turn.

In the first place, he depends on his world view, his general knowledge, his existing beliefs, his values, and his attitudes. A few years ago, when I was working in Khartoum with some Sudanese Christians who were translating the Old Testament into various Nilotic languages, I found that they all found it very hard to understand and translate the early chapters of Genesis. It turned out that the beliefs they already held, which were enshrined in the words of their languages, gave them no clues to help them understand such terms as "firmament," "windows of heaven," or "great deep." Even when, with the help of diagrams, they finally were able to make out what Genesis 1 was saying, they found it almost impossible to express in their languages. This kind of difference between the world of S and the world of R leads to very serious misunderstandings unless pains are taken to bridge the gap.

In the second place, R interprets M against the background of the relationship he has or is establishing with S (if there is no relationship, there is no reason for R to pay attention to M). The kinds of possible relationships involve their relative ages and sexes, kinship, social class, caste, race, nationality, occupational and special interests groups, and so on. In all societies, such relationships are normally loaded with expected attitudes and prescribed behaviors that strongly influence how people receive and interpret messages from each other. For instance, Jesus of Nazareth, because he fully identified with the poor and oppressed, could urge his disciples to "turn the other cheek" (Matt. 5:38-42); but if a Roman soldier, even one converted to Christ, had offered the same counsel, R would have interpreted it very differently. These relationships involve such matters as who is above and who is below socially, whether the relationship is friendly or hostile, close or distant, and so on. A little reflection on personal experience will show how heavily they influence how we interpret each other's messages. There are also in some cases strictly personal relations between S and R, which are added to but do not completely eliminate the more socially structured relations.

In the third place, there is a time and place for everything, and not all times and places are suitable for all kinds of M. The particular time and circumstances under which M is communicated affect how R will interpret it; in fact, R may reject M simply because it comes to him under inappropriate circumstances.

In the fourth place, R's interpretation of M will be affected by what he thinks he will get out of it. In the West, for instance, an R who attends a church as a means for personal economic advantage will interpret the sermon quite differently from an R who is seeking release from guilt or anxiety, even when it is the same sermon heard on the same occasion. The same thing is true of the ways in which people approach the Bible with certain expectations already in their minds as to what they will gain from it.

In the fifth place, R will not fail to notice what kind of text he is dealing with. Is it poetry or prose? Does it tell a story, or does it explain something in a matter-of-fact way, or does it present an argument, or does it simply express S's feelings? In all languages, there are different types of texts which have specific properties and which are used for different kinds of M. Think, for instance, of how you would treat the stories in the Gospels if they began in English with "Once upon a time. . . ." Now the kinds of texts that are available and how they are used to convey different kinds of M are not the same from language to language, so that there is room for much misunderstanding. For that matter, it is possible for R to misunderstand a text in his own language if he fails to see what kind it is; some people derive strange doctrines by reading biblical poetry as if it were literal prose.

In this regard, it is important for us to realize that in the original languages, very little of the Bible is in what might be called technical language. Most of it is either in ordinary everyday language or in poetic language. As a result, when some scholars ask of the Bible technical questions, they either fail to find answers or else read false answers into the Bible. This kind of flattening out of the differences between the parts of the Bible and reading it all as if it were everywhere the same kind of text leads to much error, much disagreement (some of it as pointless as the medieval argument about how many angels could stand on the head of a pin), and much division between Christians.

In the sixth and final place, the whole set of presuppositions about language, meaning, and so on which underlies R's hermeneutical principles is itself part of his context, and is not the same for all human beings in all contexts. Thus, our tendency in the West to read the Bible in a technical way, even when this distorts the biblical M, comes from our feeling that truth, truthfulness, objectivity, precision, and verifiable fact are all pretty much the same thing. But this belief is an assumption which is not shared by people everywhere; and it is not at all evident that it was shared by the biblical writers themselves.

4. One useful way of examining these factors which affect the way R interprets M is to see them all as parts of R's *culture*. This concept helps us to keep in mind certain important features of the process of interpretation.

Culture is *learned*. It is helpful to contrast the behavior patterns of animals, which are largely determined by their genes, with those of human beings, which are largely learned. The animal way makes for much greater security: the individual animal is not as helpless as the human infant. The human way makes for greater flexibility and adaptability: it takes many generations for a genetic pattern to be significantly changed, but it takes only one generation or less for learned patterns to change as necessary. This is very important for our topic, which is the problem of interpreting in one cultural context messages which were originally given in other contexts.

Culture is *shared;* it is the social heritage of a group, and it is an important part of the group's self-awareness, self-definition, and pride. It makes communication possible by assigning meanings to the environment and its parts and aspects. Culture is also socially transmitted from generation to generation.

Culture is *integrated*. Its various parts tend to fit together into a more or less coherent overall pattern. Integration, of course, is neither perfect nor static; but it is good enough so that one cannot readily alter one part without setting off a chain reaction of change.

Culture is *adaptive* and *adaptable*. This means that it is designed to allow people to make the best possible life out of the environment and its resources, and to change when the environment changes.

In listing all of these properties of culture, I want to underline how much culture develops the intelligence, imagination, and flexibility of human beings. It is not a prison but a flexible guide.

There are a few other things that need to be said to round out the picture. First, no one individual knows all that can be known of his own culture; each person knows a part, large or small according to his intelligence, experience, and place in society. This is especially true in large, complex societies with many specializations; in such cases, each person knows the basic core of his culture, some knowledge relevant to his specialty, and a smattering of knowledge of other areas gained in school and from the press and media. In very large, complex societies, there may well be a number of different world views, which only partly overlap.

All possible social relations and situations are culturally defined. In fact, each unequal relationship has at least two definitions, one from the point of view of each person involved. This also applies to relations with aliens.

5. I said earlier that R uses all kinds of clues from the context to discover implicit information in M. But even explicit information can be misunderstood, because S and R assign meanings to the words and sentences independently. R can see in M only meanings that are known to him. This is the occasion for much confusion in interpreting the Bible, even among people who are familiar with it, because translators often use terms of their languages in senses which are quite unusual or unfamiliar to ordinary readers.

For example, the Greek word *sarks* is often translated by the English word "flesh" even though the two words have the same senses in only a few cases; the only sense in which they genuinely coincide is that of "soft tissue of the body." A reader who sees the English word "flesh" standing for *sarks* where it does not have this meaning will almost automatically be misled.

6. *Understanding* results when the interpretation R gives to a text is essentially the same as S's intention. Five things must be said about this.

First, since R has to assign to explicit terms meanings that he knows, and to discover implicit information, understanding is never automatic. It often happens that R in fact assigns to a word a meaning different from the one intended by S, or fails to reconstruct the right implicit information; in such cases, R has misunderstood M.

Second, it follows that understanding is partly dependent on R and S sharing similar contexts and points of view. If they do not, it becomes necessary for R to do a good deal of research to discover what he can of S's context, through studies in history, culture, and so on.

Third, R will understand best when he considers the text as a whole, and least well when he tries to understand each word separately. This is because of the way the whole text throws light on the meaning of each of its parts. Each word, taken separately, is capable of carrying several meanings (see the entry under *head* in an unabridged dictionary). But as each word is used in a real M, surrounding words work to select that one among its possible meanings which best fits in with all the rest. This works so quickly and so effectively that R is seldom aware of other possible meanings of each word as the context leads him directly to the right one. Take the word *stock,* which in the dictionary will have at least five senses: (a) farm animals, (b) shares in a corporation, (c) broth, (d) type of paper, and (e) inventory of merchandise. If we use the word in the small context *He watered the stock,* we have eliminated senses (d) and (e), since they do not fit with *watered,* but the other three senses remain possible, so that the sentence is still ambiguous. But if we say *He watered the stock by filling the trough,* we leave only sense (a). Exactly the same thing should take place in our interpretations of the Bible.

Fourth, understanding is never instantaneous, if M is at all complex. It takes time, sometimes a great deal of time. What usually happens is that we approach a text for the first time with little or no understanding, but as we become more familiar with it and with its larger context, we understand better and better. This can be a lifelong process.

Fifth, understanding is never perfect or total. It can and does improve with time, and becomes sufficient for all practical purposes; and one can understand parts of M very well. But there is always room for growth and correction in our understandings. And yet through this humanly imperfect process, the marvel is that God speaks to us with power and clarity from the Scriptures, so that one can learn to know him, and to discern and do his will.

7. In the communication process, culture is not static. While it conditions R's understanding of M, M also has an impact on R's culture. This two-way effect is particularly clear in the case of the biblical message. For once R has understood the Bible or part of it, he will be led to new ways of thinking and behaving that will end up transforming his culture. (Remember that R stands not only for a single person, but also for a community of people.) In

other words, a hermeneutic that takes most seriously the human context of R has the best chances of leading to a transformation of that context, while a hermeneutic that ignores or denies the role of the cultural context ends up being ineffective.

CASES

We now move on to a number of cases, in which we will apply the principles outlined above to the study of problem passages or themes from the Bible. The problem is to find a way of bridging the great difference between the contexts of the biblical writers and ours today, in such a way that the essential biblical M comes through loud and clear with transforming power. In other words, we need to take culture seriously without being trapped by it.

My discussions should be taken as only suggestive; they need to be filled in with a great deal of material from biblical scholarship for which I do not have space. I emphasize certain linguistic and cultural factors both because they represent my own specialty and because most readers will be more likely to have at hand pertinent biblical helps than pertinent anthropological helps.

1. *Cosmology*. It is quite clear to anyone reading the opening chapters of Genesis that the writer(s) thought of the universe as being composed of three layers: the earth *(ha-aretz)*, which was a more or less flat surface comprising both water and dry land on which plants grew and animals and humans lived; the "firmament" *(raqiyâ)*, which was pictured as a great dome supporting large masses of water, and to which were fixed the heavenly bodies; and the "deep" *(tehom)* under the earth, containing the rest of the water. The Days of Creation were the successive stages during which these things were created and set in their places. The Flood saw a partial reversal as the "windows of heaven" were opened and the "fountains of the deep" broke up, letting water cover the earth again.

Are we bound to accept this understanding of the universe literally, in spite of all we have learned since? Or are we free to reject its outer form, recognizing its primitivity and its appropriateness to its own time but not to ours?

It should be pointed out that even during the period of the Bible itself, this view underwent progressive change. At some stage between Genesis and New Testament times, the concept of *Sheol* came into use, a place considered to be the abode of the dead, located under the earth. This was later divided into "Abraham's bosom" and the "place of torment." Similarly, the heaven was elaborated into a structure of several stories, with God's dwelling in the top one. Though many of the relevant passages are poetic (and therefore not necessarily to be interpreted literally) they show that by New Testament times the Jews had a much more complex picture of the universe than is shown in Genesis 1-11; and they do not appear to have been bothered by the difference.

Later, when the Gospel moved into the pagan Hellenized world, Christians apparently accepted without difficulty the cosmologies of the pagan world, though they did insist that God was the Creator. At least they did not seem to have debates about the differences between Genesis 1-11 and the views they had learned as pagan children. Among scholarly gentiles, it was the view of the philosopher and mathematician Ptolemy that became prevalent, with the earth in the center and the heavenly bodies circling it. Ironically, it was this view rather than any biblical view that the Roman Church defended against Galileo. But as evidence accumulated, Galileo's view prevailed.

Now a new model is gradually coming into our awareness, a view associated with names like Einstein, Planck, and others. I see no reason why this view cannot be accommodated as its predecessors were. And the same goes for many cosmologies in non-western parts of the world. The Bible is not a book intended to teach us science.

Some may fear that if we do not hold to a universe in several stories, we will lose our sense of the greatness and otherness of God. But surely the Scriptures, even though they speak of "the most high God" and use other expressions of height to emphasize his greatness, also use figures of speech involving depth and breadth. In fact, the Bible emphasizes that any dimensional term, in either space or time, is really inadequate, since God is always and everywhere (Ps. 139:7-12; I Kings 8:27). The very idea that we might with one single metaphor be able to grasp the wholeness of God is a contradiction. We dare not confuse devices that are used to help our feeble understanding with truths about the nature of God himself.

The same thing, by the way, is true about other figures which are used to describe God, figures borrowed from family or politics (''father,'' ''king''), as well as the expressions which assign to God human body parts and human feelings. All of these together can help us get a general idea of God, but cannot define or describe him fully.

2. *Women in the church.* In these days of women's liberation, some are arguing that we must get rid of the old-fashioned pattern of relations between the sexes that is found in the Bible, as if the Bible were no longer to be authoritative in this area. Others defend traditional interpretations of the Bible which assign a very subordinate position to women. Does our approach to hermeneutics shed any light on this problem? Is it possible to come to sound and legitimate understandings of the Bible which are not so hard on half of the human community?

It seems to me that there are four kinds of materials in the Bible on this topic. First, there are descriptions, usually embedded in stories, that show us what the role of women was in ancient Israel. Second, there are passages which describe the actions and attitudes of Jesus and some apostles in relation to women. Third, there are apostolic teachings that are intended to be universal and permanently authoritative. And fourth, there are passages that give instructions for specific situations and circumstances.

With respect to purely descriptive Old Testament passages, I find it hard to see why they should be normative for us today, unless we believe that the ancient Israelites were miraculously infallible. As for the other three categories, I think it should be clear that passages of the fourth type should be interpreted as less crucial than those of types two and three.

The passage which best illustrates Jesus' own attitude is the story of Mary and Martha (Luke 10:38-42), in which he insisted that women were just as welcome as men to be involved in spiritual and theological issues, and that the prevalent notion of ''woman's place'' expressed by Martha was invalid; this was truly revolutionary. As for Paul, it is clear from a number of passages (e.g. Acts 18:26 and Rom. 16:3, with respect to Priscilla) that when he met a woman of appropriate gifts and character, he recognized and encouraged her to serve to her fullest capacity.

As for universally authoritative passages, I cite only Galatians 3:28, Colossians 3:11, and Ephesians 5:21 ff. The first two passages state emphatically that for those who are "in Christ," invidious distinctions based on sex are no longer valid, any more than distinctions based on race or social status. In the Ephesians passage, the universal statement which heads the entire section is verse 21: "Submit yourselves to one another because of your reverence for Christ" (TEV). The remaining verses spell out the implications of this universal command: not only how a wife should submit to her husband, but how a husband should submit to his wife. This has two revolutionary consequences: first, it destroys any notion of supposed superiority of men over women, since it is based on reverence for Christ; second, it makes the submission mutual, not one-way.

We are now ready to approach one of the controversial passages, which I take to be teaching relevant to a specific context: 1 Timothy 2:9-15. Surely, whatever Paul is teaching here should not contradict either his universal teaching or his own practice, unless we want to accuse him of gross inconsistency. I suggest that a proper *contextual* understanding is as follows: in that social and cultural context, in both Jewish and gentile circles, women were not given much education. They were conditioned by the whole process of feminine up-bringing to be dependent, ignorant, childish, and even frivolous and silly. From verses 9-10, it seems that the typical woman was preoccupied with clothes and jewelry rather than with more important things. But it was not universal "feminine nature" that made them that way, it was their up-bringing; they were, like women in many another society, intellectually crippled by their society's ideas of "femininity" and "woman's place." A woman so handicapped would not be able to teach in a congregation of men who were better educated; she might well cause confusion if she became involved in a discussion in church. But in those cases where women, in *defiance* of social stereotypes, achieved intellectual maturity, both Jesus and Paul gave them every encouragement.

Paul's obscure argument in verses 13-14 weighs against this interpretation. But any other interpretation makes Paul very inconsistent. As for verse 15, there are so many interpretations of it that I think it is wiser to admit we do not know what it means; and it surely is unsafe to build a case on a shaky foundation.

3. *Footwashing.* It happens that I grew up in a denomination that practiced ritual footwashing as an integral part of what is called the threefold communion. I am therefore in a position to appreciate the weight of arguments that John 13:8b, 10 invest Jesus' action with theological and ritual importance. In a broader sense, two questions are implied by this passage: was Jesus' action indeed the inauguration of a rite, or merely a moral example? And whichever answer one chooses to the first question, what ought we to do as a result in twentieth-century America?

In favor of the ritual interpretation are three arguments: the washing of the disciples' feet was closely associated with the Last Supper, which was clearly ritual; Jesus commanded that they ought to follow his example, and he apparently gave this act theological significance in verses 8b and 10. Against this interpretation is the fact that footwashing is nowhere else mentioned as a rite in the New Testament (though some would so understand 1 Tim. 5:10), and in particular not in the Synoptics, which would make it the only rite supported by only one Gospel. My own view is mildly in favor of the interpretation that Jesus was giving a moral example.

The second question is more relevant to our topic: what are we supposed to *do* to obey Jesus' clear command in verses 12-15? Here an understanding of the way footwashing functioned in the first century gives us a clue: in a day when people wore sandals and walked on rough dusty roads, washing the feet upon arrival was an important part of being cleansed and refreshed. But the feet are not the most exalted part of the body, and ministering to another's feet requires a humiliating posture. Thus, the normal custom seems to have been for the host to provide water for a guest to wash his own feet (Luke 7:44). However, if a guest was especially honored, or the host wished to express extraordinary hospitality, a slave would be assigned for the unpleasant chore. Nothing could be more disgusting to a free person, nothing could better symbolize the non-human status of a slave, than this occasional duty. This can be inferred from Peter's shocked reaction to Jesus' action (John 13:8). But Jesus insisted, and added that he was setting an example which his disciples should follow. I therefore interpret this passage to mean that each Christian is to subject himself voluntarily to every other Christian, both in attitude and in conduct; and that it is especially important for leaders to accept humiliation if by doing so they benefit others (cf. Matt. 20:25-28; Mark 10:42-45; 2 Cor. 6:3-10). Perhaps this is the biblical teaching which is more than any other uncongenial to the natural human being in any sociocultural context; which is no doubt why it is so commonly ignored or distorted.

4. *The Logos.* I will discuss this topic only briefly, because it is so vast and involves much research into biblical scholarship that I do not have time to get into. I will therefore focus only on the contribution which my own disciplines can make to this subject.

It is often debated whether the concept of the *Logos* in John 1 rests primarily on a Greek philosophical foundation or upon a Hebrew Old Testament foundation. But I think a prior question is whether it is a technical term at all in the modern sense, or whether it is in fact a symbol. If it is a technical term, we would be obliged to discover its precise conceptual content and to pin down its exact origin in either-or terms. But if it is a symbol, it would be perfectly normal for it to vibrate at several wavelengths at once. It is interesting that two studies of the topic which I consulted (Sanders 1962; Howard 1952) find it impossible to choose.

It seems to me likely that John used the term in senses that resemble both the Old Testament one, the traditional Greek one, and the synthesis of these two strands which was accomplished by the Hellenized Jew Philo. John saw the *Logos* as a divine creative Word (John 1:3), as an intermediary between God and creation; but he went further in identifying this *Logos* with Jesus of Nazareth. In other words, for John the *Logos* is neither an abstract principle nor a personification, but a human being of specific history and location. But such a large synthesis of meanings is possible only if we are dealing, not with a technical term, but with a comprehensive cover symbol, ready to be filled with any congenial content.

I suggest that this gives us considerable freedom, in the contexts of today, to assign to Jesus Christ whatever compatible ideas we have concerning the origins of the universe, its maintaining principles and laws, and so on. Thus, for most educated westerners, what John would be saying is that natural law is not just a set of inferences from cases, not an impersonal determining force, nor merely a property of energy/matter; but rather that before and under and behind all of these is the Creator God, incarnate in Jesus of Nazareth. For non-westerners, a similar process of interpretation is of course equally available in relation to their cosmologies.

CONCLUSION

I have only a few things to add by way of conclusion. First, this is only an initial stumbling effort by one man, and it is subject to correction by the whole Body of Christ. Second, it is a serious and sincere effort, arising out of faith in Jesus Christ as Son of God and Lord of the Universe and in the Scriptures as the inspired record of God's self-revelation. Third, it is based on a glimpse I have had of the enormous difference between the great God and finite human minds. Fourth, it also reflects my conviction that while our cultures and languages do not give us perfect tools to understand the ways of God, they are all we have; and God has sanctified them by using them fully in the incarnation of his Son and in the inspiration of the Scriptures. Fifth, Christians in all contexts must enjoy the same freedom we claim in this endeavor. Sixth, while we can never fully transcend the limits of our contexts, we can by the use of imagination guided by the Spirit of God both grasp and be grasped by God and so be transformed into the image of his Son. And after all, is that not the point of the whole thing?

Part

II. Culture, Evangelism, and Conversion

7. The Gospel: Its Content and Communication —A Theological Perspective

by James I. Packer

JAMES I. PACKER, *former associate principal of Trinity College, Bristol, England, is Professor of Historical and Systematic Theology at Regent College, Vancouver. He is author of* Knowing God *and* I Want to Be a Christian.

THEOLOGIANS FREQUENTLY DISCUSS THE CONtent of the Gospel. Less often are they asked to speak as well about the communication of the Gospel.

Three specific insights may be derived from reflection on the themes of the content and communication of the Gospel, joined together as a single topic.

CONTENT CONTROLS METHOD OF DELIVERY

First, we are reminded of the ever relevant truth that the *content of the gospel message must always control the method of its communication*. This principle might seem to be challenged by the modern communications industry, which tends to proceed as though any technique can be made suitable for a given communications task, irrespective of the message to be conveyed. But this is not so; a technique may bring formal clarity at the surface at the cost of in-depth understanding, and it is the latter that we want here.

So, we must judge the value of the various techniques pro-posed for use in evangelism by asking how far they can and do suc-ceed in getting the message across. The content of the Gospel in-cludes a diagnosis of the hearers' state and needs before God, value-judgments on the life they live now as compared with that which might be theirs, and a call to judge themselves, to acknowl-edge the gracious approach and invitation of God in Christ, and to respond by a commitment more radical and far-reaching than any other they will ever make. The Gospel is not fully communicated unless all this occurs.

Therefore, the Gospel must be *verbalized* and in its verbal form it must be *preached,* that is, set forth by a messenger who, whether *viva voce* in the flesh or on film or tape or radio, or in print, interprets and applies it to those who are addressed in a way which makes its existential implications for them plain. Such media of expression as instrumental music, pictures, sculpture, or dance may reinforce the Gospel by the mood or vision they express, but they cannot, strictly speaking, communicate it; only preaching can do that.

Teaching the Christian faith as an academic discipline (as may be done in schools and universities) is not strictly communi-cating the Gospel, for although the relevant themes are analyzed the thrust of the application is not present. Preaching is teaching plus application.

It cannot be too strongly stressed that since the Gospel is a personal message from God to each hearer, the only appropriate and effective way of communicating it is for a messenger to deliver it on God's behalf, ambassador-style (cf. 2 Cor. 5:20)—that is, identifying with God's concerns and expressing, by the way he uses words, God's mind and heart: how he hates sin and loves sin-ners, and what he has done, is doing, and will do for the salvation of those who turn to him. "Truth through personality" (Phillip Brooks' definition of preaching) has always been God's main way of communicating the Gospel, as the Incarnation itself shows.

When Thomas Goodwin the Puritan wrote, "God had but one son, and he made him a preacher," he was echoing an authentic note in the New Testament witness. The writer to the Hebrews introduces the Son as a God-sent preacher of the Gospel before saying anything about his role as priest, sacrifice, and mediator (Heb. 1:1 ff.; 2:1, 3), and the Evangelists show Jesus' preaching of God's Kingdom as the context of all else in his public ministry.

DIFFICULTIES IN COMMUNICATION CALL FOR CONTENT ANALYSIS

Those who find that they cannot convince others of the truth and relevance of the message which they announce as offering life to all will naturally ask themselves whether they have yet understood it correctly. *Problems in communicating the Gospel ought to raise questions about our grasp of its content.* But here wrong turns are easily taken.

For example, Rudolph Bultmann saw the biblical miracle-stories, and the supernaturalist view of the cosmos which they implied, as an obstacle to acceptance of the Gospel by contemporary Germans. So in 1941 he proposed his demythologizing program, which removes the stumbling-block of miracles by abolishing the divine and miraculous Christ who performed them. In similar fashion, J. A. T. Robinson in *Honest To God* (1963) posited "the end of theism" because, as he urged, "supranaturalism," that is, the idea of transcendent personhood, could no longer communicate any sense of God's presence to modern western man, and he offered instead a notion of God formed exclusively in terms of depth, immanence, love, and moral claims.

I cite these familiar examples as cautionary tales. Both Bultmann and Robinson aimed at effective communication, but their way of getting round the stumbling blocks was to reduce the message in a way that threw out the baby along with the bath water. It is never safe for the Christian communicator to conclude that the less you commit yourself to assert, the easier it will be to assert it, or to treat objections to a particular tenet as a sign that it is dispensable.

But for communicators who hold to historic Christianity, problems in making it seem true and relevant can be salutary. What they may show is that, as a J. B. Phillips book title once told us, "Your God is too small." What we may be failing to do, or at least to do clearly and thoroughly enough, is to highlight those absolutes of God's self-disclosure which show up the preconceptions and preoccupations that impede communication.

If these absolutes are not rigorously presented, sooner or later the biblical Gospel, in which God the Creator appears in judgment and mercy reconciling the world to himself, will itself be relativized and thereby distorted through being assimilated to man's prior interests. The world will write the agenda. It happened before in old-style liberalism, which turned the Kingdom of God preached as Gospel by Jesus into the kingdom of ends taught as ethics by Kant. It seems to have happened at Bangkok in 1973, where the word "salvation" became the label for many things that men desire, but which are not salvation in the revealed and regulative biblical sense.

Running up against ideas about God or the world or man which challenge the Gospel can be good for us, by prompting us to anchor our message more explicitly and robustly in the divine ultimates, as did Paul when on the Areopagus, facing polytheism, he spelled out basic Christian theism at length and with emphasis. Thus, being stirred to strengthen the foundations, we may end up presenting the Gospel a good deal more adequately than before.

CULTURALLY CONDITIONED ASSUMPTIONS CAN HINDER COMMUNICATION

We all tend to equate our own culture-bound understanding of Christ with the Gospel itself, and this leads to trouble. All understandings of the Gospel, whether British, North American, Latin American, African, Indian, or what have you, are in the nature of the case culturally conditioned. I cannot jump out of my own cultural skin, nor can you, nor can anyone.

Yet, we must strive to be sensitive in this matter because *our own assumptions about the content of the Gospel can become an obstacle in communicating it.*

Equally, of course, the presentations of the Gospel in the New Testament itself are culturally conditioned; but there we may believe that the Palestinian and Hellenistic cultural settings, so far from being distorting or limiting or obscuring factors, were providentially shaped so as to be wholly appropriate vehicles for expressing and exhibiting God's last word to the world—the word spoken once for all in the Jew who was his incarnate Son, and through his chosen witnesses, the apostolic theologians, in whose minds Rabbinic and Hellenistic culture so remarkably met and blended.

God's revelation of himself in Christ is culture-bound, in the sense of being culturally particularized (being historical, it had to be), but not at all in the sense of being culturally distorted. This seems to me to be a crucial truth for hermeneutics today, one which urgently needs some fresh exposition and defense. I assert it here in order to make the point that there is no other culture of which this can be said.

We may be sure, therefore, before we ever sit down to look, that any version of Christianity produced anywhere at any time will bear marks of one-sidedness or myopia, not only because of imperfect exegesis and theologizing but also for reasons of cultural limitation. A culture operates as both binoculars and blinkers, helping you to see some things and keeping you from seeing others. So we shall need to be consciously critical of whatever form of the Christian tradition—in our case, the evangelical tradition—we have inherited; just as we shall need to be aware that from the great smorgasbord of international evangelical tradition no two of us are likely to have ingested quite the same meal.

Being unaware of our own blind spots, we shall be tempted to ascribe to those expressions of the Gospel in the theology, liturgy, and behavior patterns which we know best a finality, fullness, and universality which may only be claimed for the Gospel itself, and for the Christ of whom it speaks. Then the danger will be that in seeking to proclaim the Gospel in cross-cultural situations we shall impose on people our own cultural forms for expressing the Gospel, forms which to them are alien and unauthentic, and which when accepted become badges of a dependence that is not healthy.

When a version of Christianity developed in one cultural setting is exported in this way to another, the major trouble is likely to be not that it includes idiosyncrasies but rather that it ignores matters of importance. To give one example, which comes near home for us all: the western evangelical tradition is weak on the doctrine of *creation*. This doctrine was highlighted in the almost mortal second-century conflict which established (against the

Gnostics) that God the Redeemer is also God the Creator and sustainer of all that is. But since the Reformation, evangelicals, concentrating all attention on the doctrines of grace to the neglect of creation, have developed a five-fold weakness in this latter area.

First, we lack any magisterial counter to the deist, pantheist, and materialist versions of the uniformitarian myth of the universe which grips so many minds these days, and which modern technology is widely though erroneously thought to confirm. Second, evangelical discussions of the appropriate way to relate the witness of Holy Scripture to that of natural science (on, for instance, the origin of things, the flood, and the constitution of the human organism) remain almost discreditably naive. Third, we regularly ignore the cosmic dimensions of God's reconciling work in Christ, and of the renewal that is promised at Christ's return. Fourth, an atomic individualism, really a product of European rationalism and romanticism two centuries ago, has crept into our thinking about individuals before God, making us unable, it seems, to take seriously enough the family, racial, national, and Adamic solidarities which Scripture affirms as part of the created order, and which the so-called "primitive" mind grasps so much better than most of us. (Hence come theological fumblings when interpreting the phenomenon of "mass" or "people" movements into the Christian faith.) Fifth, we are short of a theology of nature and the natural, and so we have constant difficulties in convincing our critics that the biblical positivism which is our regular theological method as evangelicals is in fact genuinely attuned to the nature of things as God made them.

Now, should any individuals take over any version of the western evangelical tradition in theology as a final standard, they would be buying along with many strengths this chronic and often overlooked weakness on creation. So it is important that such purchases should be outlawed, lest in retrospect some individuals should feel themselves to have fallen victim to a confidence trick.

In cross-cultural Christian communication the right course will be neither to impose on folk of other cultures forms of Christian expression belonging to our own, nor to deny them access to our theological, liturgical, ethical, and devotional heritage, from which they will certainly have much to gain. Instead, we should encourage them, once they have appreciated our tradition, to seek by the light of Scripture to distinguish between it and the Gospel it enshrines, and to detach the Gospel from it, so that the Gospel may mesh with their own cultures directly. Thus among younger nations with distinct cultural styles and, perhaps, some touchiness about cultural imperialism, the Gospel may be set free to do its job.

If it is true (as I for one believe) that every culture and subculture without exception in this fallen world is a product not just of human sin but also of God's common grace, then respect for other cultures and desire to see them reanimated by gospel grace in their own terms, must undergird all particular admonitions we might be led to offer. And if Christians of other cultures criticize sub- and post-Christian elements in our heritage, we must not mishear this as cultural imperialism in reverse. The *koinonia* which is the church's proper life is two-way traffic, taking as well as giving, and it requires us both to share what resources of Christian insight we have and to take gratefully any further insights that others offer us. Only so can we avoid canonizing the clumsiness, blind spots, and poverties of our own tradition, which actually misrepresent the content of the Gospel which we seek to make known.

THE CONTENT OF THE GOSPEL

Thus far we have explored in general terms three preliminary points: first, that the Gospel, being what it is, must be communicated by preaching; second, that establishing its truth and relevance involves not diminishing it at the points of difficulty, but countering directly any preconceptions which oppose it; third, that the Gospel may not be equated with any post-apostolic formulation or cultural embodiment of it, but must be distinguished from them all. Now we move on to look at its content in more precise terms.

A glance at the relevant lexicography shows that the Gospel (*euaggelion,* or ''good news''), a term used sixty times by Paul, is the message that God has acted and acts now in and through Christ for the world's salvation. God's saving action was the burden of ''the Gospel of the Kingdom'' which Jesus preached (*euaggelion* appears seven times in Mark); and Jesus' incarnation, death, resurrection, reign, and return was the theme of the Gospel according to Paul. Sometimes "the Gospel" in Paul seems to signify the evangelistic *kerygma* which C. H. Dodd isolated long ago in Acts, sometimes it embraces the whole Christian message as such.

Laying out the contents of the Gospel in full is a complex task, for the material is abundant, varied, and occasional. There is the *kerygma* of the speeches in Acts and such passages as Romans 1:3 f. and 1 Corinthians 15:3 ff., detailing the fulfillment of prophecy in Jesus' life, death for sins, resurrection and kingdom, and the promise of pardon and the Spirit to those who repent and believe. There are the four accounts of Jesus' ministry, highlighting his death, resurrection and expected return in glory, each so angled as to present a different facet of his identity and role. There are also many presentations of Jesus Christ in the epistles with the thematic changes rung according to what the writers thought their readers needed to hear. All this material is rooted in Old Testament beliefs and hopes, and has a "between-the-times" perspective, looking back to Christ's first coming, forward to his reappearing, and upward to his present heavenly reign.

An effective way to analyze the material, for our present purpose, is in terms of six distinct (though overlapping and complementary) "stories," each of which is the Gospel just as all six together are the Gospel. Two of the stories are about God, two about Jesus Christ, and two about man.

1. God's Purpose: The Kingdom

The Creator has judicially subjected all mankind to sin and death, and the rest of creation to "futility" and "corruption" in consequence of the guilty disobedience of the "first Adam," in whom all now die. But from all eternity it has been his gracious plan, purpose, and pleasure to restore this situation and bring the cosmos to perfection at the end of the day through the mediation of the "last Adam," the God-man Jesus Christ. All the decisive events in God's plan save the last have now been played out on the stage of world history. The key to understanding the plan, as it affects mankind, is to see that by God's appointment each person's destiny depends on how he or she stands related to the two representatives, Adam and Christ.

What God planned was to exercise his kingship (sovereignty, an ultimate fact) over his rebel world by bringing in his Kingdom, a state of bliss for sinners who, penitently returning to his obedience, should find under his sway salvation from sin's guilt, power, and evil effects. In this Kingdom Jesus Christ should be God's vice-gerent, and trusting and obeying Christ should be the appointed way of returning from sin to God's service. God prepared the way for the Kingdom by making himself king of a national community created out of the family of Abraham: to this community he gave territory, his law, a national life, prophets and kings as his spokesmen and deputies, and promises of the Messiah who would come to reign over them in the new era of peace *(shalom)* and joy. When at the appointed time Christ came, Israel the prepared nation rejected him and compassed his crucifixion; but God, having achieved world redemption according to his plan through Christ's death, raised him to life and set him on the throne of the universe, where now he reigns, furthering his Kingdom by sending the Spirit to draw men and women to himself and by strengthening them for faithful obedience in face of mounting opposition till the day dawns for his return to judge all nations and finally to renew all things.

In this story, the goal of God's action is to glorify himself by restoring and perfecting his disordered cosmos, and the gospel call is to abandon rebellion, acknowledge Christ's lordship, thankfully accept the free gift of forgiveness and new life in the Kingdom, enlist on the victory side, be faithful in God's strength, and hope to the end for Christ's coming triumph.

2. God's People: The Church

In this fallen world where men and women are alienated through sin from both God and each other, God has acted to create for himself a new people who should live with him and with each other in a fellowship of covenant love and loyalty. He acted thus: First he made a covenant with Abraham and his descendants, thus binding himself to bless them and them to worship and serve him. When later he brought Abraham's family out of Egypt, he renewed the covenant and gave them, along with the law which showed what behavior would please and displease him, a cultus which had sacrifice at its heart, whereby sin might be put away and communion between him and them maintained. When subsequently Israel fell into unfaithfulness, a recurring pattern of divine action emerged—judgment on all, followed by deliverance and renewal for a faithful remnant. When Christ came to set up a new and richer form of the covenant relationship by his priestly sacrifice of himself, Israel spurned his ministry, and he was then the true Israel, the faithful remnant, in his own person. In him God's Israel was reconstituted out of believers as such, and in it Jew and Gentile are together as fellow-citizens, branches of one olive tree and brothers in one family. Thus reconciliation to both God and each other takes the place of the alienation that was there before. In glory the church will remain one city, family, and flock together.

Christ's death as sin-bearer under God's judgment, followed by God's affirmation of him in resurrection, was the definitive fulfillment of the judgment-and-renewal pattern, and resurrection out of death (in union with Christ's dying and rising) is the appointed and abiding shape of life for God's people, as the symbolism of their baptism shows. It is a pattern which their physical resurrection at Christ's return will finally complete.

God's covenant people, the church, lives a public life of humiliation, dispersion, opposition and distress, but its inner, hidden life is one of union and communion in the risen Christ with him and each other, as the Lord's Supper regularly proclaims. Loving ministry to one another and to needy folk everywhere is the lifestyle which properly expresses this hidden reality, in which connection Paul pictures the church as Christ's body, with each limb animated and equipped by his Spirit for the service which he through it will render.

In this story the goal of God's action is to have a people who live with him in love, and whose corporate life shows forth to the watching angels the ''many-stranded wisdom of God'' (Eph. 3:10). The gospel call, from this standpoint, is to accept a share in the life and hope of God's forgiven family by bowing to the Lord whose death redeemed the church and whose risen life sustains it. This is not to put the church in Christ's place, but to preach Christ as the answer, through the church, to every man's problem of isolation and alienation from God and men. The church does not save, but as the redeemed society it is certainly part of the Gospel.

3. The Grace of Christ

In Jesus Christ God has given the world a Savior whose great salvation more than matches our great need, and whose great love (which we may gauge from the cross) will not be daunted or drained away by our great unloveliness. Jesus is set forth as prophet, priest and king; teacher and guide; mediator and intercessor; master and protector; and the focal point of his saving work is identified as his cross, concerning which each Christian can say, "he loved me, and gave himself for me" (Gal. 2:20). Christ's death was an act of righteousness, for he endured it in obedience to his Father's will. As such, it wrought redemption, freeing us from the curse of God's law, that is, exposure to divine judgment, at the cost of Christ's own suffering. His death was redemptive because it achieved reconciliation, making peace between God and man. It made peace by being an act of propitiation, quenching God's wrath by dealing with the sin that evoked it. It propitiated God by being an act of substitutionary sin-bearing, in which the judgment which our sins deserved was diverted onto Christ's head. From the cross flows the risen Christ's gift of a permanent new relationship with God, which Paul analyzes as justification (pardon plus a righteous man's status) and adoption (a place in the family, with certainty of inheritance), and the writer to the Hebrews calls sanctification (acceptance by God, on the basis of consecration to him). With this new status is given new birth, the indwelling Spirit, progressive transformation into Christ's image, and glorification—in short, comprehensive subjective renewal. God's goal in all this is the perfect bliss of sinners, and the gospel call is an invitation to faith in Christ, through which all these gifts come to us, from the Savior's own hand, "for free."

4. The Glory of Christ

From eternity the Father loves the Son, and delights to give him glory and see him honored. The Son, for his part, loves the Father and delights to do his will. As the Father gave honor to the Son in the work of creation and providence, so he has now resolved to make him preeminent in the economy of redemption. So he has rewarded the Son's obedient self-humbling to the point of death by not only restoring to him the glory that was his before the Incarnation, but also by making him head of the church and Lord of the worlds, giving him "the name which is above every name, that at the name of Jesus every knee should bow . . . and every tongue confess that Jesus Christ is Lord, to the glory of God the Father" (Phil. 2:9 ff.). Though Christ's mediatorial kingdom as such will end when the work of grace is done (see 1 Cor. 15:24-28), the doxology, "worthy is the Lamb," shall be sung forever. In this story, God's goal is the praise and glory of Jesus Christ his Son, and the gospel call is a summons to join those who, acknowledging that all their hope is in Christ, are already resolved to spend all eternity honoring his name.

5. God's Image Restored

We were made to display God's image and likeness by practicing righteousness in fulfillment of our creaturely vocation. God's image is more than the rationality which makes such righteousness possible; it is the actual achievement in human life of that which corresponds to God's own moral goodness and creativity. But full God-likeness failed to materialize in Adam personally, and the same is true of all who are in Adam. Thus we fall short of our true human destiny, as God planned it. But as Jesus Christ's own earthly life exhibited God's image to perfection, so now he restores that image in his disciples, by leading us through his word and Spirit into the life that actualizes it—the life, that is, of active, habitual, creative response to the calling of God. This is what Paul refers to when he says that we are being renewed in knowledge (specifically, of God) after the image of the One who first led us to "put on the new man" (Col. 3:10; KJV). In this story, God's goal is to see his own character fully reflected in us, and the gospel call, quite simply, is to let ourselves be remade so that we at last become human!

6. Man's Joy Begun

Finally, those without Christ are in a pitiable state, whatever may or may not appear on the surface of their lives. They are guilty, lost, without hope as death approaches, short of self-mastery, pulled to and fro by conflicting allurements and distractions; there are skeletons of sensuality, callousness, arrogance, and other unlovely things in their closets; they regularly find frustration and discontent partly because their reach exceeds their grasp, partly because they feel thwarted by circumstances, partly because they are so largely unclear as to what is worth their endeavor anyway. The various things wrong with the folk to whom Jesus is seen ministering in the Gospels—hunger, chronic illness, fever, epilepsy, blindness, deafness, dumbness, lameness, leprosy, lunacy, organic deformity, and in three cases actual death— vividly picture these spiritual needs (and were undoubtedly included in the Gospels for that purpose). But Jesus Christ gives peace—with God, with oneself, with circumstances, and with other people— plus his own presence and friendship, plus a call to witness and service as the prior concerns of life in this world, plus a promise of enabling by the Holy Spirit, plus an assurance of final glory in the Savior's own company, and this brings integration, purpose, contentment, and joy such as one has not known before. And the promise is that as one travels the road of discipleship, so these things will increase. In this story, God's goal is to impart to us the joy for which we were made; and the gospel call is a summons to enter through faith and obedience into the joy that Christ gives.

As each strand of a rope is a little rope in itself, so each of these six stories is itself authentic Gospel, though the fullness of the message only appears when all six (and perhaps more) are put together.

WHAT "TRUTH" DO THE GOSPEL STORIES EXPRESS?

But what precisely are we to suppose that these biblical declarations are telling us? There is widespread agreement today that such "stories" as we have been reviewing should be seen as theological "models," on the analogy of models in physics. This is to say, they are thought-patterns which function in a particular way with their own particular "logic," helping us to focus one area of reality (relationships with God) by conceiving of it in terms of another, better known area of reality (relationships with each other). But when we ask how far these models correspond to ultimate reality, sharp disagreement appears, for modern theologians fan out across a broad spectrum between two extremes. The one extreme is to say that the models are humanly devised notions for focusing empirical apprehensions of ourselves and our position in

God's presence and cannot be trusted to yield any definitive truths about God. The other extreme is to say that they are divinely revealed anthropomorphisms which God uses to tell us facts about himself in terms meant to be normative for our subsequent thinking. Bultmann and exponents of the "new hermeneutic" like Fuchs and Ebeling stand at the one extreme, evangelical and Catholic conservatives stand at the other, and there are many halfway houses.

As for me, I view the models which make up this six-fold gospel story as revealing factual truths about God, not of course exhaustively (that would be impossible) but truly and trustworthily so far as they go. I urge that these models should never be treated, as some treat them, as contigent conceptualizations in ancient cultural terms which we today would do well to unshell and repack in other terms. Rather, the conceptualizations themselves should be seen as divinely given modes of instruction. When it comes to the substance of teaching, we may not cut loose from the biblical categories in which God teaches us to think.

THE BASIC POINTS OF CONTENT

So if asked the content of the Gospel for today in England, Chile, Borneo, Bermuda, Tibet, or wherever, I shall offer a formula based on and referring back to the six-theme analysis, setting forth five main points, as follows.

First, the Gospel tells us of *God* our maker, in whom we live and move and are, and whom we have been made to worship and serve, and in whose hands, for good or ill, we always remain, and whose will and purpose should always determine ours. Like Paul at Athens, we must introduce folk to the Creator whom they have forgotten to remember, and go on from there. Not till the Creator's claim is seen can we ever grasp the sinfulness of sin.

Second, the Gospel tells us of *sin,* defining it as failure to meet the holy Creator's claim, first by seeking to be "as gods" in his place and then by fighting him. The Gospel depicts this as rebellion against his authority, lawlessness in relation to him as our lawgiver, missing the mark which he gave us to aim at, and becoming guilty and unclean in his sight in consequence. The Gospel tells us that we are helpless slaves of our own rebelliousness and cannot put ourselves right. Not till we begin to grasp these things can we ever appreciate the dimensions of the declaration that Jesus Christ saves us from sin.

Third, the Gospel tells of *Christ,* and we must teach both the facts and the meaning of his life, death, resurrection, and reign. We must spell out who he is and what he has done, and we must teach folk to interpret the meaning and purpose of human life in terms of him. It is sometimes said that it is the presentation of Christ's person, rather than of doctrines about him, that draws sinners to his feet, and it is certainly true that a theory of atonement, however orthodox, is no substitute for the Savior: it is the living Christ who saves, not any theory about him. But Jesus of Nazareth cannot be known as the living Christ unless we are clear that he was the eternal God and his passion was really his redeeming action of bearing away our sins; nor shall we know how to approach him till we have learned that he is now God's king on the throne of the universe. Not till we are aware of these things can we see what the response for which Christ calls really means.

Fourth, the Gospel tells of *faith, repentance, and discipleship,* and so must we. Faith is credence and conviction regarding the gospel message, and a consequent casting of oneself on the promises of Christ and the Christ of those promises as one's only hope. Repentance is a change of heart and mind, leading to a new life of denying self and serving the Savior as king in self's place. Discipleship is a matter of relating oneself to the living, exalted Christ as both learner and follower, and to the rest of Christ's disciples as one who longs both to learn from them and to give to them, knowing that being in their company is the master's will. These things must be clearly taught, or the nature of the Christian life will surely be misunderstood.

Fifth, the Gospel tells of *newness:* new life in the Spirit, who assures and enables; new relationships in the body of Christ, where love expressed in fellowship through mutual ministry is the rule; new goals in the world for all disciples, who find that although they are no longer of it, Christ leaves them in it to render service to it; and new hope for both one's personal future and that of the world as such, inasmuch as Christ is publicly coming back. When, where, how, and with what measure of discontinuity with what has preceded Christ will come back we should not claim to know. But the certainty that he who now reigns invisibly will one day show himself and in doing so create new heavens and a new earth, wherein dwells righteousness, and that meanwhile he stands at the end of the road of our earthly life to meet us and take us home, brings a radiancy of hope to which secular optimism cannot hold a candle.

COMMUNICATION OF THE GOSPEL

Some brief points about the communication of the God-given Gospel may now be made in summary.

First, we should bear in mind that Christian communication cannot be made easy, and there is not necessarily anything wrong with what we are doing if in a particular situation at a particular time the task proves cruelly hard. Our Lord Jesus Christ was a prince and a paragon among communicators (nobody, I think, can ever dispute that), yet even he failed constantly to anchor his message in his hearers' hearts, as his own parable of the sower declares. His mighty works were clear proof in themselves of his messianic identity (cf. Matt. 11:1-6), yet Chorazin and Bethsaida saw them and did not repent. In a world satiated with communication of one sort and another, as today's world is, and with human hearts no less hard than in Jesus' day, the same negative response can be expected again in many cases.

Second, there are procedural guidelines in communicating Christianity which cannot be ignored. If we do not stay with the biblical story, and the scriptural text, and most of all with the person of the Savior; if, while observing the distinction between milk and meat, foundation and superstructure, we do not labor to make known the whole revealed counsel of God; if we do not seek, as part of our communicative strategy, to show the Gospel shaping relationships in home and family, in imaginative gestures of neighbor-love, and so on, and to ring the changes on *both* the "Christianizing" of existing culture *and* the forming of an alternative culture as true and necessary modes of Christian expression; if, finally, we decline to show any respect for cultures, however pagan, other than our own; then there is no reason to expect communication to proceed well in any context, whether in our local church down the road or on the other side of the world.

Finally, the key to persuasive Christian communication lies less in technique than in character. Paul was a great communicator, not because he was eloquent (by the standards of his day he was not, as he tells us in 2 Cor. 10:10; cf. 1 Cor. 2:1-5), but because he knew his own mind and had a great capacity for identifying with the other person. It is clear that though he had looked to the Holy Spirit to make his communicating fruitful, he knew that the Spirit works through appropriate means, and so was very conscious of the human factors in persuasion, namely cogency of statement and empathetic concern, and was always most conscientious in laboring to achieve them. With that, he set no limit to what he would do, however unconventionally, to ensure that he did not by personal insensitiveness of cultural inertia set barriers and stumbling blocks in the way of men and women coming to Christ.

> I have made myself a slave to all, that I might win the more. And to the Jews I became as a Jew, that I might win Jews . . . to those who are without law, as without law . . . that I might win those who are without law. To the weak I became weak, that I might win the weak; I have become all things to all men, that I might by all means save some. (1 Cor. 9:19-22).

Paul was a man who could, and did, share himself without stint. From his letters we know him well, and we can appreciate the trauma that lies behind the autobiographical passage of Philippians 3, where he tells us how Christ stripped him of cultural pretensions. "Here was a man," F.W. Dillistone comments,

> who possessed all the marks of privilege within a particular historical tradition. His pedigree, his tribal status, his religious dedication, his formal education, his personal commitment, had been such that by every standard of Jewish orthodoxy and by every sanction of national tradition he was justified in regarding himself as successful, superior and secure. . . . Yet he had submitted every part of his historical inheritance to the judgment of the Cross. Nothing could be removed but everything could be re-interpreted. Those things which seemed most positive gain could be judged as of no account in the service of Christ: those things which had

seemed to be hindrances and handicaps might well prove positive assets in the new order of living. . . .

Paul's loving, imaginative adaptability in the service of truth and people is a shining example to all who engage in evangelistic communication, and cannot be pondered too often or taken too seriously.

8. The Gospel: Its Content and Communication
—An Anthropological Perspective*

by Jacob A. Loewen

JACOB A. LOEWEN *has worked for many years with the United Bible Societies in anthropology and linguistics, assisting missionaries engaged in translation of the Bible in South America and Africa.* He is author of Culture and Human Values: Christian Intervention in Anthropological Perspective.

THE GOSPEL OF JESUS CHRIST IS GOD'S GOOD news for all mankind. On the personal level, its aim is to set people free from the power of sin and give them new life under the authority and power of Chirst. On the societal level, the Gospel aims to

*This article builds on two earlier articles: "Evangelism and Culture," which appears in *The New Face of Evangelicalism,* edited by C. René Padilla (Downers Grove, IL:Inter-Varsity Press, 1976), as a part of a symposium on the Lausanne Covenant; and, "Mission Churches, Independent Churches, and Felt Needs in Africa," *Missiology* (October 1976). The former indicates some of the limitations and problems that western culture creates for believers and missionaries from the West. The latter gives case studies showing how independent African churches are meeting various deeply felt needs which are uniquely African and which western-inspired national churches generally neglect or disallow.

establish a new society of citizens of the Kingdom of God in which justice and brotherhood shall flourish. Thus the Gospel is designed to bring glory to our Creator, enrichment to our fellows, and fulfillment to our own lives.

Unfortunately, this simple but far-reaching message sometimes gets distorted. Some years ago I came across an unusual example of this when a South American Indian gave me the following testimony: "It is wonderful to be a Christian," he said. "Now we have ever so many more 'hard' words than before. You can heal your friends, or you can kill your enemies, whenever you want to. All you have to do is kneel behind them in a prayer meeting and while everyone else is praying out loud you just whisper the appropriate 'hard' words, breathe on the person, and it happens just like that. For example, if you should say words like *tutechan, wikik, kisimasi* ("temptation," "wicked," "Christmas") or any of the other bad 'hard' words, the person will die like a fly. If, however, you use words like *kang, epong, klaiki* ("God," "heaven," "Christ") or any of the other good 'hard' words, the person will be well before you know it."

How in the world did this indigenous and syncretistic adaptation of Christianity come about? First, the preaching of the missionaries was done in English, with local Indians interpreting from English into their own language. Second, the tribe had a repertoire of "hard" words—magic words—that their creator-culture hero taught them so they could heal the sick. The local interpreters, faced with many Christian technical words which they did not know how to handle in translation, simply made "hard" words out of them. Those words that seemed to be associated with evil became bad "hard" words, and those associated with good became good "hard" words.

Distortion of the Gospel, especially in cross-cultural situations, is more common than many imagine. Every human activity has its difficulties, and the communication of the Gospel is no exception. Furthermore, in the history of western missions, the source of the problem sometimes lies in the messengers themselves.

To what extent can anthropological insights help us overcome such problems?

PRESUPPOSITIONS

Since success in communication depends to a large extent on understanding and, hopefully, sharing one another's presuppositions, I had better begin by stating my own presuppositions:

God's Good News is for all mankind. For me the simplest statement of the nature and the content of the Gospel we are to share with all the peoples of the world was given by Jesus on that historic sabbath in the synagogue of Nazareth when he unrolled the scroll of the Prophet Isaiah and read:

> "The Spirit of the Lord is upon me,
>> because he has chosen me to bring
>>> good news to the poor.
>> He has sent me to proclaim liberty to
>> the captives
>>> and recovery of sight to the blind;
>> to set free the oppressed
>> and announce that the time has come
>>> when the Lord will save his people."
> (Luke 4:18-19, TEV)

The life-changing power of the Gospel comes from God. It can never be generated by human effort, no matter how dedicated, how consecrated, or how anthropologically sensitive the messengers may be. On the other hand, no one can stop it no matter how hard he or she tries.

As in Jesus' day, so today there is more faith among the "gentiles" than there is in "Israel." I have to confess that my experience with so-called animistic peoples in South America and Africa, and with western missionaries who are bringing the Gospel to them, has convinced me that the capacity to believe among animists is far greater than among missionaries who have been conditioned by secularism and materialism, and who today find it almost impossible to believe in a spirit world. I am still chagrined to remember the occasion when a fellow missionary and I were pushed out of a circle of Indian believers who were praying for the healing of a sick person. I will never forget their words: "We're sorry, God's power cannot heal when there are unbelievers in the circle."

Sad to say, western missionaries not only suffer from infection by this virus of unbelief, but they are also carriers of it. In the interests of fighting ''superstition,'' they train national pastors to become similar disbelievers! (See my article in *Missiology,* Oct. 1976, ''Mission Churches, Independent Churches, and Felt Needs in Africa.'')

Anthropology does not have any ultimate answers for the communication of the Gospel. I am firmly convinced that the science of anthropology can provide us with tools to understand culture and cultural problems. It can give us insights into our own behavior and the behavior of people in different cultures. But it can never write *the* foolproof formulae for communicating the Gospel. Just as our Lord refuses to be confined to temples built by the hands of men, so his ongoing work will not be confined by any human intellectual structures, be they theological or anthropological.

On the other hand, when we stand in the Great Judgment, ignorance of the insights of anthropology will not serve as a valid excuse for not having done correctly what God committed us to do.

Communicators of the Gospel must have personal experience of its power. This experience must include both the transforming power of the Gospel in one's own life and in one's own culture. Only persons who can testify how the Gospel met their deepest needs, and how ''the new Spirit'' from God provided them with the resources to overcome the personal devils that held them chained, can be believable witnesses on the Gospel's behalf.

THE SCOPE OF THE GOSPEL

My use of ''Gospel'' embraces not only the New Testament but the whole Bible, which I accept as the Word of God, valid universally and eternally. This broad use of ''Gospel'' may strike some readers as simplistic ignorance. I have been asked, for instance, ''Do you mean 'Gospel' (with a capital), that is, salvation through Jesus Christ? Or do you mean the 'gospel' (no capital), that is, the practical outworking of God's Word in a specific culture?'' Others have been puzzled by the fact that I treat personal salvation and the solution to cultural problems as equally central to the Gospel.

Though I am aware of all of these distinctions and more, from my anthropological perspective there is little practical value in maintaining them. In many Third World societies, the solution to a painful local cultural problem can be as much a part of salvation as the individual's forgiveness of sin. For instance, for those African countries which in recent years have undergone their own "exodus" liberation experience, the biblical example of how God formed the nation of Israel out of twelve separate and often competing tribes may, in actual fact, be a far more relevant and meaningful message than one that singles out individuals for "personal salvation." Here, we need to be aware of the sharp contrast between, for example, western individualism and African groups that still practice consensus. For the latter, a highly individualistic approach to salvation may be seen as socially disruptive, rather than contributing in a God-given way to the building of a nation that will provide justice and equality for all.

These are several reasons for highlighting the broadest dimensions of the Gospel:

1. The biblical message is, after all, a multifaceted one. Not only did God's people get it over a long period of time, but it was given to men living within differing cultural settings and operating on very different presuppositions and world views.

In addition to radical differences in world view between the Old and New Testaments, within the Old Testament itself we find that the presuppositions of Abraham, Isaac, and Jacob were very different from the presuppositions of David and Solomon, or of Ezekiel and the prophets in exile. We also need to recognize that the Bible does not hesitate to emphasize both sides of an issue; for example, in Romans, faith alone without works is stressed for salvation, while in James, faith without works is considered dead and useless. The implication of the multifaceted nature of the Gospel is that not all facets will be equally in focus for one person or one people at one point in time.

Interestingly enough, Africans say that the New Testament has more or less a western world view, while the Old Testament is founded on a world view similar to their own. In this light it may be significant to point out that at the present time about 75 percent of all Bible translation work in Africa includes the Old Testament. The identification of the Africans with the Old Testament is so strong that up to World War II (after which so many of the African countries became independent and the authority of foreign missions eclipsed) the arrival of the Old Testament again and again split the existing church. Rebelling against what they viewed as the western wrapper in which the missionaries had given them God's message, many African believers started separatist movements boldly proclaiming: ''The African Gospel—the Old Testament—has finally arrived; the missionaries have kept our Gospel hidden and have preached only theirs.''

2. Different facets of biblical truth come into prominence for us at different times in our spiritual pilgrimage. The most important thing for me in my boyhood days in the Mennonite Brethren community in which I grew up was ''to escape from hell and to be saved.'' Later, in my university days, I was excited by the insight that God's truth was like a giant piano keyboard, capable of many new chords. Even my unbelieving professors, I realized, were allowed by God's grace to discover some of his truth, while there were church people who insisted on playing in one key only, as though they possessed the whole truth.

Then, as anthropological awareness grew upon me, I became deeply aware of how my western material-oriented culture, with its total cleavage between the material and the spiritual, was actually stifling my capacity to believe in the spirit world. More recently it has been the Incarnation—the truth that God himself, in order to communicate his Good News to men, found it necessary to limit himself to human nature and to a specific culture. This is the big truth in my life and thinking today.

3. Different cultures, facing the Gospel for the first time, will find different facets of it more meaningful than others. A missionary statesman recently asked Bakht Singh, the beloved evangelist of India, what dimensions of the Gospel he found most useful in witnessing to his own people.

''Do you preach to them about the *love* of God?''

''No, he said, the Indian mind is so polluted that if you talk to them about love they think mainly of sex.''

''Well,'' the missionary said, ''Do you talk to them about the wrath and judgment of God?''

''No, they are used to that,'' he replied. ''All the gods are mad anyway. It makes no difference to them if there is one more who is angry.''

''About what do you talk to them? Do you preach on the crucified Christ?'' the missionary guessed.

''No, they would think of him as a poor martyr who helplessly died.''

''Then what is your emphasis? Eternal life?''

''Not so,'' he said, ''if you talk about eternal life the Indian thinks of transmigration. He wants to get away from it.''

''What then is your message?''

Listen to his answer: ''I have never yet failed to get a hearing if I talk to them about the forgiveness of sins and peace and rest. That's the product that sells well. Soon they ask me how they can get it, and then I can lead them to the Saviour who alone can meet their deepest longings.'' (George W. Peters, ''Is Missions Homesteading or Moving?'' *Mennonite Brethren Herald,* April 15, 1977.)

4. Differing cultural backgrounds and their concomitant presuppositions will cause people to hear a *differing content* from the *same* message. This was forcefully driven home to us when my wife and I tried to serve as resource persons to a group of missionaries and nationals who were trying to develop a Sunday school curriculum ''that would really speak to the African people.'' To our disappointment we discovered that the Scripture passages and the truths they were to teach had already been chosen by the parent church in North America. When my wife and I objected, suggesting that we should let the Africans decide which truths should be taught and also let them select which stories taught those truths, the missionaries were incensed. After all, they were seminary-trained people, they knew the Bible and what it teaches!

In order to help them become more aware of how different cultural perspectives cause different people to hear very differently, we reviewed a number of Bible stories, and asked both the missionaries and the nationals to write down what they thought the central messsage was. The first example was the story of Joseph. The missionaries wrote that here was a man who was loyal to God even to the point of resisting the most fierce of sexual temptations. The Africans wrote that here was a man who, in spite of his brothers' mistreatment, was totally loyal to his family.

5. The believing community in each culture must assume the ultimate responsibility for contextualizing the Gospel in its own setting. That is, it must be allowed to develop its own patterns of translating the Gospel truth into daily life and worship, applying it to the felt needs, problems, and contradictions of the culture.

However, for a people to be motivated to do this, they need a deep consciousness that God is speaking specifically and directly to them. In my experience, the extensive involvement of the believing community in the translation of the Bible makes just such an impact. It is the awareness of the importance of a contemporary encounter with the inspiration of the Scriptures that has led the United Bible Societies to shift from missionary translators to mother-tongue speakers as translators. When the believing community undertakes the challenge of Bible translation, it is moved to pray: "God, how would you have said this if you had spoken in our own language in the first place?" Then, when the group experiences consensus in regard to an answer, the people's attitude towards God's Word changes radically. One retired minister in Zambia testified: "For 25 years I have told the people that the Bible is the Word of God, but deep down in my heart there was a nagging suspicion that it was the white man's God speaking to the white man. But that has completely changed now. God has spoken to us and under his Spirit's guidance we have made decisions which no white man could make."

These several factors point to the need for seeing the Gospel in its broadest as well as its deepest dimensions, rather than insisting on a "one chord" definition.

THE MESSENGERS OF THE GOSPEL

Though many people feel called to be messengers of the Gospel, there are some prerequisites that should characterize them all:

1. They should recognize that they are the products of their particular culture. Western culture is not unique in creating problems for obedient followers of the Gospel. Each culture has its own inventory of problems, and the messengers must become fully aware of them.

2. Messengers must learn to appreciate and to understand the cultural background of the Gospel in the Scriptures. Without an adequate understanding of the cultural settings of biblical times, no one can fully understand the biblical message or make a "dynamic equivalence" translation of the Gospel into a new cultural milieu. Working as a translations consultant in East Central Africa, my appreciation for the Old Testament has grown immensely. In Africa I am working with a people whose culture in many ways is more like the Hebrew culture than my own, and these people find great delight in seeing how God operated within that cultural setting. Unless one is aware of the specific cultural framework in which a given biblical message is imbedded, one can readily fall into the trap of defending nonsense, like when my church some decades ago excommunicated women for cutting their hair on the basis of the Pauline prescriptions to the Corinthians.

3. When messengers of the Gospel have occasion to witness across cultural boundaries, they need to be aware not only of the culture from which they come, but they must have an equally deep appreciation for, and an understanding of the receptor's culture. To begin with, this presupposes a thorough mastery of the local language. As a translations consultant I frequently find myself trying to help national churches extricate themselves from the meaningless jargon imposed upon them by missionaries who had insufficient understanding of and respect for their culture. Thus in one African language the missionaries rejected the local words for "spirit" as satanic, and on the basis of the Greek and Hebrew used the local word for "breath" to mean "spirit." But notice what happens, then, with the key theological concept "Holy Spirit": Since the word for "holy" in this language is a homophone for "red," the people tend to hear "red breath." (!) Likewise, "evil spirits" comes out "bad breath," and "unclean spirits" is "dirty breath." During a translator training program in this language, the nationals concluded that "the whole thing doesn't mean anything!" A hundred years of mission work without an adequate vocabulary for some very essential truths of the Gospel!

4. Messengers must approach their cross-cultural witness with expectancy. Having recognized the incompleteness of their

own understanding of the Gospel, they must be open and ready for the Spirit of God to do a "new thing." When Peter experienced the vision of the sheet being let down from heaven and was ordered to eat unclean animals, he, of course, was puzzled by the meaning of this strange experience. But it had so shaken him that he was able to break out of his Jewish restraint and racial prejudice against the gentiles and go to Cornelius' house and witness God perform a new thing—the gentiles also becoming recipients of God's Spirit.

In addition to the above principles which apply universally, there are special words of caution for messengers of the Gospel, depending on their cultural background:

The western missionary as a messenger of the Gospel. As I have written in "Evangelism and Culture" *(The New Face of Evangelism),* there are a number of negative aspects stemming from western cultural wrappings which affect the way people from the West present the Gospel. I think I am correct in saying that even today many western missionaries still consider the cultural wrapper of their home Christianity an integral part of the Gospel. I find relatively few making a conscious effort to free the Gospel from its western wrapper and even fewer who are aware of how their culture inhibits their own faith and obedience.

Local, missionary-trained pastors. All too often, if the missionaries are unable to separate the Gospel from its western cultural wrappings, the national pastors who are trained by them become twice the sons of Gehenna.

Recently a newly ordained national pastor came to me and asked: "Do you think it is true that spirits of the dead appear to the living?" He went on: "I had been in my congregation for just a few weeks when a man died. There had been considerable trouble, because this man had lent another member of the congregation some money and the debtor was refusing to pay it. On the day after his burial the dead man's soul appeared to his sister and said: 'You must go to the man who owes me the money and tell him to pay it at once. I am unhappy to leave this unsettled. If it is not settled I will not live in the graveyard alone.' "

When the family came to this pastor to ask for his blessing on their new approach to the defaulting debtor, he did not know what to say. As to whether the dead could appear to the living as the family had claimed, a retired lay preacher assured him, "That's exactly what happens." Unsatisfied, the pastor next sought out a fellow seminary-trained minister who reminded him: "We seminary-trained preachers don't believe in such things." The pastor finally told the people that he could not help them.

Then, as if suddenly remembering while talking to me, he added: "When I was living with my parents in the village, such a thing would not have troubled me. I would have believed it. But now I am a seminary graduate." In an effort to help him, I asked if there were any examples in the Bible of the dead appearing to the living. Relief flooded his face as he thought of the biblical examples.

Third World Christians as missionaries. It is a healthy sign that many Third World countries are launching missionary initiatives in countries other than their own. But sad to say, in many cases such Third World missionaries are no more sensitive to the cultures to which they are going than western missionaries were in the past.

Prophets of Independent churches. Probably the most successful witnesses (in terms of the number of members gained) on the African scene today are the prophets of Independent churches. Barrett recently observed that six out of ten conversions in Africa today are to Independent church groups. To this I would like to add from my own observation that even the members of mainline churches (Presbyterian, Methodist, etc.) again and again fall back upon these groups for healing, "dewitching," and so forth.

The prophets usually operate on the basis of a personal encounter with God who has given them a mandate to preach and teach a given way of worship. They identify very deeply with Old Testament prophets. Culturally they usually are single-mindedly African. This, often coupled with very limited Bible knowledge, leaves them very vulnerable to syncretism. Recently, however, I have observed in Zaire, Rhodesia, and Botswana an openness on the part of large numbers of such prophets to receive outside help to upgrade their knowledge of the Bible.

Culturally aware local leaders. It is gratifying to see a new kind of leader emerge on the African church scene. These usually are people who are proud of their African heritage but who have had extensive exposure to western cultures and also have gained some understanding of biblical cultures. It is men and women of this calibre who will be able to discern the western wrappings in which the Gospel came to them, while at the same time they will be aware of where the dangers of syncretism lie. They are the great hope of the church to develop a truly contextualized Christian faith that will meet the needs of the people and further the growth of God's Kingdom.

THE COMMUNICATION OF THE GOSPEL

God is always ready to meet us at the point of our greatest felt need. This, in itself, goes far in assuring that we will truly "hear" his message. I have been deeply impressed, while rereading the life of Jesus, to see how he put Isaiah's definition of the Gospel into practice according to the principle of felt need. Thus, when the four men brought the paralytic to Jesus to be healed, Jesus did not say, "My son, you are healed," but "My son, your sins are forgiven." Then, for the benefit of the Pharisees who took Jesus' statement as blasphemy, he said: "To show you that I, indeed, can forgive sin, I am going to tell this man to get up and walk." The healing almost seemed like an afterthought. Jesus began with the man's yearning for forgiveness—his deepest need. On the other hand, when the man who had been incapacitated for thirty-eight years was healed, Jesus did not even identify himself to him. That came later, and it was not until then that Jesus said, "Go and sin no more."

If we accept Jesus' definition of the Gospel—"good news for all, whatever their problems"—then it behooves us to find out what the pressing needs of a given people are, and to check whether the message we are giving them is indeed meeting their felt need, because, if not, we may be the modern Pharisees who "bind grievous burdens upon people but don't themselves lift a finger to help them carry them" (Luke 11:46).

This is not the time nor place for full-scale analysis of the problems of the communications process. However, it does seem essential to mention two crucial areas, one especially pertaining to the messengers of the Gospel and the other to the hearers of the Gospel:

Willful or unconscious misuse or skewing of the Gospel. Missionaries who accompanied the Catholic conquistadores and the Protestant colonizers did so with the highest motivation and found ample Scriptural justification for their "Christian/lord-to-pagan/servant" approach. Today we look back and say their approach was entirely wrong—it made a travesty of the Gospel. But the question that we need to ask is: Has that old attitude really died? Or has it merely taken on a new shape?

Racist white people have for generations been using the curse on Canaan quite out of context and completely erroneously to justify the subjugation of black men by white men. This interpretation may be dying out in Southern United States, but it is flourishing in Southern Africa. And what is most tragic about people having such biases is that they often are fervently religious. It is my deep and earnest prayer that the amount of skewing would decrease as we grow in grace and in the knowledge of our Lord Jesus Christ.

Syncretism. By syncretism I mean the mixing of the Christian faith and local traditional (non-Christian) beliefs and practices with the result that the Gospel is perverted, distorted, or largely voided in the process. A case in point is the South American tribal believer whose "testimony" I cited in the introduction of this chapter. Another example is found in the Kako people of Cameroon, who restructured the communion service on the model of their own *sataka* peace-making ritual, resulting in a short-circuiting of repentance and reconciliation in cases of excommunication.

Effective communication is a cooperative effort between the source and the receptor. No matter how good the source is in structuring a message, if the receptor is not receiving properly the communication will be limited. And likewise, no matter how hard the receptor tries to receive the message, if the source severely warps the message for one reason or another, the reception will be hindered or skewed. For this reason a basic attitude of *reciprocity* between the source and the receptor is fundamental. To my mind this involves at least the following areas:

1. *An honest acceptance of the validity of each other's cultures.* While some things may be new, strange, or even difficult, source and receptor will never suspect each other's motives as persons nor as members of a culture.

2. *A spirit of exchange.* Missionaries have often been so preoccupied with the greatness of the message they had to communicate that they were unpreprared to learn from their communicants. I can honestly say that during some thirty years in which I have tried to share the Good News with people in many languages, tribes, and societies, I have usually been taught more than I was able to teach.

3. *Personal and cultural self-exposure.* As they understand each other's personal and cultural reactions more fully, source and receptor will be able to serve as mirrors to each other to help each other become aware of those things that are incongruent with the tenor of the Gospel in their life-style or in their culture.

4. *Indigenous "sources of steam."* When the Gospel impinges on a culture, obviously some things in that culture are going to have to change. But culture change is difficult to effect unless there is an adequate amount of push from within. All too often in the past, missionaries have tried to provide the push from the outside, but as soon as they turned their backs, or whenever they had to leave the field, things reverted to the old way. For this reason any genuine change that is to be effected must be linked to an indigenous "source of steam" that will help keep up the momentum after the missionary has disappeared from the scene.

5. *Cooperative effort in contextualizing the Gospel.* At first blush, this may seem to contradict what was said earlier: "Each culture must assume the ultimate responsibility for contextualizing the Gospel in its own setting." But to my mind it does not. Adequate contextualization is a difficult task and the sympathetic outsider can often have a very unique role to play as mirror, source of alternative, catalyst, friend of the court, and so forth.

The outsider-as-mirror is as crucial to the established churches of the West as it is for the younger churches in the Third World. Contextualization is never a once-and-for-all event—it is an ongoing process. In fact, what was meaningful and right in grandfather's day may be utterly wrong today. I think it is highly significant that church people working overseas become deeply aware of serious problems extant in North American Christianity. For this reason we of the West will do well to consider seriously such mirror reflections as that of the South American Indians who are convinced that money, and not God, is the "axle" of our way of life. (See my chapter in *The New Face of Evangelicalism.*)

6. Last, but not least, *there must be an adequate interchange between the older and younger churches.* As a church gets established in a "receiving" society, early on there should be exchanges between it and the "sending" church. This exchange must always be a two-way street. Too often, older churches have found the criticism of younger churches quaint, interesting, or sometimes even annoying; seldom have they done anything about them. When older churches take seriously the challenges given to them by younger churches, their own communication with younger churches will be maximized.

Over and above these requirements, which are equally valid for both the source and the receptor, there are certain specific requirements for each.

In view of the sources' call to be witnesses of the Gospel, I feel that they must accept the greater responsibility for effective communication:

1. They must take the lead in cultural awareness, that is, in knowing their own, the Bible's, and the receptors' culture.

2. They must assume responsibility for establishing the proper initial channels of communication, following the communication principles outlined by E. A. Nida (see *Message and Mission,* Harper, 1960).

3. They must begin at the felt need of the receptors. Western missionaries—even the most evangelical—come from a highly secularized church situation in which God and the church have largely abdicated their concern for crop growth, human fertility, illness and health, mental health, social welfare, and so on. In the Third World, however (as in the Bible), these areas are still major religious concerns, and the Gospel will be the Good News for the Third World only if it includes such basic concerns in its focus. As I have indicated, when mission-founded churches offer no help in these areas, the people fall back on some other religion to cope with their problems.

4. They must demonstrate a humble acceptance of the fact that the receptor will establish an independent relationship with

God. Western missionaries have too long held a spiritual-father complex toward people to whom they have been privileged to bring the Gospel. (To be sure, this paternal role has often been aided and abetted by the receptor's readiness to accept the "child" role, thereby escaping personal responsibility.)

On the side of the receptors, I would like to underscore the need of an ongoing willingness to put themselves, their culture, and their unspoken world view and values under the scrutiny of the Spirit of God. There must be an implicit obedience to the truth as God's Spirit gives them new insight regarding the implications of the Gospel. In the spirit of the early church, they will submit themselves to the whole counsel of God (Acts 20:28).

9. Conversion and Culture
—An Anthropological Perspective with Reference to East Africa

by Donald R. Jacobs

DONALD R. JACOBS *is overseas secretary of the Eastern Mennonite Board of Missions and Charities. For many years he was Bishop of the Mennonite Church of East Africa.*

I WAS SLIGHTLY STARRY-EYED, A YOUNG EAGER American missionary appointed by the church to witness for Jesus Christ overseas. I was indeed humbled by the task but not consciously plagued with self-doubt. The site for my joust with the devil and myself (the two not always clearly distinguished, incidentally) was Tanzania, in a dominantly Bantu culture. As I determined to witness to Jesus Christ without reference to my Germanic Mennonite American background, I soon discovered that I had but a hazy concept of the relationship between my own culture and my Christian faith.

The issue was laid bare for me, however, when I chanced to hear another North American missionary say with obvious satisfaction, "So-and-so is really converted; he is beginning to think like we do!"

I could no longer avoid the problem. Can we assume that

conversion will result in moving a person toward ''our culture,'' the culture of the missionary? What, indeed, are the cultural expectations as perceived by the convertee and the converter? How should an experience of belief in and of walking with Jesus Christ affect a person's relationship with his own culture?

These became my compelling questions. Having allowed myself to form the questions, I was on a journey of discovery. It was as much a journey of discovery into myself as into the culture which hosted me.

As a Bible-honoring Christian, I carried then—and continue to carry with me now—certain theological assumptions, evangelical in nature, which underlie my anthropological approach to the subject of ''Gospel and Culture.'' These assumptions are:

1. When a man in his fallen state responds in repentant faith to Jesus Christ as revealed in the Scriptures and as known and loved by men and women through the ages, he experiences what is commonly known as Christian conversion.

2. This conversion will exhibit itself in changed behavior no matter what the cultural context. Conversion must be demonstrated in order to be recognized by the community and in order to be consolidated by the believer.

3. All levels of one's life are not changed or altered to the same extent following conversion. It is therefore helpful to understand what happens at the various levels of life as a result of conversion and why such changes do occur.

4. While it is agreed that conversion is an ongoing process (for we all have many ''turnings''), the conversion which is produced by an initial assent to the known will of God in Jesus Christ is nevertheless discernible and consequential.

5. Though conversion is an individual experience, it always occurs to persons in cultures, not in vacuums.

I have divided the subject into two parts. In the first part I will deal with what happens within a person's cultural experience upon and following conversion, and in the second I will trace what happens as Christian communities shift their relationships vis-a-vis the cultures from which they sprang.

THE HUMAN CULTURAL IMPERATIVE

Human beings are unhappy just to receive data; they have a compelling, almost relentless desire to interpret data. They do this in light of some frame of understanding which helps them to categorize and label. People therefore create cultures which are, in the last analysis, their particular group's grids for analyzing, sorting out, and tabulating data. Each group thus provides for itself a way to comprehend and to view life. People would be hard pressed to cope with life at all if it were not for the fact that when they were but children, their group molded their world view, which in effect gave them a ready-made structure for the comprehension of life.

Cultures enable groups to accumulate and tabulate the learnings of many generations in their own particular philosophical, ecological, and historical context. These cultures and sub-cultures are, to the participants, absolutely self-evident, universally applicable, and imminently "human." (Outsiders may, however, have a different view.)

THE PHILOSOPHICAL UNDERGIRDING OF A CULTURE

Each culture has a view of existence, a guide to understanding what life is all about and how to survive as happily as possible in that community. The most basic assumptions (presuppositions) a culture makes form a philosophical grid through which the group views the world. Normally, the culture assumes that the presuppositions are self-evident and therefore do not need to be stated. These presuppositions normally cover such basics as the nature of time, space, existence (ontology), and knowledge (epistemology).

An example may help to illustrate this. Suppose there is a serious bus accident, and we ask, "What caused it?" In seeking the cause, my culture leads me to inspect the steering gear, the brakes, maybe the condition of the road. While the Kuria people from Tanzania might find such bits of knowledge interesting, for them this approach does not encompass a wide enough scope of investigation to solve the riddle as to why the bus flipped over. They will probably look for "facts" which are, in their view, more important; for instance, who was angry with whom? The relational "facts" do not only describe for them more adequately the cause of the misfortune, but will then establish a scenario in which the malevolent powers are exposed and subsequently placed in a position where the community can deal with them.

Both cultures, mine and the Kurias', see relevant "facts," "the truth" of the situation, and each identifies a different set of "facts" to explain the situation. I say, "The truth of the matter is the steering gear broke and that is that." The Kuria says, "That is obvious, but that is not what ultimately caused the accident. The truth of the matter is, so-and-so willed someone's death on that bus. To know how the accident happened is only incidental. To know why it happened is essential."

All events, then, are examined in light of the prevailing world view. Every culture has its understanding of what is logical. It is obvious that cultures differ greatly in the ways they conceptualize their settings. That is at the heart of "tribalness" or ethnicity.

1. Philosophical Presuppositions and Conversion

Now we come to the question, what happens to a person's philosophical presuppositions when he is converted to belief in Jesus Christ? Or, we might ask, must these presuppositions be altered *before* conversion? Or do they change at conversion, or after conversion?

After pondering this question for many years I am slowly coming to the conviction that Jesus reveals himself meaningfully to a person "just as he is." A restructuring of the presuppositional grid is not required as a precondition for conversion.

The New Testament itself tells the story of how the Gospel which came to one particular people, the Jews, was then liberated from that culture so that it could be accepted by all men. The story plot of the Acts traces how Christ's presence became meaningful in both the Hebrew and Greek cultures. This happened in such a way that Hebrew Christians were permitted to retain their Hebrew philosophical presuppositions while at the same time the Christians from Greek cultures experienced Jesus Christ's presence in their own world.

The thrust of the Scriptures is clear; the evangelist must assume that the receptor's philosophical presuppositions form the context in which he will comprehend Jesus Christ, at least initially. Jesus' own incarnation is the basic model. Paul, in his evangelistic methodology, grasped the concept clearly. His sermon on Mars Hill, which was preached in the heart of the Greek culture, was couched in Greek rationalism. In contrast, his approach to the Ephesian occultists appealed to the miraculous. The philosophical presuppositions of these two audiences varied greatly; consequently Paul philosophically expressed the Gospel in different terms.

In order to grasp the consequences of this problem it may be helpful to consider briefly one of the philosophical presuppositions of culture, namely space. When I as a westerner think of space I think materialistically; for example, space contains only matter in a variety of shapes and weights. To think otherwise requires effort. I must almost do a "double take" every time I am required to think of that same space as the habitation of spiritual beings. It is not easy to step out of a chemistry class in Philadelphia and go to Sunday school. The Scriptures of the Sunday school admittedly pose a "spirited" universe, while western man tends to conceive of space materialistically. Therefore, when the Kuria relate to the universe of Scripture, they must shift their cultural assumptions less than the westerner to understand what the Bible teaches.

But the truth of the matter is, both cultures can and do experience Jesus Christ within the context of their own understandings. By communicating with one another in love, persons from different cultures can enlarge one another's horizons; but when it is all said and done, Kuria Christians remain undeniably Kuria in their perceptions of space and Germanic Americans remain Germanic Americans in their perceptions. Through painstaking effort they may stretch their categories somewhat, but the "stretch" will be slight—the findings of cultural anthropologists generally support the premise that shifts at the philosophical presuppositional level normally occur very slowly.

2. The "Powers" and Conversion

Within every culture certain powers are identified which impinge upon the community. Cultures go to great lengths to provide each person with a glossary of powers. The powers may be local or exotic, malevolent or benevolent, imminent or distant, demanding or indulging, complicated or simple, tractable or intractable, and so forth. Emotions are communicated when reference is made to this power and that. "He is to be feared, she is to be trusted, never do this or that power will affect you, etc." These powers interrelate, sometimes conflicting, sometimes reinforcing one another. The constellation keeps changing. The point is that the understanding of power sources is at the very center of a culture's existence. This is such a critical area for this discussion that I place it at the center of the world view (with what I call "kinetics" in the next layer, cultural themes in the next, and values in the outermost layer):

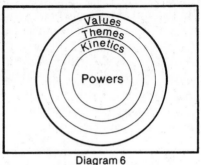

Diagram 6

When a person is converted to Jesus Christ, what happens at the level of the "powers"? I am quite convinced that for a sustained conversion experience a person must elevate Jesus Christ to a position of Lordship in his power constellation and keep him there through Christ-honoring living. In fact, one might well question a so-called conversion experience in which Jesus Christ is not exalted above all powers, when he is simply placed alongside of, and somewhat equal in power with, traditional powerful spirits and personalities. Belief in Christ does not eradicate all other powers, rather it places him *above* all powers.

Most of the world's Christians would score high on a doctrinal questionnaire as to the person of Christ. The test comes, however, in times of crisis when they require power or knowledge which they may feel Jesus withholds. Such crises bring out one's true cosmology. Conversion which does not include an experiential elevation of Jesus Christ above all other powers may well be

short-lived unless nurture or spiritual revival can quickly move in
and correct the misconception.

3. Kinetology and Conversion

Related very closely to the central core of "powers" is
another level for which we will invent the term "kinetology." This
represents a culture's attempt to understand the ways powers function and interact.

Cultures are survival conscious. We know that if we do not
constantly analyze events to determine cause and effect connections, we are in danger of annihilation. All cultures believe that it
is important to discover why things happen in order to better control their destiny. This is the purpose of kinetology, the dynamics
of power.

Kinetics defines the nature of power, as perceived by that
culture, how power operates, the concept of life-force and vital
protection, curses, blessings, the dynamics of how events are
caused and controlled and how power moves effectively from
source to point of motion.

Too often western missionaries presented the Gospel in
Africa in such a way that it had very little to do with the kinetological world of the people. That was a mistake because most of
Africa's cultures have elaborate systems which help them to detect
cause and effect relationships which in turn enable them to incorporate powers into their own life patterns. It was assumed, perhaps, that Jesus should be merely conceptualized and not *actualized*
in terms of power. If Jesus is not part of a person's cause and effect
conceptions, he remains an interesting but irrelevant figure.

I am convinced that their sensitivity to the kinetological
world has beautifully prepared Africans to comprehend Jesus
whose Name is above every name. I further believe that many
westerners miss much of God's provision in Christ by failing to
grasp Jesus as "the power of God unto salvation."

4. Cultural Themes and Conversion

Philosophical presuppositions and an understanding of
powers give rise to cultural themes which are in turn embodied in
myth systems which exist in the mind as concepts. To illustrate, a
Germanic-American theme which arises from our presuppositions

is the theme of thrift. This theme gives rise to myth systems which, on one hand, encourage accumulation of quality products, and, on the other hand, breed disdain for the free spenders, the non-savers, and people who do not take care of what they accumulate.

What happens to a person's cultural themes and myths when he or she is converted? It is my experience that thematic or mythical shift is a slow process indeed, unless the myth in question is in direct conflict with a theme of the Scriptures which the convert esteems of major importance. Cultural themes such as love and compassion (which are also biblical themes) will be strengthened and themes that give rise to avarice and pride will be rejected. For example, among the Wakuria, their strong fertility theme conflicts with the New Testament theme of self-sacrifice, which permits denying spouse, children, and property if it should be the clear will of God to do so as it was for Jesus and for the apostle Paul. In such cases the believers must clearly decide which themes they are going to give priority. Having said this I must hasten to say that prevailing themes, even after conversion, may well reflect some aspects of the pre-conversion ones.

In anthropological theory it is assumed that any one culture will seek to integrate its themes. It is highly unlikely that a culture will be able to sustain at the same level of importance two equal, competing themes. One ultimately will take dominance based on how the "powers" relate to the issue.

5. Values and Conversion

As we move to the fourth level, that of values, more shift can be expected, in fact is necessary, as a result of Christian conversion. This squares with social change theory which acknowledges that change occurs at the value level before it does at the inner levels.

We do well to pause at this point and ask an important question. When value shift occurs, will it be in the direction we would assume, that is away from previously held values to the values clearly expressed in the Scriptures? When a missionary (transcultural advocate) is involved, the shift is probably toward his or her value orientation (which may or may not be that of Scripture). There are several reasons for this. First, converts are usually well disposed toward the converter, and in symbolizing their new allegiance to Christ they may well espouse some of the converter's values.

Or, secondly, it might be that the new believers assume that the missionary has filtered out the anti-Christian factors in his or her own cultural experience and that, as a result, the advocate embodies a tried and tested variety of Christian living. So what often happens is that new believers swap some of their own cultural values for some of the cultural values of the missionary. This often serves, incidentally, to isolate the new Christians from their own cultures. This is a position which seems reasonable to the new believers because they desire a separate identity in the early stages of the establishment of a Christian community.

And, finally, new communities desire new sources of power. The believing community perceives the missionary's culture as "powerful." It therefore develops power linkages with the missionary, symbolized by a yielding to his or her value orientation.

The most obvious restructuring in a convert will occur at the value level. Hopefully the change that does occur will be toward biblical values and not simply toward the values of the missionary's culture.

6. Symbols, Ritual, Behavior, and Conversion

Up to this point we have been dealing with the conceptual aspects of culture, the world view. But culture does not remain in the head, it must be formalized in life. Both the metaphysical and cosmological beliefs will find expression in a multitude of symbols, rituals, and in everyday behavior. The process can be diagrammed:

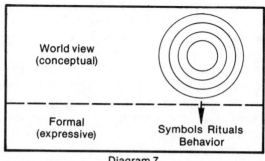

Diagram 7

Upon conversion the most obvious changes occur at the formal level. People quickly find ways of symbolizing their newly found relationship with Christ. In the minds of many, a conversion experience can thus be accomplished by a substitution of one set of rituals and symbols for another. However, such a change may be inconsequential. Unless there are significant shifts at the conceptual level the formal changes probably will not be permanent.

We have been seeking to examine the changes that occur in a person's world view as a result of Christian conversion. In any culture, we can reasonably expect change to occur at the formal level, power level, the value level, and the theme level (generally in that order). Change at any level has some effect upon all other areas but not equally so. A change at the formal level does not necessarily trigger a change at the world view level even though this is often the process one is tempted to rely on to bring about change. A change at the core of power hierarchy, however, can and does send shock waves through the entire system.

CHANGING CULTURAL EXPECTATIONS AND CONVERSION

When Christianity is introduced into a culture by advocates of another culture, several distinct stages of interaction may occur.

1. The Rejection Phase

As a small community of Christians emerges, having seen Christianity modeled by the foreign advocate living among them, the new community usually develops an antagonistic stand vis-a-vis the pre-Christian culture. Rejection might best describe this stage. Presumably cultural rejection is seen by the new minority as a way to enhance its chances of survival as a group.

The new Christian community does not reject its pre-Christian culture in its entirety; rather it selects very carefully what it wishes to reject and what it can live with. In their own way the new converts detect what in the pre-Christian culture compromises some aspect of the Christian faith and which must therefore be rejected.

In East Africa I discovered that the initial confrontation had to do with the power of Christ contrasted to the power of the other spirits, especially the spirits of the ancestors. Here the battle was joined. In order to draw clear lines of demarcation between their belief in the supremacy of Jesus Christ as a Spirit and their previously held beliefs about the power of other spirits, they disassociated themselves from any rituals in which the ancestral spirits were consulted or even assumed to be meaningfully present.

Even the paraphernalia employed in the former rituals connected with the ancestral spirits was often rejected. I was among those missionaries who thought it unfortunate that drums were abandoned for so long in regular Christian worship, but I see now that it has taken a long time to "launder" drums of their association with pre-Christian ritual.

During the rejection phase the semi-isolated community seeks deliberately to build cultural bridges to the missionary seeking in him or her potentially beneficial power sources. They participate in the advocate's ritual and symbolic life to a great extent, hoping thereby not only to demonstrate a rejection of much in their traditional culture but also to signify that they are laying new power conduits which will ultimately make the traditional power sources inconsequential.

The new Christian community may seek to link with the advocate in what the advocate might term secondary sources of power such as education, technology, and management, and miss what is to the advocate the secret of power—a vital living relationship with Jesus Christ.

Some advocates refuse to encourage a coupling of the Gospel with these secondary categories, lest they be accused of making "rice" converts. This concern must be applauded, but who in the world has sorted out the "acceptable" motivation for becoming a Christian? The advocate, whether he is conscious of it or not, is himself a beneficiary of many secondary privileges and powers associated with his or her own culture. So there is an obvious inconsistency in the attempt to withhold similar benefits from converts.

During the rejection phase the new community sees itself in contradistinction to the traditional culture; therefore new believers are expected to exhibit the proper anti-traditional stance. Persons who are converted in the context of a rejection phase will have cultural expectations placed upon them which do not apply, at least not as markedly, in later phases. So in the rejection phase much emphasis is given to the parts of the baptism formula which have to do with the renunciation of the past and the promise to begin a new life in a new community of faith. Also, in this context it is not surprising that so much is made of the ritual of renaming. For many this was and perhaps still is the public demonstration of a shift of sociological base from the traditional society to an exotic one. The renaming consolidated the conversion stance, perhaps even more than the ritual of baptism itself.

The effect of this radical cultural shift may not only be self-imposed isolation. In reaction the dominant society may encapsulate the new community. The Christian community is then forced to become a sub-culture which stands at a distance from the dominant culture. While the process of forming a sub-culture may contribute to a Christian community's stability, it also creates genuine barriers to evangelism.

2. Accommodation Phase

Various sources ultimately come to play upon a Christian community both from within and without to effect a shift in its culture stance. When the prevailing national mood, for example, is integrative rather than innovative, as it is in many parts of Africa today, a "stand-offish" group is made to feel quite uncomfortable. Many African churches, therefore, have moved into a new phase in which they attempt to accommodate themselves to the national or ethnic expectations.

This move toward accommodation often accompanies a renewed interest in evangelism on the part of the churches. Since evangelism is basically an exercise in communication it is clear that some of the "petty separation" must go. Thus the sharp edges of radicalism are dulled, some cultural innovations which were a bone of contention are modified and the Christian community rejoins society, perhaps two generations after the initial rejection.

The theological perils of this phase include the temptation toward syncretism. For this is the time when the Christian community tries to integrate its own themes, values, and cosmology with that of the traditionalists. Precarious though this period may be, it is nevertheless quite a significant one if the Christian community is to evangelize effectively.

During this phase the power conduits are relaid. Many channels which had formerly gone to the missionary's culture are now directed toward local power sources. This explains in part why political rapprochement marks this era and why a moratorium is called on the aggressive cultural expansion of impinging cultures.

Persons who are converted during this era are expected to be respectable citizens as well as keen Christians. If the prevailing mood is accommodation they will, of course, display signs of this attitude by, perhaps, getting involved in social issues, entering politics as Christians or by empowering the Christian community by some other means, usually laying the conduits to local power sources.

3. Reestablishment of Identity

A third stage is marked by a renewed desire on the part of the Christian community to come to terms with the dominant culture in a relevant, more dynamic way, in which case symbols of separation are again sought. Usually they choose some social evil which they feel threatens their Christian values. Then they seek to express their new boundary of separation by employing symbols of rejection which everyone in the culture can understand.

The search for new boundaries is often destructive of harmony in the church. Because of varying interests in the Christian community, it is hard to reach a consensus on a particular issue. The outcome is usually a new rejection movement on one hand and on the opposite side, a more complete accommodation movement. The accommodation movements tend to fuzz their boundaries with the dominant society, laying their power conduits to it without apology. The community of rejection withdraws many of its power conduits from the dominant culture and turns these conduits in on itself, yet remaining a part of the cultural ethos. They accomplish this by rejecting specific parts of the dominant culture but employing meaningful local symbols so that the not-yet-believing people can see clearly what the Christian community's agenda is. In this way it differs from the rejection community in stage one.

As the rejection community readjusts its relation to the dominant culture it becomes a sub-culture. When a person is converted he is expected to join this group, displaying signs of conversion by submitting himself to the discipline of this sub-culture. Phase three then conceives of conversion as "domesticating" a person culturally whereas phase one conversion was supposed to exhibit itself in a liberation from traditional culture.

For the group seeking even more accommodation to the dominant culture, conversion is not marked with such radical intent. In fact, other than participating in certain Christian rituals from time to time and paying their dues regularly, nothing much is expected. Converts in these groups tend to take a line of accommodation in their own lives.

These stages are not always generational. They can all be operating at one and the same time, yet if a particular Christian community is examined it will be found that such a sequential development is not unusual.

What are, therefore, the universal signs of conversion? This question is vexed by problems of cultural evolution and social change. When, for example, an Amish Mennonite young man in Eastern Pennsylvania in the United States in converted, he knows at once how his community will expect him to exhibit his conversion; in fact his conversion occurs in the context of cultural expectations. On the other hand, if a Roman Catholic in Eastern Pennsylvania is converted, an entirely different set of cultural expectations come into play.

SUMMARY

We have examined the phenomena of Christian conversion from two angles—the first by asking what occurs in a person's world view and formal system upon conversion and the second by tracing the way cultural expectations may change as the Christian community readjusts its stance in relation to the dominant culture.

The cultural and psychological variables which go into the believers' understanding of conversion vary widely. It is impossible to make very many general statements. Yet a few may be helpful:

1. Conversion takes place in the context of cultural expectation and is greatly influenced by that fact.

2. Unless Jesus Christ enters the convert's cosmology in a

meaningful way as a primary source of power, the experience of conversion will be brought into question as alternative power sources dominate life.

3. It is presumptuous for persons of one culture to dictate the "normal" cultural signs of conversion for another culture. The culture in question is equipped by the Scriptures and the Holy Spirit to make these judgments.

4. Even within one culture the signs of conversion may differ, depending upon the extent of the formation of Christian subcultures within it.

5. Conversion must be symbolized. The symbolization is determined largely by the particular group the person is in.

6. While conversion may be accompanied by a significant shift in behavior, the preconversion, culturally defined philosophical presuppositions will be minimally affected.

In summary, getting converted and witnessing about the experience are largely culturally controlled.

10. Conversion and Culture
—A Theological Perspective with Reference to Korea

by Harvie M. Conn

HARVIE M. CONN *is associate professor of missions and apologetics, Westminster Theological Seminary, Philadelphia, Pennsylvania. He is editor of* Theological Perspectives on Church Growth.

IN 1908, HORACE UNDERWOOD, A PRESBYTERIAN pioneer in Korea, spoke of the growth of the church there as "almost like a fairy tale, and veritably it has seemed like a chapter from the Acts of the Apostles." On the other hand, China seemed impenetrable. And even in Japan today, the Christian community has never exceeded one percent. Why?

In answering that question we seek for answers to other questions as well. What is world view and its relation to "religious change"? Does conversion affect world view? How? Should missionaries, out of respect for other cultures and to avoid cultural imperialism, seek to accommodate the Gospel to the cultural world view of their hearers?

CULTURE AND RELIGION

Part of one's answer to these questions depends on how one sees culture and its relationship to "religious decisions." Some

Christian commentators, like Donald McGavran, insist on culture as a conglomerate of components, as "aggregates rather than as organisms because, while a high degree of interrelatedness is observable, the components are seldom essential to the culture. Most components," he continues, "can be changed or even abandoned without trauma" (McGavran 1974:38). The majority, however, are reluctant to segment culture in this manner and see it rather as a kind of roadmap made up of various forms designed to get people where they need to go. Often borrowing language and ideas from the functionalist school of anthropology popular since the 1920s, definitions speak of culture as "that in terms of which our life is organized" (Kraft 1977:109-110), "the integrated system of learned patterns of behaviour, ideas and products characteristic of a society" (Hiebert 1976:45). Running through these attempts are common themes—culture as an integrating force, a dynamic organism that patterns our way of "seeing" reality.

Within this cultural structure, forms, functions, meaning, and usage remain distinctive but interrelated. Every cultural form serves particular functions, conveys meaning to the participants of a culture and, since relatively passive in and of itself, is dependent for its meaning and function on how active human agents use it in their cultural framework. So meat as a culturally satisfactory way of fulfilling the human need for food is religiously neutral in itself (Rom. 14:14; 1 Cor. 8:8). But, dedicated in sacrifice to an idol, its ties with the demonic world from which the new believer is now withdrawing may represent to "the weak" a supernatural power drawing him back into the "old age" from which Christ has been extricating him. Its old function and usage transform it into a stumbling block to the Gospel. That meaning cannot be forgotten even by "the strong" (Rom. 15:1). Within a Hindu culture a hamburger from McDonald's takes on religious dimensions.

Culture, then, by virtue of this interrelationship, is never simply a religious neuter. It is "that complex of spiritual, moral, technical and agricultural forces wherein a tribe or a people tries to express its basic feelings towards God, towards nature, and towards itself. The culture of a people is in its common attitude of life, its style of living and thinking, rooted in its apprehension of reality" (Bavinck 1949:57). Culture's forms remain per se neutral building blocks. But their ties with the functions, meaning, and usage given to them by the culture never leave them absolutely neutral. "All elements have their secret ties with the religious faith of the people as a whole. Nothing is to be found anywhere that can be called a 'no-man's land.' Culture is religion made visible; it is religion actualized in the innumerable relations of daily life" (Bavinck 1949:57).

The relation of the religious dimension of human life to world view and culture may be illustrated as follows:

Diagram 8

In this model, religion is the crucial allegiance dimension. Admittedly, this approach is problematic to much contemporary usage in anthropology. The functionalist school has been willing to include religious phenomena within the cultural matrix of society (van Baal 1971:165), one of many needs demanding satisfaction in culture's "vast instrumental reality." But even this concession is not enough. Behind it lies the functionalist conception of culture as "an instrument serving man's biological and psychological needs" (Hatch 1973:320).

We seek to stress the core place of religion in the structuring of culture's meaning and usage. Religion in culture is response to the "supracultural" God. Fallen Adam does not escape the covenant obligations of culture building (Gen. 1:28-30). Even his painful labor in subduing the earth is given religious dimensions by God. The building of a city by Cain the murderer to bear his son's name (Gen. 4:17), the erection of a tower on the plains of Shinar, is given religious significance by its meaning, the exalting of man's name, an invitation to divine judgment. When metals can be smelted, swords can be made, and Lamech can sing his boastful song of hate (Gen. 4:23 ff.), "the demonic dynamic of the 'abominations' of the heathen begin to appear. The kingdoms whose cultural riches Satan will show to Jesus begin to rise like beasts out of the sea" (Clowney 1976:5). Culture's forms are universal—poetry (Gen. 4:23-24), music (4:21), forging metals (4:22). But they do not share necessarily a religious commonality of meaning and usage across cultures. Culture's forms are shaped by our self-service as "sons of Cain" or by our "spiritual service" (Rom. 12:2) as "sons of God." The "spiritual" dimension every Christian wishes to guard in its cultural role is not simply one human universal among others (safety needs, love and belongingness needs, esteem needs). Nor is it even a synonym for the cultural commonality of religion. It is not an area of life, one among many, but primarily a *direction* of life, and even more specifically, a Christian direction of life. The entire scope of man's living in Christ in his culture is "spiritual service."

Religion, then becomes the "heart" of culture's integrity, its central dynamic as an organism, the totalistic, radical response of man-in-covenant to the revelation of God (Prov. 4:23; Jer. 29:13; Matt. 12:34). The world's religions are not simply complex entities, containing much that is beneficial. They are powerful, life-controlling entities, indivisible structures, each element cohering with all the others and receiving its meaning from the total structure (Bavinck 1960:172-173).

The task of Christianity vis-a-vis any given culture or subculture thus becomes primarily the possession by Christ of that culture's functions, meaning, and usage, calling for a transformation of its forms in Christ. The cultural forms of sexual needs that once demonstrated the "darkening of foolish hearts" (Rom. 1:21, 26-28) in Christ become analogs of Calvary's self-sacrifice (Eph. 5:25, 32). "Eating and drinking and whatsoever we do" become expressions of the glory of God (1 Cor. 10:31), not sacrifices to the god who is our belly (Phil. 3:19).

Both Catholic and Protestant histories in Korea illustrate these points, but in opposite directions. Both came at times of social and cultural disorientation. Confucianism, the stabilizing cultural core of the peninsula from the fourteenth century, had become the symbol of social exploitation. But in this cultural vacuum of turmoil, Catholic mission policy had turned to an ''uncompromising attitude . . . against traditional culture and customs'' (Park 1970:156), whereas the Protestant apologetic was one of identification with Korean cultural selfhood. Catholicism in Korea became deeply identified with western, foreign alliances. The government persecutions against it that began in 1785 and ended in the 1860s were as much against its identification with the West as against Christianity. In 1801, this identification was reinforced when Hwang Shi-yung, a Catholic from the Korean noble class, composed a letter to the Bishop at Peking, asking for armed intervention to end persecution of the Christian community. The letter was intercepted by Korea's then-isolationist government and taken as a mark of Christianity's solidarity with alien forces. The church's policy of baptizing converts with foreign names (Andre Kim, Pierre Lee) and sending French priests secretly into the country further fueled fears of foreign intervention. Church growth came to a standstill and Catholicism became a ''catacomb'' or ''ghetto'' community (Biernatzki, Im, Min 1975:5).

The Protestant movement, begun in the late nineteenth century, was much more successful in ''naturalizing'' the Gospel. In China, Christianity was seen as ''the unwelcome face behind the iron mask of western imperialism'' (Palmer 1967:48). In Korea's encounter with Protestantism, however, it was Japan, not the West, that was perceived as the imperial oppressor and it was the Protestant missionary who was ''the representative Westerner, not the merchantman nor the official'' (Gale 1909:130). Koreans perceived Protestant Christianity as ''an agent of continuity'' with their cultural destiny.

A number of events symbolized that identification. The decision to translate the Bible into Korean script was highly significant. The alphabet had been the product of the Yi dynasty's ''Golden Age of Culture'' and its patron, King Sejong (1418-1450). But it was spurned by the educated class as a ''vulgar script,'' and the Chinese ideographs (in use from the early second century B.C. in Korea) had remained the language of society and

Yi culture. Unlike China where more than fifty years elapsed between the arrival of the first Protestant missionaries and the printing of the Bible, the Korean script Bible was smuggled into the country in 1883, two years before the first preaching missionaries arrived. "It can be said that the missionaries and the church popularized the people's alphabet and brought it into general use even in non-Christian circles" (Kay 1950:116-117).

This revival of the vernacular formed the basis of a new literature closely associated with a reformist-nationalist movement. Korea's first vernacular newspaper appeared in 1896. Its editor, Philip Jaisohn, a convert to Christianity, saw the paper as a call for Korean national independence and for "the moral and spiritual regeneration of Korea" (Palmer 1967:75-76). Christian secondary schools became seedbeds for the incubation of ideas of nationalism and independence. Many of the early Korean leaders in the struggle against Japanese colonialism were trained in such schools.

Nationalist sentiment, with its strong identification with Christianity, climaxed in 1919 with the March First Movement. Nationwide peaceful demonstrations took place upon the public reading of a Declaration of Independence from Japan by thirty-three Koreans of national prominence. Fifteen of the signers were Christians, and of the 19,525 who were arrested in connection with the demonstrations, 3,428 of the 6,312 with "religious affiliations" were Christians. Again, by way of contrast between Catholicism and Protestantism, there was strong Catholic reluctance to participate in the 1919 Independence Movement.

The adoption of the celebrated Nevius mission method of self-government, self-support, and self-propagation by Korea's Presbyterians reinforced the image of Christianity as a transformer of culture, not a destroyer. Behind the three-self formula was a confident assurance that Protestant Christianity was not only relevant to Korean culture but that Koreans themselves would spontaneously promote the Gospel without distorting it. Typical of missionary sentiment may be the words of Mary F. Scranton, founder of Ewha Girl's School in 1886. The girls, she said, "are not being made over again after our foreign way of living, dress and surroundings. We take pleasure in making Koreans better Koreans only. We want Korea to be proud of Korean things, and more, that it is a perfect Korea through Christ and his teachings" (Paik 1929:119).

Even the missionary approach to Korea's religions was not one of wholesale condemnation. Horace Underwood, responding to the hypothetical question, "What religions are chiefly attacked by the missionaries?" perceptively writes,

> I think no attack upon any religion is usually made. The missionary who goes to a foreign field has not the time to spend in attacking its old faiths. His work is simply to hold up Christ and Him crucified, and in His presence no other faith can live. . . . We found that God, by His spirit, had been at work throughout the length and breadth of this land before we reached here, however; that all over it men and women were being led to lose faith in their old religions. (Underwood 1908:90-91)

Preeminently the link was forged with the culture in the choice of the Korean term, *Hananim,* "Spirit of Heaven," to communicate the Christian idea of God. It was apparently borrowed from Shamanism which, with the queen's support, was enjoying a revival during the early Protestant years. The missionaries rendered it as "the one Great One," thus implying (somewhat naively) a connection with a "primitive pure monotheism" (Underwood 1910:103-111). *Hananim,* in the Shamanistic legend, had given life to the people and their culture by sending his divine son, Tan'gun, into the world. His grandson had been the first Korean king. Comments Gale, "Immediately when the Bible is read, 'In the beginning some One created the heaven and the earth,' they answer 'Hananim' . . ." (Gale 1906:78-79). Thus it was that when the Korean, "standing by his simple altars, where, with neither image or spirit tablet his fathers have for generations worshipped the God of heaven, learns that God is a spirit and truth, he believes that this is the God of his fathers" (Underwood 1910:261).

There were other benefits in the choice besides what the missionary took to be the "strong possibility" of its monotheistic implications. Park Pong-bae suggests that the original term was drawn from a Shamanism syncretized not with Buddhist pantheism but with Confucian heaven-worship and its ethical implications of kindness and love, filial piety, purity and chastity (Park 1970:40-46). This would help explain why the *Hananim* myth carried a social or ethical dimension of "man for the public interest" (Park 1970:52-53), the Confucian "mandate of heaven." Thus, the original context of the term could only reinforce the identification of Christianity with Korea's high regard for the western ethic. It goes far to explain the remark of a prime minister who, although not a Christian himself, hoped that his king would become a believer: "Only with a God-fearing king who knows that he must render account as to how he rules this country, can we have a good government" (Underwood 1908:40).

The anthropologist Homer Barnett has said that new ideas will be accepted only if (1) they satisfy a want better than some existing means, (2) they connect in part with the previous life experience of the people, and (3) pervasive dissatisfaction has already gripped a portion of the people (Barnett 1953:378 ff.). Korea, providentially prepared by the Spirit to meet those conditions, had begun to taste the transforming work of Christ. The remarks of a public magistrate who attended an evening service of a Bible training class reflected it. "He expressed a sentiment which shows the present attitude in many minds towards Christianity. 'There is nothing left for us to do now but to put our trust in the Christians' God' . . ." (Shearer 1966:54).

WORLD VIEW AS THE CHANGE CENTER AND THE KINGDOM OF GOD AS THE CHANGE-MAKER

Where must culture change begin to be the most meaningful? With world view change, what Eugene Nida has called the "deep structures" (a culture's presuppositions regarding time, space, supernatural power sources, etc.). World view, to modify the language of Charles Kraft, is a paradigm, a deep-rooted "map" of reality ordinarily unquestioned by the culture. Through the particularity of the world view, its proponents perceive and structure reality. By means of that same uncriticized world view they generate theories to justify their constructions of reality. A world view is an integrated, all-encompassing perspective, a storage shed of presuppositions about the world. Its value system is a bank vault, "both the repository and the generator" of those conceptual models through which its subscribers will perceive and interact with reality (cf. Kraft 1977:78).

As "the central control box" of a culture, the world view, as outlined by Kraft, performs a five-fold function: (1) It explains how and why things got to be as they are and how and why they continue or change. (2) It validates the basic institutions, values, and goals of a society. (3) It provides psychological reinforcement for the group. (4) It integrates the society, systematizing and ordering the culture's perceptions of reality into an overall design. (5) It provides, within its conservatism, opportunities for perceptual shifts and alterations in conceptual structuring.

That central control box is changed by a sovereign act of divine grace, what J. H. Bavinck has termed *Possessio,* God in Christ capturing the stronghold of change. And when that divine work is initiated, people begin to change their world view. In the language of anthropology, there is (1) a change of allegiance that issues in (2) a concomitant change in the evaluation principles within the person's/group's world view, and (3) a resultant series of new habits of behavior (Kraft 1977:279). This is the open-ended process of reevaluation, reinterpretation, and rehabituation the theologians call conversion.

One of the biblical images used to describe this work of God in redemption is that of the Kingdom of God. The prophetic promise of the "return" to the land is the promise of the return of the remnant of God, those to whom the Lord would manifest his kingly redemption (Pss. 22:27-28; 72:8-12). At the heart of the Kingdom dimension to conversion will be the initiative of God's grace (Ps. 80:3, 7, 19), God's "turning again" to his people (Kittel 1971:724). The message of the New Testament is the announcement that the Kingdom has come in Christ, the day of repentance and conversion begun (Luke 1:16; Matt. 3:2). So, Jesus heralds the Kingdom come by calling men to "turn" and "repent" (Luke 5:32). "Repentance and faith are simply the two main aspects of the kingdom, righteousness and the saving grace of God, translated into terms of subjective human experience" (Vos 1972:91). So, Peter's sermon in the temple points to Jesus' death and resurrection as the fulfillment of the prophetic word and concludes with a call to "repent and return" (Acts 3:19). The Pauline commission to preach to the Gentiles is outlined in terms of a call for "repentance and turning to God" (Acts 26:20). Conversion is to Christ and his Kingdom.

The Kingdom dimension of conversion calls for a totalistic approach to culture which has not been characteristic of missions. J. H. Bavinck notes that the Pietistic movement of the seventeenth and eighteenth centuries displayed "a remarkable hostility to the cultural side of the missionary task" (Bavinck 1949:45). Cultural anthropology has refuted the popular separation of religious from cultural life, of the sacred from the secular. But the traditional fixation on the personal dimensions of salvation has hindered the church from incorporating the cultural obligations of personal redemption into mission methodology. "Jesus Christ is Lord of everything. The whole of life ought to be subjected to the royal authority of Him who has redeemed us by His precious blood. It is noteworthy that the missionary command in Matthew 28 follows upon the declaration of Christ Himself that all power in heaven and on earth has been given unto Him" (Bavinck 1949:30). Jesus, the second Adam, is the fulfiller of culture and the refashioner of its world views. The work of the Kingdom is not narrowly cultic or "religious" in the narrow sense in which it is used by cultural anthropologists. Conversion to the Kingdom is commitment to world view change, to bring our culture under the authority of the King, into conformity to the Kingdom and its fullness.

The impact of the radical Kingdom rule of Christ will do more than merely "modify" a world view or "accommodate" itself to an existing one. If true transformational change (as opposed to merely external alteration) is to take place, the change must occur not merely at the behavioral edges of the world view's manifestations but at its center. Here begins the process Kraft has called reinterpretation, reevaluation, and rehabituation. Out of a world view now Christ-possessed at its root, the convert starts the lifelong habit of Christ-transformation. World view reformation begins with the convert evaluating and interpreting each aspect of life in the Spirit in terms of the Kingdom claims of his new allegiance. From this comes "rehabituation," "changes in habitual behaviour issuing from the new allegiance and the consequent reevaluational process" (Kraft 1977:103).

In this process, the missionary will "seek to encourage a minimal number of critical changes in the world view, rather than a larger number of more peripheral changes" (Kraft 1977:290). Peripheral changes run the risk of encouraging "culture conversion'' rather than "conversion to Christ." Missionary resistance to polygamy has often had this effect. Polygamy, a peripheral issue, is given central significance as a mark of faith, and baptism is delayed or given on the basis of the convert's willingness to break with it.

Korea's history illustrates this misunderstanding. After much debate in the 1890s, both the Methodists and the Presbyterians adopted policies that denied full fellowship in the church to those who had not broken all polygamous relationships. From it flowed a heated discussion among the missionaries as to requirements for church membership and what constitutes a credible profession of faith. The outcome was much more rigorous demands for membership. The Methodists separated the rite of baptism from the reception of church membership, and set up four classes of church adherents: full church members, baptized probationers, probationers, and inquirers. The Presbyterians adopted a prebaptismal probation, known as the catechumen class. After six month's probation, the candidate for baptism was reexamined, and either admitted, continued, or dropped. The failure to distinguish between world view change and peripheral change had altered the significance of baptism from conversion sign to sanctification sign.

Another term to describe this core change of the world view, used in other contexts by Alan Tippett (Tippett 1973:88-91), is "power encounter." It is that clash in cultural world view between the redeeming, liberating power of the Kingdom of God manifest in Christ, and his victory over the powers (Eph. 6:10-12, 1 John 3:8), and the kingdom of Satan in which the world lies (1 John 5:19). It is the elenctic call in which cultural world view becomes the battleground on which the Gospel communicator proclaims the defeat of sin and death through the resurrection of Christ and his consequent authority (Matt. 28:18).

Power encounter is not simply "point of contact." It is "point of attack." This is seen in Paul's attitude toward the altar to the unknown god in Acts 17:

> In this altar heathendom experienced its impotence and helplessness, its endless multiplication of gods and goddesses. Paul knew very well that this altar had nothing to do with the worship of the God who appeared to us in Christ

Jesus, but Paul here heard the cry of despair and misery, and this made it possible for him to sketch boldly the sole way of escape. (Bavinck 1960:141)

The Kingdom power encounter always will be shaped by the varieties of cultures' world views. But it must always retain its dynamically equivalent shape as the godward side of conversion, God's saving power motivating man's turning from and turning to.

That power encounter may be traced in the impact of the Christian concept of sin on Korea's Confucian world view. In the Confucian model, there is no concept of radical sin or evil. In Confucianism, opposites (including good and evil) are constantly blending into a complementary and mutually necessary harmony of "becoming." The Confucian world view speaks of "impropriety or offenses against traditional authorities, parents, ancestors and superiors in the hierarchy of office" (Park 1970:213). Against this background, the Christian concept of sin was perceived as extreme and undignified.

Yet it was precisely here that a decisive power encounter occurred in Korea. The Gospel message "destroyed the self-asserting and self-righteous attitude of Confucianism. For the first time, Koreans were forced to reflect upon the religious and ethical meaning of humility. The new awareness of the radical nature of sin made Korean Christians deathly afraid of the divine judgment . . ." (Park 1970:219). That power encounter manifested itself most visibly in the Great Revival of 1907. In Korea's shame-oriented culture, the desperate prayers of confession and petition signaled a "collapse of the self-righteous attitude, the deepening of the concept of sin, the internalization of ethical motivation, and the elimination of rigid exclusivism" (Park 1970:220). James Gale, an observer, comments, "Old conservative Koreans who had drunk deep of Confucius . . . , whose pride of spirit made them un-approachable were among the broken-hearted and the contrite" (Gale 1909:213). From it flowed "a deep impression of the exceeding sinfulness of sin and of the everlasting obligation of righteousness" (*Korea Mission Field* 1908:70).

The patterns of prayer and contrition continue. Prayer is accompanied by weeping and often shrill pleading, quickly stopped by the ring of the pastor's bell on the pulpit. The forms of prayer have been shaped by a profound shift in world view.

THE PROCESS OF CHANGE AND CONVERSION

Up till now, we have mentioned world view change as a process. Any number of things may short circuit that process—cultural overlays held by the Gospel communicator or by the hearer, inability to differentiate between the cultural forms of conversion often developed by ecclesiastical tradition and experience, and conversion as a biblical "given." There may be a lack of sensitivity to the "constants" of biblical conversion—conscious allegiance to God in faith and repentance, the dynamic interaction between God and human beings that issues from man's conscious allegiance to God, growth or maturation in Christ, the community nature of the maturation process, the cultural appropriateness of the conversion process (Kraft 1977:604-613). The end result of one or more of these inhibitors can be "culture conversion" as much as it is conversion to Christ.

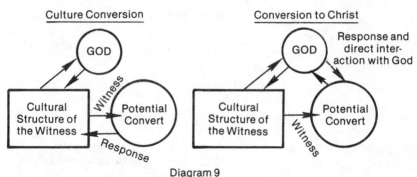

Diagram 9

One of the most serious short circuits is too much focus on conversion as a single act of initiation into the Kingdom, what anthropologists would call conversion as a "rite of passage" rather than as also a "rite of consolidation."

That danger is very real in the evangelical community where, in the development of theology, conversion has lost its comprehensive meaning for the entire renewal of man. Under the impact of Protestant scholasticism and its syncretistic accommodations to western rationalism, the study of the nature of conversion became controlled by a desire for precise, clear-cut cognitive categorizations. Conversion began to lose the fluid sense Calvin gave it and was confined to one, logically isolatable, narrow activity in the so-called "order of salvation" *(ordo salutis)*. Along with such scientifically fixed categories as justification and sanctification, conversion became a separate act of initiation into the Kingdom. Calvinist and Arminian disagreed over whether it preceeded regeneration or followed it. Since it was an act and not a process, debates arose over whether that act could be repeated or not. "Once saved, always saved?"

The impact of Pietism, later Puritan preparationism (Allison 1966; Pettitt 1966), and moralism reinforced the emphasis by underlining conversion as an individual appropriation of the salvation given in Christ. The convergence of all these influences produced a severely narrowed concept of conversion, controlled by western culture's excessive emphasis on the individual and leaving us with a concept of conversion as a simple step of repentance and faith somewhere very near the beginning of our Christian life, sharply distinct from sanctification as a process. The words of the Reformed theologian, Louis Berkhof, are typical of the results of this approach: "If we take the word 'conversion' in its most specific sense, it denotes a momentary change and not a process like sanctification" (Berkhof 1949:485).

This leads to arbitrary distinctions commonly made between, for example, national revivals and conversion. So, examples of "national conversion" in the Old Testament may be dismissed as "merely of the nature of moral reformations. They may have been accompanied with some real religious conversions of individuals, but fell far short of the true conversion of all those that belonged to the nation" (Berkhof 1949:483). Thus, "true conversion" is reserved for initial one-time experiences, on an individual level. The fact that the Bible "speaks of the Christian's return to God, after he has fallen into sin, as a conversion" is acknowledged by Berkhof—and then set aside in favor of the western preference for more precise definition.

Two streams are coming together now to alter this restricted picture of conversion. Christian anthropologists, like Alan Tippett and Charles Kraft, are calling attention to "conversion as a dynamic process" (Tippett 1977:218-220), conversion as "a multitude of (often very small) decisions by human beings in interaction with God" (Kraft 1977:606). Even with strong differences as to how this process should be interpreted, there remains a relatively common avoidance of identifying conversion with one point on a Kingdom continuum. No one is concerned to deny the place of conversion as that verbal symbol pointing to the obligations of faith and repentance for entrance into the Kingdom, the human "rite of initiation" as it were. It is simply that the anthropologist is stressing as well the conversion process, the intensification and increasingly meaningful nature of the change conversion makes in the growing world view change.

Especially within the Reformed theological community, this perspective on conversion is being underlined by a new sensitivity to conversion, not as merely a single step in the order of salvation, but conversion as a dynamic and comprehensive designation of man's response to the coming of the Kingdom of grace in Christ. Conversion is thus recognized as an eschatological sign of the beginning of the last days in Christ's coming (1 Cor. 10:11; Heb. 1:1-2, 1 John 2:18). The age-to-come has been inaugurated by Christ's resurrection, and conversion is a sign of our resurrection already in Christ (Vos 1930, 1952:42-61). Like justification, adoption, and sanctification, conversion is not a distinct act but an aspect of our solidarity in Christ's resurrection and our new existence in the new creation age, inaugurated by his resurrection (Gaffin 1978:140).

The uniqueness of conversion as "turning to God" lies in its sign character of "the great change experienced by him who was translated from the power of darkness into the kingdom of the Son of God's love (Col. 1:13)" (Warfield 1952:362). In describing that change from its godward side, a whole group of terms are used in the New Testament ("to be born," "from above," "from God," "from the Spirit," "regeneration," etc.). And in describing its manward side, says Warfield, are such terms as "to repent" and "to turn." "We must set over against 'repentance' as the inward word its complement in 'turning' as an outward word, denoting the changed course of life" (Warfield n.d.:95). Warfield's emphasis in this is on conversion as process, "and a process which has two sides. It is on the one side a change of the mind and heart, issuing in a new life. It is on the other side a renewing from on high issuing in a new creation" (Warfield 1952:369). The entirety of that process, viewed as the work of God in man, is what the Scriptures designate as "renewal." It is the change of vesture, the process of laying aside the old Adam-like soiled clothing, and putting on the new Adam-like clean raiment (Eph. 4:24; Col. 3:9-10). It is a metamorphosis, becoming transformed beings by the renewing of our minds, freeing ourselves more and more from the fashion of this world (Rom. 12:1-2). So deeply does this idea of change-process control the language that even repentance as the heart's change of direction can be distinguished from its decisive deeds of expression. "Repentance is known by its fruits, but it is not its fruits. John called on his hearers to show their repentance by their deeds: 'Bring forth, therefore, fruits worthy of repentance' (Luke 3:8, cf. Matt. 3:8)" (Warfield n.d.:94).

In all this we do not seek to ignore the point of entry into the Kingdom as emphasized in the traditional western approach. On the other hand, we seek to emphasize the eschatological significance of conversion, the consummation of conversion not simply in "turning to God from idols to serve a living God" but "in waiting for His Son from heaven . . . who delivers us from the wrath to come" (1 Thess. 1:9-10). We underscore also the transformational, eschatological, forward dimension of the process. "Raised with (or in) Christ," the believer, even while situated in the cultures of the present age, lives "in the heavenly places" and participates in the new creation begun by Christ. In the process of the ongoing response of faith to the Kingdom reality already initiated by Christ, the believer moves in increasing depth from the point of entrance into the Kingdom to the future age and the final regeneration.

We leave open the matter of the precise steps, and the order of the steps, which will be taken in that Kingdom transformation of culture and world view. In so doing, the western propensity for instant perfection and for identifying the cultural marks of conversion with his own are diminished. It becomes more necessary to acknowledge "the distinction . . . between what *makes* a person a Christian and what *shows outwardly* that he is a Christian" (Taber 1976:1). In identifying conversion change, we do not look for an absolute degree of attainment as proof that one is a child of God but for discernable progress in the *right direction* (Taber 1976:3).

Thus, in an animistic culture, the earliest evidence of conversion change might very well be a sense of communion with God, not the individualistically motivated self-reflection the westerner is accustomed to expect. Biernatzki and his colleagues would seem to write of early Catholic conversions in Korea this way:

> Without ignoring the role of supernatural faith, it seems reasonable to suppose that they initially turned to Catholicism to seek consolation and refuge from their earthly suffering in much the same way that their pagan counterparts sought shelter and salvation in animism, popular Buddhism, or in the new religions which bloomed in such profusion during the troubled final decades of the Yi dynasty. (Biernatzki, Im, Min 1975:22-23)

Similarly George Paik describes the experience of early Protestant converts: "There was a fellowship among converts that was attractive to an outsider. The Christians were sympathetic toward each other and stood together in sorrow and joy" (Paik 1929:284).

In the same way, among those Koreans whose world view was deeply motivated by their political and social interests, the most visible signs of conversion might carry a political flavor not normally considered by evangelicals as a sign of Kingdom change. Yi Seung-hoon, who was suggested as a signer of the 1919 Declaration of Independence, was a dissatisfied Confucian who had "wanted, from his youth, to eliminate social differences between yangban and sangnom (high and low classes), but had no Biblical conception of God as the Creator who had made all men equal" (Clark 1971:429). As Clark notes, Yi "was first converted to popular reform, then to Christ" as he came to realize "that the Christian Church had the real power needed for the future."

At the same time, these cultural variations in identifying conversion and its process, unless carefully perceived, can open the way for the believers to lose sight of the eschatological tension between the Kingdom's "now and not yet," lapsing simply into a "this world's now." "Christian churches were involved in politics to such a degree that Korean religious institutions became virtual political institutions" (Park 1970:163). This distortion reflected the pull of a Confucian social ethic of involvement, unchecked by Kingdom realism about the powers of this age. On the other hand, the Shamanistic, Buddhistic escapism, unreconstructed by the radical demands of the Gospel, turned other churches inward, towards a noninvolvement with this world, eyes set only on heaven.

When conversion loses its eschatological integrity as a process, liability to blindness regarding cultural pressures grows more real.

COMMUNAL CHANGE AND COVENANT SOLIDARITY

Culture-building is a communal activity, a pattern for living shaped by the collective solidarity of a people, its forms shaped by a people's understanding of its covenant relationship to God, the world, and one another. Insensitivity to that communal, covenant character to culture can be a major hindrance to the change process. This danger is especially strong for the missionary change agent whose enculturated western individualism makes it hard for him to conceive of conversion except in an individual-oriented way. We have already drawn attention to an example of this in Berkhof's treatment of "national conversions" in the Old Testament.

By way of contrast, the conversion process described in the Bible is in terms of the "turning" of a people to God in covenant. This is clearly the case with Israel. Her reaction to defeat by the Amorites at Ai is described in terms of "returning and weeping before the Lord" (Deut. 1:45). Her banishment among the nations will one day mean "a return to the Lord, your God," mirrored in "obeying him with all your heart and soul according to all that I commanded you this day" (Deut. 30:2, 8).

Associated with this eschatological promise of Israel's "return" (Deut. 30:3) is the conversion of the nations. Egypt will be numbered among the remnant who "return" (Isa. 19:22). "All the ends of the earth" will turn to the Lord and be saved (Isa. 45:22). In the last day "many nations" will "go up to the mountain of the Lord" (Micah 4:2).

The communal dimensions of conversion are not lost in the New Testament. The church is the covenant community, the fellowship of the Spirit formed by the gifts of the Spirit (1 Cor. 12:12-27). The instances of household baptisms among the Gentiles recorded in Acts become testimonies of this same covenant solidarity of grace, expanded now to include Gentiles as well as Hebrews. The narrative of Cornelius' conversion particularly underscores this. It is prefaced by Peter's reluctance as a Jew to associate with a Gentile (Acts 10:2 ff., 34 ff.). It is concluded by the church's admission that "God has granted to the Gentiles also the repentance that leads to life" (Acts 11:18). God is building in the day of the new covenant one new remnant from Jews and Gentiles (Eph. 2:1-14).

Conversion, then, becomes turning from the community shaped by the sin of the first Adam to the community shaped by the redemption of the second Adam, "Turning *from* ethnicity, tribalism *to* open covenant based on Jesus' Lordship (within the church) and *from* geographic and temporal parochialism (nationalisms) *to* the universal (present and coming) Kingdom" (Shank 1976:6). The covenant community broken in the garden is restored in Christ.

Donald McGavran and his colleagues have done western missions a great service by reminding us of the importance of communal, covenant solidarity in the work of converting the peoples of the world. They warn of the limitations of western-style evangelism which seeks out converts "one by one against the social tide" (McGavran 1970:299; Kraft 1977:620). Kraft reminds us of what this means for our missionary methodology. "Transformational change is accomplished more efficiently and effectively if *advocated by groups* than if advocated simply by individuals. 'Social change of any magnitude at all cannot be made by individuals.' This is why movements are of such great importance in cultural transformation" (Kraft 1977:293). So, Kraft concludes, appeals for both conversion and cultural transformation should, for maximum effectiveness, be directed primarily to socially homogeneous groupings of people and to leaders who will influence such groups. That advice seems eminently practical.

However there is one qualification I wish to make. It is that the basis of homogenity runs deeper than merely sociological or cultural bonds. Cultural solidarity ultimately reflects a people's relationship to God, the religious direction of the heart (Conn 1977b:15-19). "In one way or another, obediently or disobediently, all men give expression to what lives in their hearts" (DeGraaf 1976:7). That heart commitment, even in a secularized culture, does not leave untouched any of culture's dimensions.

Only by recognizing the religious basis of all human life can we account for the depth of the demonic side of cultural solidarity. The church's struggle to transform the cultural unit is always a concrete manifestation of its ongoing struggle with the powers (Eph. 6:12). ''Mulit-personal decisions,'' even with the aid of the insights of sociology and anthropology, are not easily made. They also are part of ''the spiritual warfare in which the church is engaged for the ruling Christ between the 'decisive battle' of the resurrection and the final victory of Christ's second coming'' (Knapp 1976:20). Men, to use McGavran's language, do like to become Christians without crossing racial, linguistic, or class barriers. But each of these barriers has religious dimensions, flowing from man's integrity as image of God.

Covenant solidarity is most visibly expressed in the family, ''the *only* divinely instituted natural social unit'' (Boer 1961:176). Though distorted by sin, modified by historical forces, reduced by western individualization from extended to nuclear, the family remains the pattern for covenant expressions of conversion. In this light, the ''biological growth'' of the church is much more than sociologically defined potential pool for the expansion of the people of God. The family, together with its ''clan'' and ''people'' extensions, is a covenant-structured means of conversion. Accordingly, baptism signs and seals more than potential commitment to covenant. It is the real introduction of disciples into the communal jurisdiction of the new covenant (Matt. 28:18-20), the mark of consecration of a people into the solidarity of allegiance to the Great Suzerain of the Kingdom (Kline 1968:79-81).

These communal, covenant dimensions of conversions were abundantly evident in the early mission history of Korea. Roy Shearer reports that the ''web of family relationships'' was

> the means by which the Korean Church multiplied ahead of the missionaries. Because of the close-knit web of family relationships and the interfamily relationships through the clan, no one wished to make a great step in accepting a new religion which would break down these family ties. A person hearing the Gospel of Christ . . . would go back to his own village, talk it over with the members of his family and clan, and if a positive decision was made, the entire group often quite naturally became Christian, still holding fast to its family relationships. (Shearer 1966:148-150)

The identification of Christianity with Korea's national aspirations would quite naturally reinforce this decision-making process.

At the same time, the dark side of the principle of man-in-solidarity was also displayed. In the Confucian world view that defined Korea's attitudes toward the family, filial piety was the "supreme virtue and the basis of general morality." This religious character to the family was expressed in what is popularly called the practice of ancestor worship. The final criteria for ethical decisions was the "sake of family" or "the honor of family." By the twentieth century, that had solidified into personal loyalties which "usually did not go over the lines of family, clan, locality, and faction" (Park 1970:114). Unfortunately, except for its overt manifestation in ancestor worship, these religious tendencies of Confucian enculturation were not radically challenged by the missionaries. The result is seen in the Korean church's sad history of regionalism and factionalism along clan and regional lines. The church has not developed adequately the principle of an open community of grace and service. Its structures and understanding of the ecclesiastical authority has too often been oriented along familial and regional lines. All this stands as a warning. Too simple an appeal to family ties as "the bridges of God" may not be wholly adequate for reorienting, transforming, these social structures for Christ.

CULTURE'S CONTEXT AND GENERAL REVELATION

Our emphasis on conversion as an eschatological, covenant process demands that we pay the most serious attention to the cultural context in which conversion takes place. That requires much more than simply understanding the original situation in the original frame of reference, the Bible. We must also develop sensitivity both to the context through which the hearers interpret the message and also to our own cultural context, to the context which formed the way we first heard and interpreted the message and which, in many ways, continues to shape the present state of our (ongoing) conversion. Our own narrow enculturation can inhibit appreciation of those very cultural themes and needs which may provide the key for the authentic communication of the Gospel to non-western peoples.

Simply put, this means we must be constantly asking four questions: (1) To whom am I bringing the Gospel? Paul addressed himself differently to Festus than to the crowd at Lystra. "The different way in which God spoke at different times is so essential in the history of revelation that it constitutes a controlling element. The revelation of God does not hang in a vacuum, it is not an abstract universal truth that descended upon us, but God's revelation entered into our history" (Bavinck 1960:83). (2) What person brings the Gospel? Elijah is different from Elisha, Matthew presents the Gospel in a completely different form than does John. "The milieu in which the bearer of the gospel is born, his development, his cultural background, his personal characteristics, his age all play a part and are used in the hand of God" (Bavinck 1960:84). (3) What is the time of the power encounter? "Each moment has its own particular opportunities and difficulties, its *kairos*" (Bavinck 1960:85). (4) What is the place of encounter?

How does one reconcile an emphasis on the radical effects of sin on cultural world view and still speak of culture as the gate through which the call to conversion enters? How can we turn felt needs, "points of contact," into "points of attack"?

The answer is found in the biblical insights associated with "general revelation." Even in the indivisible unity of cultural solidarity "there is a hidden crack. The culture of a nation is a product of human work, but there is an untraceable influence in it that cannot be scrutinized because it has it origin in the mercy of God" (Bavinck 1949:77). Culture's patterns display the chisel marks of those "who suppress the truth in unrighteousness" (Rom. 1:18) and also the dimmed glory of God who has fashioned boundaries of habitation and determined appointed times that men and women "should seek God, if perhaps they might grope for him and find him" (Acts 17:26-27).

Does God ever use the stained and mutilated knowledge which the Gentile has at his disposal to do his wonderful work in the heart? What part did the shattered politics of Korea's nineteenth century and the bitterness of the Japanese protectorate play in the conversion of men like Philip Jaisohn and Syngman Rhee? Why did a 1907 newspaper correspondent write, "The whole country is fruit ripe for the picking. . . . If the Christian Church has any conception of strategy and appreciation of an opportunity, . . . she will act at once" (Paik 1929:353)? Did the Nestorian influence on China play its part in the shaping of the Tan'gun myth of Korea and the creation of a term, *Hananim,* later to be transformed by the Christian Gospel? Was Korea's culture in the powerful grip of God before it was aware of it?

What does God do with those fragments of knowledge in a Gentile's life? Does He sometimes overcome that suppressing and superceding force that is always at work in his heart? Does He sometimes stop the hidden machinery of unbelief and rebellion by the unconquerable power of His holy Word, even if that Word reaches the heart in disguised form? Here we suddenly feel ourselves confronted with the deepest of all mysteries, the mystery of the power of God. (Bavinck 1949:106-107)

Should not this alertness to the providential creation of context also require us to recognize that conversion as turning from and turning to must be shaped by a variety of themes and needs in a variety of cultures? David Shank provides a very provocative list of the dimensions conversion might take in response to a variety of felt needs and cultural themes:

Context of Experience	From	To	Through Jesus
Acceptance	Rejection	Acceptance	Love
Direction	to err about	to aim at	Call
Festival	Boredom	Joy	Feast-giver
Meaning	the absurd	the reasonable	Word
Liberation	Oppression	Liberation	Liberation
Becoming	Nobody	Somebody	Invitation
Fellowship	Solitude	Community	Presence
etc.			

(Shank 1976:5)

In all this, are we not reflecting the willingness of a Paul to be "all things to all men, that I may by all means save some" (1 Cor. 9:22)? Paul could not modify the Gospel itself according to the particular characteristics of his hearers. At the same time, being "under compulsion" (1 Cor. 9:16) of the Gospel empowers him to be free to make its full impact felt in each culture's unique setting and historical place. Religious tradition and social position are relativized by the Gospel's universal absolute. At the same time, those Gospel universals must be communicated in and to those particular life situations and contexts.

An impossible job? Only if we forget that "the Chief Actor in the historic mission of the Church is the Holy Spirit. . . . He is a destroyer of barriers, a bridge builder, one who enables each to see the other. He opens the eyes to see Christ, but also . . . to know in order to understand. . . . He makes us aware and sensitive" (Oosthuizen 1977:60-61). It is the Spirit who enables us to listen and learn until one sees the world of the person in another culture through his eyes. It is He who opens that culture to the powerful entrance of the Gospel. And it is He who enables the missionary advocate to be freed from the cultural imperialism that inhibits him from being all things to all men.

BIBLIOGRAPHY

Allison, Christopher F., 1961. *The Rise of Moralism.* London: S.P.C.K.

Barnett, Homer, G., 1953. *Innovation: The Basis of Cultural Change.* New York: McGraw-Hill Co.

Bavinck, J. H., 1949. *The Impact of Christianity on the Non-Christian World.* Grand Rapids: William B. Eerdmans Publishing Company.

_____, 1960. *An Introduction to the Science of Missions.* Philadelphia, Pa: Presbyterian and Reformed Publishing Company.

Berkhof, Louis, 1949. *Systematic Theology.* Grand Rapids: William B. Eerdmans Publishing Company.

Biernatzki, William, Im, Luke, & Min, Anselm, 1975. *Korean Catholicism in the 70s.* Maryknoll: Orbis Books.

Boer, Harry, 1961. *Pentecost and Missions.* Grand Rapids: William B. Eerdmans Publishing Company.

Clark, Allen D., 1971. *A History of the Church in Korea.* Seoul: The Christian Literature Society of Korea.

Clowney, Edmund P., 1976. "Contextualization and the Biblical Theology of Culture." Unpublished paper delivered at the Contextualization Study Group, Fourbrooks, Pa., January 29-31, 1976.

Conn, Harvie M., 1977. "Reactions and Guidelines: The Praxis of a Covenant Ethnos." Unpublished paper delivered at the Consultation on the Homogeneous Unit Principle, Fuller Theological Seminary, May 31 - June 2, 1977.

DeGraaf, Arnold, 1976. "An Alternative to Our Traditional Anthropological Models." Mimeographed paper distributed through the Institute for Christian Studies, Toronto, Ontario.

Gaffin, Richard B., Jr., 1978. *The Centrality of the Resurrection: A Study in Paul's Soteriology.* Grand Rapids: Baker Book House.

Gale, James S., 1906. *Korea in Transition.* New York: Eaton and Mains.

_____, 1909. *Korea in Transition.* New York: Laymen's Missionary Movement.

Hatch, Elvin, 1973. *Theories of Man and Culture.* New York: Colombia University Press.

Hiebert, Paul, 1976. *Cultural Anthropology.* Philadelphia: Lippincott.

Kay, Il-seung, 1950. "Christianity in Korea." Th.D. dissertation submitted to Union Theological Seminary, Richmond, Va.

Kittel, Gerhard, editor, 1971. *Theological Dictionary of the New Testament, Vol. VII.* Grand Rapids: William B. Eerdmans Publishing Company.

Kline, Meredith G., 1968. *By Oath Consigned.* Grand Rapids: William B. Eerdmans Publishing Company.

Knapp, Stephen, 1976. "Contextualization and Its Implications for U.S. Evangelical Churches and Missions." Mimeographed paper distributed through Partnership in Mission, Abington, Pa.

Kraft, Charles, 1977. "Theologizing in Culture." Pre-publication manuscript distributed through Fuller Theological Seminary, Pasadena, Calif.

McGavran, Donald A., 1970. *Understanding Church Growth.* Grand Rapids: William B. Eerdmans Publishing Company.

_____, 1974. *The Clash Between Christianity and Cultures.* Washington, D.C.: Canon Books.

Oosthuizein, G. C., 1977. "The Holy Spirit and Culture," *The Holy Spirit Down to Earth,* Paul. G. Schrotenboer, ed. Grand Rapids: Reformed Ecumenical Synod.

Paik, L. George, 1929. *The History of Protestant Missions in Korea 1832-1910.* Pyeng Yang, Korea: Union Christian College Press.

Palmer, Spencer J., 1967. *Korea and Christianity: The Problem of Identification with Tradition.* Seoul, Hollym Corporation.

Park, Pong-bae, 1970. "The Encounter of Christianity with Traditional Culture and Ethics in Korea: An Essay in Christian Self-Understanding." Ph.D. dissertation submitted to Vanderbilt University, Nashville, Tennessee.

Pettitt, Norman, 1966. *The Heart Prepared: Grace and Conversion in Puritan Spiritual Life.* New Haven: Yale University Press.

Shank, David A., 1976. "Towards an Understanding of Christian Conversion," *Mission-Focus,* 5:1-7.

Shearer, Roy E., 1966. *Wildfire: Church Growth in Korea.* Grand Rapids: William B. Eerdmans Publishing Company.

Taber, Charles, 1976. "When Is a Christian?" *Milligan Missiogram* 3(3): 1-4.

Tippett, Alan R., 1973. *Verdict Theology in Missionary Theory.* South Pasadena: William Carey Library.

_____, 1977. "Conversion as a Dynamic Process in Christian Mission," *Missiology,* 5:203-221.

Underwood, Horace G., 1908. *The Call of Korea.* New York: Fleming H. Revell Company.

_____, 1910. *The Religions of Eastern Asia.* New York: The Macmillan Company.

van Baal, J., 1971. *Symbols for Communication. An Introduction to the Anthropological Study of Religion*. Assen, the Netherlands: Van Gorcum and Company.

Vos, Geerhardus, 1930, 1952. *Pauline Eschatology*. Grand Rapids: William B. Eerdmans Publishing Company.

_____, 1972. *The Kingdom of God and the Church*. Nutley, N.J.: Presbyterian and Reformed Publishing Company.

Warfield, B. B., n.d. "New Testament Terms Descriptive of the Great Change." Reprint from the *Presbyterian Quarterly*, 90-100.

_____, 1952. "On the Biblical Notion of 'Renewal,' " *Biblical and Theological Studies*. Philadelphia: Presbyterian and Reformed Publishing Company.

11. Conversion as a Complex Experience
—A Personal Case Study

by Orlando E. Costas

ORLANDO E. COSTAS, *former director of the Latin American Evangelical Center for Pastoral Studies (CELEP), San Jose, Costa Rica, is professor of missions at Eastern Baptist Seminary, Philadelphia. He is the author of* The Church and Its Mission: A Shattering Critique from the Third World.

CONVERSION, IN THE TRADITIONAL EVANGELical understanding, is a static, once-for-all, private experience. Furthermore, it is viewed as a transcultural, non-contextual event, as though it were the same everywhere for all believers, at all times.

I would like to explore what I believe to be a more biblically, theologically, and socio-historically sound view: conversion as a dynamic, complex, ongoing experience, profoundly responsive to particular times and places and shaped by the context of those who experience it.

I approach the subject as a Latin American from the Hispanic Caribbean. It is natural, therefore, that I should refer to Latin American and Puerto Rican cultures. To be sure, there are diversities of cultures in contemporary Latin America, but even so, there is a common cultural heritage that gives a unique character to the peoples who live or come from south of the Rio

Bravo and make up the islands of the Hispanic Caribbean.

However, what gives Latin America its homogeneity is not so much its common cultural heritage as its common historical situation: it is the offspring of a civilizational process which incorporated into exploited nuclei the aborigines and their descendants, the slaves from Africa and their children, as well as the half-breed and creole offspring of the Spanish *conquistadores*.

As a Puerto Rican I represent one of the last overt colonies in the hemisphere. As one who lived for many years in the greater New York area, I represent the internal and external migratory process, which has characterized the life of many of the peoples of the region during the present century, largely as a by-product of their socio-economic (and in some cases political) situation. I reflect, therefore, not just the colonial and neo-colonial socio-historical reality of the region, but a migrant sub-culture, concretely that of Hispanic-America, and stand as a counterpart to the many ethnic groups that have emerged out of the fantastic urban migration that Latin America has experienced since the 1930s.

Starting from this rather complex situation, I would like to deal with the meaning and distinctiveness of Christian conversion by means of the case-study method, using my own conversion experience as a basis for reflection.

AUTOBIOGRAPHICAL NOTES

I was born in Puerto Rico, the son of a God-fearing Methodist family. I was baptized into the Christian faith when I was forty days old and was consecrated to God's service by my mother even before birth. I received a high moral example from my parents, a sound Christian upbringing and fairly good care from the church. Yet I lived a most restless and turbulent childhood. I was (and I suppose still am to a degree) hot-headed, egocentric, rebellious, ambitious, proud, and boastful.

When I was twelve my father failed in his grocery business and (as did many Puerto Ricans) decided to migrate to the continental United States. We lived with an aunt in the Bronx who was married to an Anglo-American. Since I had been brought up in a middle-class family with many privileges and freedoms, I was very confident and did not think that the experience would be as traumatic as it turned out. The encounter with my aunt's childless cross-cultural marriage in a very rough Irish-Puerto Rican neighborhood, and in a school situation which can only be described as a "Blackboard Jungle," produced such a profound culture shock that I do not think I have ever recovered.

My father went to Chicago but was not able to find a job. (It was in the mid-1950s when jobs were hard to come by, especially if you were an unskilled Puerto Rican.) A job finally turned up in a small grocery store in Bridgeport, Connecticut, where a small Puerto Rican community had begun to emerge. I went to live with my father in December 1954, and three months later the entire family was reunited. Our first home was in a run-down, unheated flat across from the school my sisters and I attended.

For three years I suffered the impact of a strange environment, full of hostility and prejudice. I developed strong feelings of shame and self-hatred. I tried to overcome the stigma of being Puerto Rican through an aggressive social behavior which bordered on juvenile deliquency. When I saw that this was not getting me very far, I tried new roads to personal status. First came music; I was discovered as a teenage tenor by the Police Athletic League Talent Theater Group and was awarded a scholarship with a teacher from New York. Then came sports; I became very active in basketball. And third, personal leadership; I joined a local boys club and within two years I had been designated "Boy of the Year," the first Puerto Rican in the United States to receive such an award.

From the moment of our arrival, we became part of the Hispanic Evangelical Mission, which was sponsored by the local Protestant Council of Churches. This Mission became a sort of social refuge for the family. Very soon, however, I began to branch out into other (English-speaking) congregations. Thereafter my religious universe would encompass both the Spanish Mission, where the family interacted with other Spanish-speaking families, and the English-speaking congregations, where I interacted with Anglo-American peers.

In spite of regular church attendance, I was rebelling against the family and my parents' expression of the Christian faith. For example, whenever I heard my mother praying I would enter into her room, interrupt, and ridicule her to the point that she would often stop her prayer and begin to cry. I made life miserable for my sisters, bullying them around and mistreating them. Though I was only fifteen years old, I thought myself old enough to come home very late, to hang around with anybody I chose, to go anywhere and do anything I pleased. My father tried disciplining me, lecturing me, getting me to read the Bible, and even going into my room early in the morning and praying out loud for me. None of these things worked. I would not listen, I would not respond, I would not turn around in my attitudes and behavior.

In the midst of that situation, I attended Billy Graham's 1957 New York Crusade. That night something strange occurred in my life which I can only describe as the beginning of a long spiritual pilgrimage. Looking back, I can easily recognize lines of continuity with earlier stages of my life. How much continuity I cannot say, but consciously, at least, there was a new beginning; something unique did happen on June 8, 1957, in Madison Square Garden, and has been happening ever since.

A CONCENTRIC MODEL OF CONVERSION

This pilgrimage can be described in three concentric circles. The center is Christ, of course, and the first circle represents my conversion to him.

1. Conversion to Christ

An exact reconstruction of this event is, of course, impossible. The exact moment when I became a true follower of Christ, I cannot identify with certainty. June 8, 1957, was not the first time that I had made a public profession of faith in Christ. Neither can I assert the exact reason why I went forward. Certainly it was not because of the sermon, since I had hardly paid any attention to it. Yet, as the choir sang "Just as I am, without one plea . . . O Lamb of God, I come, I come," I could not help but recall many of the things I had read in the Bible, the prayers and exhortations I had received from my parents, and the lessons I had been given in Sunday school. I was also conscious of my complex personal spiritual situation: the way I had been trying to push God out of my existence, my rebellious, uncourteous, and aggressive relations with my family, my pride, and egocentrism. I decided to respond affirmatively to the invitation that was being extended by the evangelist and *make the words of the hymn my own.*

The quasi-sacramental act of going forward and the personal prayer of confession I made later became the outward means through which I expressed my commitment to Christ. The evidence that something positive and unusual had occurred was the change of attitude I began to demonstrate several hours later. When I arrived home that evening, the first thing I did was tell my mother that I had been converted to Jesus Christ and that I had begun a new life. There was a change in my attitude toward prayer and Bible reading. No longer was I offended by my parents' religious practices. I began to be more considerate with my sisters. I abandoned my irresponsible behavior outside the house and disciplined myself to act as a member of a family and not as a solitary individual. And I began to think of my future not in terms of personal aggrandizement, but rather of what would contribute to the enrichment of others.

Yet as I reoriented my life I began to encounter a number of difficulties, the chief of which was the tremendous demand placed upon my life as a result of my musical contacts. Because of my emotional and religious immaturity, these militated against my new Christian life. My parents and I decided to seek advice from the pastor of the Spanish Mission, who suggested that perhaps I should complete my schooling in the Christian setting of Bob Jones Academy.

2. Conversion to Culture

It was at Bob Jones that I began to experience the second great crisis of my life, which led eventually to what I have identified as a cultural conversion. Bob Jones Academy and University, located in Greenville, South Carolina, was (and still is) a center of North American southern fundamentalism. I arrived there in 1958 at the height of the neo-evangelical-fundamentalist controversy. There was strong opposition to Billy Graham for his practice of cooperative evangelism, which he introduced in the New York Crusade. Accepting the backing of so-called ''Protestant liberals'' was considered by Bob Jones, John R. Rice, and others to be a compromise of the fundamentals of the faith. They set out to combat Billy Graham and all those who reflected such ''soft'' attitudes toward liberals. As with many of my classmates, I soon began to take, without understanding all the issues involved, a similar stand against liberals and neo-evangelicals. I became a fundamentalist.

Not only did I discover North American fundamentalism at Bob Jones, but I came face to face with Anglo-Saxon culture in its worst form. The annual Shakespearian productions and the exaltation of Anglo-Saxon literature; the weekly vesper services, which focused, for the most part, on the Anglo-American religious heritage; the daily chapel services, saturated by the North American revivalistic and crusading spirit; the puritanical value system, manifested in such things as the chaperon-controlled dating system and the rigid disciplinary procedures; the shameless defense and justification of racism, so characteristic of Anglo-Saxon culture; and the triumphalistic belief in the divine destiny of the United States—all of these cultural configurations led me to ask myself whether I had any part in such a world. Later on I concluded that I not only did not belong to that world, but that I did not want to, even if allowed.

This feeling of not being part of the cultural milieu at Bob Jones was intensified by my discovery of the Latin American world, for there were many students from Latin America at Bob Jones. As I fellowshiped with them, I began to discover how different I was from the average white Anglo-Saxon Protestants who made up the overwhelming majority of the student body. That experience not only kindled a passionate love for the lands south of the Rio Bravo but became the beachhead for the rediscovery of my hidden Latin American identity.

At Bob Jones I also discovered the Christian imperative of evangelism. Through the testimonies of friends who had gone on evangelistic missions to Mexico and Central America and, especially, through the inspiration of a Puerto Rican colleague who had the gift of evangelism, I developed a passionate concern for the communication of the Gospel to those who live outside the frontiers of the faith.

Finally, I discovered the church as something larger than myself and my family, or as a place where one goes to meet other people or hear someone preach. Partly as a result of my contacts with peers who had a more dynamic understanding and commitment to the church, and partly as a result of the ecclesial consciousness of some of the religious activities on campus (the Sunday school program, for example, was organized according to the different church traditions), I became convinced of the need to become an official part of a visible church *fellowship*. I therefore decided to join a local Congregational church in Bridgeport. This act was accompanied by the decision to give public witness to my commitment to Christ through baptism. Though I had been baptized as a child, I felt (at that time) that I should give outward evidence of my new relationship with Christ and that the most scriptural way to signifiy it was through what in some free church traditions is known as "believer's baptism."

My studies at Bob Jones had given me not only an evangelistic passion for my people but a deep concern for preaching. So while fellowshiping at the Black Rock Congregational Church I became actively involved in ministry among the Spanish-speaking people of Bridgeport and New York. I took my first pastorate at the age of nineteen, in a small store-front congregation affiliated with the Christian Church (Disciples of Christ) in the heart of the Latin neighborhood. The work prospered, but after a short period I decided that I needed biblical and theological training. I enrolled at Nyack Missionary College.

While at Nyack I took a short student pastorate with an Evangelical Free Church in Brooklyn where I met my wife and organized a Latin American evangelistic team. My wife and the team members enrolled at Nyack and from there traveled to New York every weekend for meetings in Spanish-speaking churches.

One summer we made an evangelistic tour of Puerto Rico, and during the trip I became aware of the need to study more closely my cultural heritage and to become part of a larger fellowship of churches. I concluded that in order to minister effectively to Latin Americans I had to understand their history and culture. I decided to inquire about the possibility of working with the Puerto Rico Baptist Convention and of studying at a local university. Both possibilities became a reality when I was invited to become pastor of the First Baptist Church of Yauco, a town in the southwestern part of the island and only thirty minutes from the main campus of Inter-American University (IAU).

Several things occurred during my three-year ministry in

that church. For one thing, I discovered the church as an *institution;* that is, as a complex system of distinctive beliefs, values, rites, symbols, and relationships which maintain a line of continuity with the past and through which the Gospel is communicated and lived. I became fully integrated into the Baptist fellowship, and especially into the Puerto Rican and American Baptist Conventions, when I was ordained to the ministry at the age of twenty-one.

For another, I had a chance to finish my undergraduate studies at IAU, majoring in Latin American history and politics. These studies led me to rediscover my Puerto Rican identity, to affirm my Latin American cultural heritage, to begin to question the political hegemony of the United States in Latin America, and to *consciously* break with its culture.

That did not mean that I had become hostile to North Americans as persons. It meant rather that I was becoming increasingly aware of the political oppression and economic exploitation which their *nation,* as an imperial and neo-colonial power, was exercising over Latin America as a whole, and in particular, over my own country. It meant, further, that I had finally come face to face with the fact that I was not an Anglo-American; that I did not need to be one, for I had a rich cultural heritage of my own which I should accept joyfully; and, therefore, that I should aim at getting rid of any Anglo-American influence which stood in the way of the full expression of my Puerto Rican and Latin American heritage.

3. Conversion to the World

After completing my university studies, I returned to the continental United States to further my theological preparation at Trinity Evangelical Divinity School and later at Garrett Theological Seminary. I also studied during the summer at the Winona Lake School of Theology. In order to support my family I accepted the call to pastor an inner city Mexican-American and Puerto Rican Baptist congregation on the south side of Milwaukee.

No sooner had I settled in at the *Iglesia Evangelica Bautista* than I was called upon by people of the Spanish-speaking community to represent them in the Social Development Commission, which administered the so-called War on Poverty through the County of Milwaukee. I immediately discovered that I was in a loaded political situation. The Latin community was a minority among a minority. Not only the white majority, but also the blacks were consciously marginating our people from the programs and social benefits of the War on Poverty. It soon became obvious that the reason for this was the lack of political organization in the Latin south side as against the sophisticated organization of blacks in the north side and the institutional power of the white majority. From the blacks we learned how important it was to put together a cohesive organization. So I got involved in community organization, helping to organize the Latin American Union for Civil Rights.

In this political praxis I never lost my Christian and pastoral identity. On the contrary, this process led me to reflect critically on my ministry and on the nature and mission of the church. This led me to discover the world of the poor and the disenfranchised as a fundamental reference of the Gospel. I came to realize that the Christian mission had not only personal, spiritual, and cultural dimensions, but also social, economic, and political ones.

My ministry in Milwaukee had led me to experience a missiological (and socio-political) conversion. My conversions to Christ and to my culture had been complemented by a conversion to the world, *especially the world of the forgotten and exploited.* Interestingly enough, this enabled both the church and me to deepen our understanding of our relationship to Christ and to our cultural heritage. The church experienced a well-rounded, healthy growth. As for me, the fruit of that experience became evident in the decision of my wife and me to go to continental Latin America as missionaries and in the publication of my first book, *La iglesia y su misión evangelizadora,* in which I began to rehearse an integral concept of mission and evangelism.

A SPIRAL MODEL OF CONVERSION

I was lecturing in Hong Kong when I first thought of interpreting my spiritual pilgrimage in a concentric model. From Hong Kong I continued my journey through Africa. While visiting Cameroon, I had the occasion to share my three-fold conversion experiences with an African friend and theologian. His reaction was a straight look and a "So?" I asked him, "What do you mean 'so'?" He answered: "So you think those will be your only conversions? If they are, then their validity will have been denied. For if you are to continue to grow as a person and as a Christian, you will have to experience one turn after another.''

These words made me think . . . and change my concentric model into a *spiral* one. For the complexity of conversion does not lie in a fixed number of experiences but in the fact that it is a plunge into an ongoing adventure. Christian conversion is a journey into the mystery of the Kingdom of God which leads from one experience to another. Initiation in the journey of the Kingdom implies a plunge into an eschatological adventure where one is confronted with ever new decisions, turning points, fulfillments, and promises which will continue until the ultimate fulfillment of the Kingdom. It also implies that one is confronted with the need to make ever new returnings to the fundamental point of reference, a signpost that accompanies one throughout the journey, like the traveling tabernacle in the Old Testament or the ''recalling to mind'' that the children of Israel engaged in year after year in the Passover: a celebration and living again, at whatever point of their pilgrimage, of the Passover experience.

THEOLOGICAL EVALUATION

My analysis leads into a theological evaluation. Can my three conversions be considered legitimate Christian conversions? What biblical and theological basis do I have in referring to my cultural and socio-political conversions as part of an ongoing spiritual process? Does the newness of the Kingdom ushered in by Christ warrant such a dynamic, dialectical understanding of conversion?

To respond to the question, I shall briefly survey three biblical terms and their uses: the Hebrew *shub* and the Greek *epistrepho* and *metanoeo,* which stand behind the notion of conversion.

In the Old Testament, the Hebrew verb *shub* meaning ''to return'' appears over one thousand times (Holladay 1971:362-69). It is linked with the prophetic call to Israel to turn from its sins, to return to Yahweh, and to renew its vows. It also appears in connection with God's acts towards Israel and the nations.

In the New Testament, *epistrepho* stands out. It is often used in the Greek translation of the Hebrew Scriptures, the Septuagint, to translate the verb *shub* (Bertram 1971:723, 724). It means "to turn, bring back, or return." It is often used in relation to the turning of unbelievers (for the first time) to God (Acts 3:19; 26:20) from their sins (Acts 14:15; Barclay 1964:21, 22). But sometimes it is linked to erring believers (Jas. 5:19 f.) who are brought back into a right relation with God (Bertram 1971:727).

The third term, which is often used in the New Testament, is *metanoeo* which means "to change one's mind," often feeling regret, and "to adopt another view" (Behm 1967:980-82). It is used both in the context of the call to forgiveness from sin and liberation from future judgment (Acts 2:38; 3:19; 8:22; 17:30; 26:20) and in reference to the problem of apostasy inside the church (Rev. 2:5, 16, 21, 22; 3:3, 19).

Metanoeo is closely connected with *epistrepho,* as in Acts 3:19, where Peter calls the multitude to "Repent . . . and turn again. . . ." It also appears in connection with *pisteuo,* which means "to believe," or "to adhere, to trust or rely on." Thus Jesus summoned his hearers to "Repent and believe in the gospel" (Mark 1:15).

The uses of these different words in Scripture underscore several aspects of the biblical concepts of conversion. First, conversion means a turning from sin (and self) to God (and his work). Second, this act involves a change of mind, which implies the abandonment of an old world view and the adoption of a new one. Third, it entails a new allegiance, a new trust, and a new life commitment. Fourth, it is but the beginning of a new journey and carries implicitly the seed of new turns. Fifth, it is surrounded by the redemptive love of God as revealed in Jesus Christ and witnessed to by the Holy Spirit.

Let us explore further these biblical perspectives in three propositions which demonstrate the theological complexity of conversion.

1. Conversion as a Distinct Moment and as a Continuous Process

Conversion as a distinct moment and as a continuous process seems to be self evident when Paul states:

but when a man turns to the Lord the veil is removed . . . . And we all, with unveiled face, beholding the glory of the

Lord, are being changed into his likeness from one degree of glory to another. (2 Cor. 3:16-18)

In this passage, Paul is referring to Israel's incapacity to understand the old covenant because of spiritual blindness. Only "through Christ" can this blindness be removed and Israel come to see the truth of the covenant (v. 14). This is true not only of Israel, but of all people. We are all unable to see God, because we have before us the veil of our sins. But when we turn (or are converted) to Christ, that veil is removed. This turning to the Lord puts us in the sphere of the Spirit of Christ, who not only enables us to see "the glory of the Lord," but constantly transforms us "from glory to glory." Conversion is then both a distinct moment and the first in a series of transforming experiences.

The continuing process of conversion is seen elsewhere in the New Testament (e.g., Mark 1:15), as conversion is connected with the Kingdom of God. This is the new order of life which the Father offers in Jesus Christ through the enabling power of the Spirit. It is a future reality which is, nevertheless, anticipated in the present. It is a reality that we experience both personally and in the community of faith. It is a reflex of what God has done, is doing, and will do, but it is basically discernible in the obedience of faith. Christian conversion revolves around this future-present, socio-personal, reflection-action reality. In the words of José Míguez-Bonino, it is "the process through which God incorporates [women and men], in [their] personal existence, into an active and conscious participation in Jesus Christ" (Míguez-Bonino n.d.:5).

This process, which has a distinct, though not a consciously uniform beginning, implies a constant turning from self to God. Obsession with the self alienates women and men from their human vocation, from their calling in creation to be at the service of one another. The self is the idol which separates them not only from their vocation but from their creator. In turning to God, they are reconciled to the true source of life and are renewed in their vocation. Conversion is, therefore, a passage from a dehumanized and dehumanizing existence to a humanized and humanizing life. Or to put it in other terms: it is the passage from death and decay to life and freedom. In conversion, women and men are liberated from the enslavement of the past and given the freedom of the future; they are turned from the god of this age, who passes away, to the God who is always the future of every past (Pannenberg).

Such a passage cannot be limited, therefore, to a single moment, for this would mean reverting to the static existence from which the Gospel liberates. Rather the dynamic life which is appropriated in conversion implies new challenges, new turnings, and new experiences. It is a life, on the one hand, which is appropriated in history, in the midst of history's precarious and evil reality. As historical beings, believers are always assailed by evil and are always tempted to go back to the past and fall into sin. Thus the biblical reminder to be on the lookout, to resist temptation, to constantly turn away from evil and commit themselves to God.

On the other hand, the new life is part of the "new creation" which God in Christ is bringing into being. Believers have been set on the course of God's coming Kingdom. They have been made the pilgrim people of God, called to set their hopes on "the city which is to come" and to participate in the afflictions of Christ in the world (Heb. 13:13, 14). Accordingly, they are not to escape from history, but rather to participate in its transformation through their witness and service. In so doing, they will encounter ever new challenges and should expect ever new turnings. This, says Paul, "comes from the Lord" who has "put his seal upon us and given us his Spirit . . . as a guarantee" (2 Cor. 3:18b; 1:22).

2. Conversion as a Socio-Ecclesial Reality

In the second place, we should think of conversion as a socio-ecclesial reality. Social, because it is historical. It is not something which occurs in a vacuum but takes place in particular social contexts which bear witness and are witnessed to by conversion. Conversion constitutes both a break with and a new commitment to society. It places believers in a dialectical relation with their environment. Free from its absorbing power, believers can give themselves completely to its service. Perception of this new relationship often requires "new turnings." In fact, Christians are *always* in need of more clarifications from God in their relation to society, and often need, as Peter did, to be transformed in their outlook in order to fulfill their calling.

Also, conversion is an ecclesial reality. It is the result of the witnessing engagement of a visible community which leads to incorporation into that community. This implies a new set of relationships, participation in a new fellowship, witnessing with others to a new social reality, and sharing in the hope of a new future, similar to what Luke tells us occurred at Pentecost:

> And all who believed were together and had all things in common; . . . And day by day, attending the temple together and breaking bread in their homes, they partook of food with glad and generous hearts, praising God and having favor with all the people. And the Lord added to their number day by day those who were being saved. (Acts 2:44, 46, 47)

This community, however, is affected by the tensions of history. It is constantly threatened by what the New Testament calls the principalities and powers. Hence, the situation described in Acts 5:1 ff., where the fellowship of Pentecost was broken by the cheating of Ananias and Sapphira. Situations like this are repeated throughout the New Testament and the history of the church, and can be witnessed everywhere today. Not only individual believers but the church as a whole in a given geographical area can be trapped in sin. The reminder to resist evil goes, therefore, to every believer and to the whole church everywhere.

As an ecclesial reality, conversion is the means by which the church is brought into being and is constantly being brought back into right living. It is also the way to growth and maturity. Was this not what happened at the Council of Jerusalem (Acts 15)? Or was this not the case with the Protestant Reformation or with so many other periods in the history of the church? Indeed, conversion is God's way of renewing and changing the face of his church, so as to lead it through new paths and enable it to cross new frontiers.

3. Conversion as a Missional Commitment

In the third place, we should think of conversion as a missional commitment. Conversion has a definite "what for?" Its goal is not to provide a series of "emotional trips" or the assimilation of a body of doctrines, nor to recruit women and men for the church, but rather to put them at the service of the mission of God's Kingdom. As Míguez-Bonino has observed:

> The call to conversion is an invitation to discipleship . . .
> whether it takes the direct form of Jesus' call to follow him or
> the apostolic form of participation through faith in the Mes-
> sianic community. . . . It revolves around the kingdom.
> Consequently, it involves a community which is engaged in
> an active discipleship in the world. (Míguez-Bonino n.d.:6)

In the Matthean account of the Great Commission (Matt.
28:19, 20), the call to discipleship is *mediated* by baptism (which is
the outward sign of incorporation into the body of Christ) and
teaching. The *goal* of discipleship, however, is the observance of
everything the Lord had commanded to do. All of these things can
be summed up in the great commandment: "love the Lord your
God . . ." and "your neighbor as yourself" (Mark 12:30, 31).
Christian conversion aims at putting women and men at the service of God and neighbor. It is that process by which they commit
themselves to loving God and neighbor in "deed and in truth." It
can only be verified, consequently, in concrete situations, in the ef-
ficacy of love. Here the words of John are extremely pertinent:

> This is the message which you have heard from the begin-
> ning, that we should love one another. . . . We know that we
> have passed out of death into life, because we love the
> brethren. By this we know love, that he laid down his life for
> us; and we ought to lay down our lives for the brethren. But
> if anyone has the world's goods and sees his brother in need,
> yet closes his heart against him, how does God's love abide
> in him? Little children, let us not love in word or speech but
> in deed and in truth. (1 John 3:11, 14, 16-18)

The foregoing argument, I think, validates the notion of
conversion as a complex experience. While not everyone experiences conversion in the same way, there is ample evidence in
Scripture and in Christian theology to substantiate the idea of a
qualified (by the return of Christ) open-ended process, grounded
in a vital, initial encounter with and acceptance of Christ as Savior
and Lord.

This perspective, to be sure, does overlap somewhat with the
concept of sanctification. But there does not seem to be any hard
biblical or theological evidence for the neat, clear-cut distinction
between conversion and sanctification which has been made in the
formulation of the *Ordo salutis* in traditional Protestant theologies.

On the contrary, sanctification seems to be implicit in conversion and vice versa.

PRACTICAL IMPLICATIONS

1. Importance of the Socio-Historical Setting

It can be inferred from what has been said that the socio-historical context plays an important role in conversion. The forms which conversion takes vary in accordance with the situation of the person(s) that is (are) converted. Thus, for example, Jesus said to the adulterous woman, "Go and do not sin again" (John 8:11), but to the rich young ruler he said, "Sell all that you have and distribute it to the poor . . . and come, follow me" (Luke 18:22). It was not that Jesus had a double evangelistic standard, but that different contexts demanded different forms of the call to conversion and of response to it. The woman had nothing and she knew it. The rich young ruler was also helpless, but his socio-economic situation inhibited him from recognizing his true need. Míguez-Bonino has rightly commented that

> Evangelism must . . . be related to the forms in which human groups place themselves in the world, their world-vision, their forms of social representation, their class- and group-consciousness. And, on the other hand, it must be related to the way in which people act, their course of conduct. This means also that "conversion" may arise within the recognition of a verbally articulated message or through the engagement in a new form of conduct . . . . (n.d.:6)

2. Creative, yet Critical Involvement in Society

Second, the understanding of conversion implies both a creative and a critical role for the convert in his or her social milieu. As the Gospel is filtered through a person's socio-historical configuration, so conversion should arise in forms which correspond with that person's reality. Such a person will always be in a dialectical relation with his or her environment. It is true that the Gospel frees Christians to fully identify with and participate in the joys and hopes, the values and life struggles of their society, but at the same time, they must maintain a critical distance so as to be able to detect any form of idolatry or any attempt to absolutize a given practice, person, group, institution, or vision.

3. Imperative of Engagement

A third implication of what has been said is the imperative of engagement for an adequate differentiation between Christian and other types of human conversion. Christian conversion can only be verified in the concrete manifestation of a distinctive quality of life. This does not mean that there is a uniform pattern of behavior which corresponds to all believers in all socio-historical circumstances. But it does mean that there is an "ethical minimum" which, though expressed differently in different contexts, maintains, nevertheless, a distinctive quality, easily recognizable everywhere. This "ethical minimum" has been located in the course of our discussion in the command to love God and neighbor. Christian conversion can be said to be taking place whenever people are turning to God and neighbor through faith in Christ and when that turning is continually translated in outward signs of loving service. Thus, for instance, whenever the rediscovery of one's cultural values or the acceptance of a political challenge enables one to deepen and make more efficacious one's service to God and neighbor, a new conversion can be said to have taken place. Likewise, conversion can be said to take place whenever believers fall away from this missional imperative (or "ethical minimum") and then "return" to their vocation.

4. The Challenge of Conversion inside the Church

Finally, what has been said implies that conversion not only confronts the church with an activity that takes place outside its walls in the world, and for which its witness is vital, but with the challenge of change in its inner life. A centrifugal theology of mission has enabled the church to come to terms with the biblical imperative of the "church for others." But it has also robbed it of the centripetal dimension of mission; that is, the fact that mission is always a two-way street, a going-coming, outer-inner reality. The church can only be *inside-out,* if it is *outside-in.* In order to minister, it must be ministered to; in order to call others to conversion, it must be converted itself. We have seen how sin and evil are a constant threat to the church. Whenever the church falls into this trap, it enters into a situation of (functional) disbelief, its life and mission become corrupted, it becomes deaf to God's word, and it loses touch with the Holy Spirit. In such situations, the call to conversion inside the church becomes a missional priority. For, as I have said elsewhere,

> . . . a church which loses touch with its source of strength (the Word and the Spirit), a community which loses sight of the object of its mission (the world and, particularly, the poor); a people that are un-responsive to the demands of the gospel, "cannot be the salt of the earth . . . [and] the light of the world. . . ." Indeed, such a church "is trapped in its own blindness, its own captivity . . . [and therefore], has to be liberated in order to be a liberating agent in the world." (Costas 1976:350)

In all of this, however, we should not forget that though the church might be unfaithful, God remains faithful, and that though conversion involves our human responsibility, it is made possible because of the sovereignty of God's grace. "Turning" and "returning" are thus gifts which God invites us to accept in Jesus Christ and enables us to appropriate by the liberating action of his Spirit.

BIBLIOGRAPHY

Alves, Rubem, 1975. *O Enemiga da Religiao.* Petropolis: Editora Vozes.

Barclay, William, n.d. *Turning to God: A Study of Conversion in the Book of Acts and Today.* Grand Rapids: Baker Book House.

Barth, Christopher, 1967. "Notes on 'Return' in the Old Testament," *Ecumenical Review,* Vol. XIX:3 (July), 310-311.

Behm, J., 1967. "Metanoeo, Metanoia," *Theological Dictionary of the New Testament,* Vol. IV, ed. by Gerhardt Friedrich, translated and ed. by Geoffrey W. Bromiley. Grand Rapids: William B. Eerdmans Publishing Co., pp. 975-980.

Bertman, 1970. "Epistrepho," *TDNT,* Vol. VII, pp. 722-729.

Costas, Orlando E., 1976. *Theology of the Crossroads in Contemporary Latin America.* Amsterdam: Rodopi.

Fackre, Gabriel, 1975. *Word in Deed: Theological Themes in Evangelism.* Grand Rapids: William B. Eerdmans Publishing Co.

Green, Michael, 1970. *Evangelism in the Early Church.* Grand Rapids: William B. Eerdmans Publishing Co.

Heikkinen, J. W., 1967. "Notes on 'Epistrepho' and 'Metanoeo,' " *Ecumenical Review,* Vol. XIX:3 (July), pp. 313-316.

Holladay, William L., 1971. *Concise Hebrew and Aramic Lexicon of the Old Testament.*

Marsh, J., 1962. "Conversion," in *Interpreters Dictionary of the Bible,* Vol. I, ed. by George A. Buttrick. Nashville: Abingdon.

Míguez-Bonino, José, n.d. "Notes on Conversion—For a Critical Rethinking of the Wesleyan Doctrine," unpublished paper prepared for the Roman Catholic-Methodist Dialogue.

Nissiotis, Nikos, 1967. "Conversion and the Church," *Ecumenical Review,* Vol. XIX:3 (July).

Packer, James I., 1976. "What is Evangelism?", in *Theological Perspectives on Church Growth,* ed. by Harvie M. Conn. Nutley, N.J.: Presbyterian and Reformed Publishing Co.

12. *Conversion and Convertibility*
—With Special Reference to Muslims

by Kenneth Cragg

KENNETH CRAGG *is reader in religious studies, University of Sussex, and Assistant Bishop of Chichester, England. Known as a specialist in Christian-Muslim relations, he is author of* The Call of the Minaret, Christianity in World Perspective, The Christian and Other Religions, *and other volumes.*

"THE SIMPLICITY THAT IS IN CHRIST" (2 COR. 11:13) is one of those memorable phrases in the Authorized Version which up-to-date English has to alter but which still fascinate for their older meaning. The "simplicity" Paul attributed to Christ was not the sort that prevented him speaking of Christ as "the wisdom of God" where the depth and riches are "unsearchable." "Simple" in archaic usage means "for no other sake but its own," "intrinsically and without reservations."

A modern translation would probably reach for "integrity." It is a term Paul clearly relished (see 2 Cor. 1:12, Col. 3:22, and Rom. 12:8) and the early translators of the Greek Old Testament used it for the wholeheartedness with which David's people gave their offerings for the temple building. The noun means the opposite of duplicity, dividedness, deviousness and inner contradiction; it suggests singleness of mind, wholeness of heart.

Given this integrity in Christ, there must also be integrity in conversion, a unity of self in which one's past is genuinely integrated into present commitment. Thus, the crisis of repentance and faith that makes us Christian truly integrates what we have been in what we become.

We are readily familiar with the term conversion and with the issue of its cultural context. Traditionally, it is the "newness" we emphasize, the break with the past which occurs in regeneration, leading to the transformation of the sinful self into the new man in Christ.

But that dimension is only one side of the story. For conversion takes place within a personal "continuum." There is an ongoing identity within which conversion happens, for which we need the concept of "convertibility." The convertibility of man is a glorious conviction of Christian hope and mission. It is an important dimension of study. For it focuses our thought about culture realistically, laying emphasis on that which is going to be there still (like the fabric of a washed garment) when the meaning of Christ has taken hold of it.

Nicodemus' question was a sound one. "How can a man be born when he is old?" He cannot be. The questioner had misheard Jesus' meaning. Return to the womb, which Nicodemus knew to be impossible, was not "the new birth" which Jesus meant but only a literalist hearing of his words. "Born of the Spirit" is an event within existing biography, or it is nothing. Conversion does not unmake: it remakes.

Focusing on this aspect of "convertibility," we take up here the particularities of Islam as a determinant of the cultural fabric of the Muslim world. In Islam we have a "theology" (if you will) of availability for Christ, for Islam is the determinant of the "natural birth" of Muslims. We cannot be too surprised if, like Nicodemus, they find the summons to new birth incomprehensible.

What follows draws on the background of two persons of Muslim birth and family, now baptized Christians. One is a noted Christian leader, the other an influential scholar, poet, and translator. Both came to be "in Christ" by faith and conversion, and have remained so. Both believe that their Muslim origins have found radical fulfillment and expression in Christ.

It has not been necessary for them, in mature perspective, to see their heritage as requiring repudiation. Yet their discipleship of newness in Christ is not in doubt, and, unlike many short-term converts, it has not been necessary for them to revert to their former allegiance. We will not confine ourselves to these two exemplars but allow them to indicate other aspects of the Muslim-culture/Christ-faith equation.

In the interests of examining convertibility in the Muslim context, let us consider the Christ-dimension and the culture-ground under three aspects: the mind's understanding, the soul's expression, and the will's discipleship. (These circumscribe personality, shaped by the past and coming into the faith.) These three, of course, interdepend. The first has to do with what Paul calls "the knowledge and love of God," and undergirds all else.

THE MIND'S UNDERSTANDING

There is, truly, a conversion of the mind. But what of the convertibility of its natal ideas and concepts, if they can be so described? Those of Islam and of Muslims need careful study on our part. For it is customary to stress the features of tension and even hostility that exist historically between the two theisms. Strenuous, on all counts, these tensions are the denial of the Word Incarnate, the disallowing of the Cross of Jesus, the astigmatism about what is meant by "Gospel," and the confusion about the integrity of the New Testament faith and how the Gospel *of* Jesus develops into the Gospel *about* him.

Nevertheless, the positive implications for the faith of the Christian within Islamic theology are significant and must, at all costs, be imaginatively and loyally retrieved.

But, first, it is fair to be reminded that conversion is not simply intellectual, a persuasion of the thinking part of man. In fact, one of our two representatives tells of no particular emphasis here. His sense of Christ came in the setting of a Christian school and through its influence in his boyhood. Though questions of articulate theology came later, they did not belong in the basic experience which was a response to Christian love and to the witness of unstinted friendship.

With the other representative, however, a realization of

what he came to call the "worshipability" of God in Christ was paramount, and this was a deeply theological theme pondered in a keenly philosophical mind. It stemmed from a childhood made sensitive to the mystery and dignity of suffering. His father, a very learned Muslim scholar, had become a widower in his middle years. He strove determinedly to be a double parent in loving closeness to his family despite its costly toll in diverting him from his loved books and studies. The son, as a result, lived with a growing realization of self-giving affection, and of how exacting it might be, as well as with the deep awareness of suffering in general countered by tenderness. Later, in the pursuit of his own scholarship, the son encountered the bigotry of religious obscurantism and the unfeeling exercise of dogmatic authority, crushing the spirit and the wistfulness of inquiry into truth.

Both these issues raised for him the relevance of (his Muslim) belief in God. "God is greater," says the *Shahadah,* or Creed of Islam. What should divine greatness mean, he asked himself, in the realm of compassion and suffering? How was the infinitely estimable thing he found in his father to be related to the divine sovereignty? Could the same compassion and suffering be there also, appropriately infinite and ultimate? If God is indeed greater, then clearly the human could not outdo the divine in this most crucial realm of bearing with need. It was in this context that the impact of the Gospel of the compassionate, suffering Christ came into his ken.

On the other issue in his mind of insensitive authoritarianism in religious custodians, he asked himself whether this could square with the notion of divine justice which he knew to be a deep theme in the Koran. Was suppression of liberty of inquiry a right attitude on the part of those who led the community of faith in God's revelation? Was there something in the very greatness of God which was betrayed—or at least forgotten—in an oppressive zeal for his scripture?

It was these two areas of sensitive personal experience that guided his thoughts towards the Christian faith and, surprisingly, with very little intervention, so to speak, from any Christian apologetic. His interest in Jesus as the Christ belonged with his sense of a divine counterpart to the compassion he had parentally received, while he felt constrained to claim, even within his scholarship about Islam, the intellectual integrity he had known in Christian academic friendship.

Is it not a fundamental principle of Islamic faith that not only what is not God (i.e., idols) must be denied worship, but what is divine must be adored? What then, if one finds in the love of the suffering Christ that which is truly worshipable? Will not this be the meaning and, in experience, the discovery of his divinity? "God in Christ" is then "learned" (to borrow the language of Eph. 4:20) in the context of the great Muslim obligation to "let God be God." In this personal case, the mind-conversion we are describing can be summed up in simply letting God be as God is in Christ—compassion, by this measure, addressing our liberty and reaching our hearts as the One who saves.

Of course there are familiar and entrenched Islamic disavowals of this view. It is these that make conversion necessary and right. To see Jesus crucified, to "let him suffer," or, rather, to believe that he does, is to run counter to the Islamic Jesus as Prophet-teacher, whose verbal ministry, though threatened by ill-wishers, ended in rapture to heaven out of danger. His "vindication," in the Muslim view, was by intervention of rescue, not by the wounds that save. But, in the case of the personal story before us, that disallowing of the Cross, however well-meant, seemed less fitting to divine greatness than the redeeming alternative. The converting conviction was that the greatness and power of God are supremely present in and known by the love that suffers; the mind received the history of Jesus as being, in truth, one of death for us, not of rescue for himself.

That persuasion, however, as to Jesus crucified—always a vital aspect in conversion—belongs deeply with what Islam already believes about the divine power, sovereignty, and forgiveness. Yes, the sense of forgiveness is already there: God is *Al-Rahman al-Rahim*. The question has to do with how such forgiveness avails. It may come to the heart of a man (as in this case) to see as utterly fitting to God the *redeeming* forgiveness he finds in Christ. Then to think that dimension improper to God is to impugn his being the sovereign Lord.

Moreover, the sovereignty to which Islam has loyally witnessed need not (the Christian would say, should not) be seen as a transcendence that is inhibited from any enterprise for our redemption. For then we should be implying some kind of divine imprisonment in aloofness; we should be found forbidding things to God—hardly an Islamic posture, least of all when it is a prohibition of initiatives of grace!

This is precisely what came to impress itself upon the mind of one of our examples. He writes:

> It was the fact of the Incarnation which made me fall in love with Christianity. To a Muslim the very idea of God becoming man is blasphemous, but it was this "blasphemy" that saved me from unbelief. To me it came to be the most natural thing. Stories are told of Shah Abbas (18th century ruler in Persia) and how, in order to get to know his poorer subjects, he used to dress up as a poor man—a dervish—and thus go among them. This gracious act he was able to do precisely because he was king and by such an action nothing was taken away from the glory of his kingship. If we admire such action in human beings, why should we not admire it in God?

So we may come to see that believing in Christ is believing in God. So it was for the mind of the one we are reading here. He saw in that Christ-revelation of the nature of God a kinship with implications of his own Muslim theology. Not least among these was the realization of how, in a real sense, the rule of God in human society is constituted to turn upon the human recognition of it. God, in the Koran's perspective, has created a world in which mankind is free even to have idols, to prefer false gods.

To be sure, orthodoxy claims that this does not harm God. But here orthodoxy may have to think again. For, manifestly, the Prophet's mission against plural worship matters, and matters intensely. One cannot assume that its reception is a matter of indifference. Quite the contrary: "God and His messenger"—the Koran always links them together. Man is seriously summoned to submission and obedience. We can hardly then conclude that God is not, in that sense, vulnerable to man.

What Islam calls *Shirk,* or plural worship, is "great wrong" (Surah 31.13), that is, wrong against God. The Christian faith finds this "wrong against God" measured in "the sin of the world" which the Cross constitutes. Contrasted as many things are at this point between the two faiths, they are together in the conviction of "men against God." Could there be a greater evidence of man's obduracy than the way he uses his liberty to prefer false worship to the rule of God? Is it not precisely that obduracy which Muhammad's mission is understood as sent to overcome? Surely we, and Muslims even more, would jeopardize the whole seriousness of that mission, and of the rule of God believed to be staked in it, if we allowed it to be implied that the sins which defy it do not matter. Is there not, then, a way to the conversion of the mind from the reality of man's "wrong against God" identified as *Shirk,* to the Christian belief that our wrongfulness before God is both registered and redeemed at the Cross?

The reality of man's responsibility is also clear in Islam, despite many impressions or assumptions to the contrary. For *islam* (as a common noun), namely the will to let God be God, must be a willed response. If it is inevitable it is unnecessary. If it is automatic there is no need of a mission to teach or a prophet to demand it. It takes freedom to bring an *islam* to God's claim. He is, then, the God we may ignore—as the unbeliever does—if He is to be the God we ought to worship and to serve. What rich convertibility there is here for Muslims into the Christian dimension of a divine love which suffers our obduracy and waits for our autonomy to coincide itself freely with His rule!

In any event, these are some of the considerations which led our exemplars Christward and allowed them to feel at the same time that a deep strand of their Islam had found legitimacy, so that their movement of allegiance was not wholly one of abandonment but of deeper fidelity. There is need for us, in thinking theology and culture, always to identify and enlist every discernible resource in the potential of what we find outside our own tradition. Such is the way of convertibility and such the benedictions of integrity in Christ. Let people, so to speak, persuade themselves that Christ is their own logic.

THE SOUL'S EXPRESSION

We must pass from intellectual reflections on the convertible potential towards "God in Christ" of the Islamic world view, to issues of culture when personal conversion transpires within it.

This is what is meant by "the soul's expression." Here the experience of both our chosen examples is significant.

They came to see their discipleship within their past heritage in its arts and poetry which (in later maturity if not at once) they felt free to bring within their new allegiance. Arabic, Urdu, and Persian are, of course, languages that delight in calligraphy, and calligraphy of the Arabic Koran is both the primary form of "religious" art and the mode of veneration of the word. So biblical Arabic, or Persian, or Urdu, deserves no less, if for a different reason.

This may serve as a ready illustration of the new in the shape of the old, even as the early church took over some of the features of the synagogue such as lections and psalmody. The cursive flow of letters, the elaborate overlay of words and all the ingenuities of fastidious penmanship, schooled by reverence of the Koran passed over congenially into the service of the Christian meanings. The same they found true of geometrical and floral design and Arabesque. Islam has no monopoly of graces which belong with space *per se,* or in nature as the matrix of the human arts. Angle, curve and line and sequence have no exclusive copyright. Cultural usages, as nature constitutes and nurture teaches them, are in this sense common.

That situation is confirmed by the Koranic theme of "signs" in the natural order, tokens of divine beneficence, which constantly present themselves in the earthly scene and in its social experiences. These are lost upon the casual observer but they register with the careful and evoke that gratitude which is a prominent feature of the Koran's submission call. Behind them all is the understanding of creation and of the law which charters it for man the creature. That delight in external nature and the sense of the human obligation to receive it reverently provide a validation of all that is consistent with its meaning in the diverse arts that culture affords. The disciple does not have to be imitative of others or to opt out of the patterns of his own ethos.

Even so, both the converts we have in mind have possessed and repossessed the cultural language and forms of their birthright within the critical newness they found in Christ. They have been able to express themselves in the poetry of their own heritage. Christian architecture of the last half century in Persia has shown a remarkable capacity to "baptize" to its purpose the traditions of a splendid Islamic inheritance.

But arts and poetry are the readiest of cultural forms for this sort of "baptism." There are other cultural expressions of Islam which pose sterner problems. What of the fast of Ramadan, the direction (or *Qiblah*) of prayer, the forms of prostration, the rite of ablution, the saying of *Takbir* ("God is greater"), the use of the human voice in the summons to worship? Are any of these, in any sense, transmissible from old to new, from mosque to church?

The *Qiblah* provides an intense geographical and historical focus for Muslims at prayer and on pilgrimage. It speaks of their unity. How do Christians from within Islam realize their unity in Christ? Their faith's transcendence of particular territorial locale requires them to hold together the fellowship, immediate and universal. Their *"Qiblah"* becomes the Word and the sacrament, at once local and inclusive. "At Philippi, in Christ," Paul, for example, would say. But may the convert legitimately retain a sense of the direction that physically unifies his old community, in order to care, as Paul might again say, for his "brethren according to the *Qiblah*"? (What we would give for some Pauline—or Johannine— Epistles about the Muslim setting!)

How do these thoughts square, it may be asked, with Paul's "counting all things loss" which were once gain to him? Does he not mean the new criteria, rather than a cultural negation? Pride of works, trust in forms—these, truly, were renounced. But the "familiars" of the heart, subject always to the rule of Christ, may be duly integrated and fulfilled.

So doing, the convert may be the means of mediating into his old community the arts, the signs, the symbols, of his new discipleship. It is remarkable, for instance, how the image of Jesus crucified, and even of the crown of thorns, has come into contemporary Muslim Arabic poetry in the context of the Palestinian tragedy. (So far has this been the case that it has evoked the disapproval of Muslim orthodox authorities.) Sunni Islam has no adequate cognizance of the tragic sense of life, and when events make the latter inescapable, poets, if not shaikhs, may reach wistfully towards the symbols they do not communally possess. How much more, then, may the committed disciple bring his new "in Christ" experience to the positive reckoning of his customary world.

What of the postures of Muslim prayer? (One might quote Ps. 95:6: "O come, let us worship and prostrate before the Lord. . . .") Clearly, Christian patterns of worship have their distinctive source in Christian faith, and Islam anyway would not want to have its forms borrowed. Nevertheless, is there not something latent in the Muslim form which may escape us and which it would be important to elucidate? The erect-prostrate-erect sequence in Islamic prayer ritual is a powerfully acted parable of a view of man under God. It is expressive of man's creaturely submission and liability with authority. His proudest member, the brow, is abased to the lowly earth, but only in order that he may return to the erect stance, resume his sandals and go about the business of life in the meaning of that submission. He does not grovel, or stay prostrate. Yet the claim of his humbling must be with him in the dominion he wields, of which erectness has always been the symbol.

How do Christian converts relate to this meaning? Surely they maintain its truth and develop the Christian understanding of such human dignity under God into a steady witness to the reality of the sin that blights and the grace that saves. Christians will not share the ritual, but they will recognize the significance of its reading of man, alike "humbled and exalted."

THE WILL'S DISCIPLESHIP

"Knowledge of God" and "expression" in the conversion experience into Christ from within Islam have been our concern thus far. What of the self in action, and its convertibility so that it is not lost in some mistaken, Nicodemus-like question about being "unborn when it is old"?

Here we need to remember that Islam is far other than a religious option of opinions, freely chosen or freely abandoned. It is a totality which includes a dimension very like nationality, as well as belief. There is no more tenacious community than Islam. Islam, at least in Arab and most Asian lands, is hardly yet a faith one is free to leave. Its tolerance, historically, has been limited to a freedom to continue to be what one was born, that is, Jewish or Christian (if not Muslim). Or it meant a freedom to migrate into Islam. There was no liberty for the born Muslim to migrate out of it. It was never supposed that a Muslim would desire to become anything else, and were he to do so it would be indicative of the utmost perversity.

This spells the tenacity of the *Ummah* concept, both in theory and in practice. To this day, for example, a Christian Turk or a Christian Malay is almost a contradiction in terms. Christians are Armenians or Greeks, or whatever—the other "faith-nations." There are, it is true, Christian Arabs, surviving as *dhimmis* (tolerated minorities from before the rise of Islam). So Arabism is not wholly dominated by Islamicity, though there are those who think it should be. But the role of minorities is notoriously difficult in many cultures. Islam has a better record than some, in letting "others" be. But they have to be "others." Its own denizens do not, for the most part, enjoy such freedom as might allow them to become non-Muslims.

Over the centuries, it may be said that the Christian communities within Islam have accepted this static account of themselves, as once-born identities. This has, indeed, been the psychic price of their durability. They have not lived, or been allowed to live, in any realistic expectation of conversion, from Islam, into their fellowship or faith. Emigration, and naturalization elsewhere (as in one of the two disciples here concerned) may facilitate a legal change of faith. But, by the same token, a local ex-Muslim church is not thereby generated. (Persia is one country where a small church, with ex-Muslim clergy and lay poeple, does exist. In Africa, because of the third denominator of animism, and for other reasons, the situation is more fluid and there is much more intercommunal liberty of movement and inter-penetration of ideas and usages.)

In central Islamic countries, the rigor of the situation is a primary problem besetting feasible conversion, to speak humanly. As long as Islamic solidarity is politically determined and sanctioned, personal initiatives will face stern and often impossible strains. In this sense it is probably wrong to talk of conversion and culture, since the equation goes far beyond what culture would normally connote. It might almost be phrased "conversion and treachery," or "conversion and dis-identity." For as such it has so often been seen by the human context in the *Ummah* of once-born, always, Islam.

Nor is a plea for heroism the answer if it leaves intact, or does nothing to bring into question, the pattern which calls for it. In the existing structure the ultimate hope must be the realization within Islam that a faith one is not free to leave, or question, is a virtual prison, and that no self-respecting religion can afford to maintain adherence by sheer immobility of will.

But in the meantime, what of the will's discipleship? Surely part of the answer is that convertibility means a studied effort after continuity. Hence the careful search, in our first section, for the Islamic dimensions, of a Christian sense of a divine solicitude for man, and a divine stake in human freedom to acknowledge that He is, and must truly be allowed to be, God. All our theology and conversion rationale is here—in God duly known and loved and served for the God He is, and, for us, the crucified Christ as the ultimate climax of that theism: "God in Christ reconciling the world to himself."

In this way the new disciple can affirm a genuine continuity with hope and without compromise. Only so will he really surmount the hurdle of a self-accused treachery, a deep inner feeling of having forsaken one's past and somehow disowned one's community. Both our two examples felt and suffered this acutely.

No Christian approach to questions of conversion and culture within Muslim societies can rightly neglect the necessary battle for liberty of mind to follow persuasions of truth. To believe in conversion without caring—as far as in us lies—for the circumstances preceding and attending it would be disloyal. The issues of freedom of belief are, of course, the responsibility of those inside Islamic communities, not of outsiders. But the latter may help to clarify and foster the thoughts and factors that make for liberty of belief. In some academic areas the battle has already been largely won. But legal rights, and the readiness of public opinion to make them effective, are yet to be made secure. One of the surest ways of influencing cultural patterns in this respect is simply the quality of Christian relationships as patient, reverent, and expectant.

However, it is not only the dominant culture in its attitudes to movement of religious faith that is involved. How is the converting Muslim, now willing to receive Christ, accepted in the churches? With eager warmth and ready welcome? The fact is often otherwise—with skepticism or reluctance. Among the reasons for this is in the long habituation of the old churches under Islam to non-evangelism, at least in the active sense. Churches, too, of more recent missionary planting or association, tend to stay wary of the newly baptized. Motives may be suspected or professions distrusted, so that the inquirer is liable to find a doubtful reception. (In Africa the situation is easier, in that Islam itself is less rigorous, more relaxed, and there are mixed Muslim/Christian families, such as rarely, if ever, occur in the Arab world. Africa, sub-Saharan, puts its own stamp on every situation.)

In light of this, what are we to say of convertibility in the external and "confessional" sense of discipleship *via* baptism and participation in the Christian community? "Baptized into Christ" is certainly the New Testament principle; and the commands to preach the Gospel and to make (publicly identified) disciples are linked in one. The waters of baptism are institutionally as symbolic and decisive as the Red Sea and the Jordan, those waters of history whence the imagery came.

Yet such baptism presupposes the welcoming community. Moreover, what is one to do when the spiritual meaning of baptism is obscured by assumptions that a treachery has been committed? How can it be known only and truly as a transaction in discipleship?

Around the answer to that question lurks a surmise some of us cannot ignore. Is it possible that baptism could even become a kind of Christian circumcision and so merit the strictures of the New Testament apostles? In such circumstances as we have described, should we be ready to risk community in the Holy Spirit without it? "Christ sent me, not to baptize, but to preach . . ." (1 Cor. 1:17) wrote Paul. Though he did baptize on occasion, the apostle's priority is plainly implied. He would seem to be saying that mediation of the Word has priority over the initiation of hearers, the more so if the latter became thereby partisans of a mission(ary) or a sect. For what avails finally is "neither circumcision, nor uncircumcision, but a new creation." There are no easy answers to this problem. But the worst answer of all would be to behave as if it did not exist.

Are there, perhaps, further senses, with or without the rite of baptism by which Christian discipleship can be known for what it is in action and in fellowship? Surely yes! There is a way to be in the midst of culture as would-be guardians of truth, servants of faith, and people of hope. Culture, in all its manifestations is, after all, the quality of society, the "style" of life. It is always in flux and change, needing to be leavened, seasoned, lifted, resisted, renewed.

This dimension of vocation lies deeper than discerning ways in which Christian worship can recruit cultural forms and reject the habit of alien imitation. It means more than caring for vocabulary, artifacts, music, design, and idiom in the local guise, significant as all these must be seen to be. Conversion to Christ means reaching out *via* the newness of mind, *with* the authentic idiom, but *into* the whole context, to "prove what is the good, acceptable and perfect will of God." That "proving," surely, is not a learning to accept the circumstances that befall and to find them "working for good," simply in personal safety and well-being. It is, rather, giving people around us to know for sure what God would have them and their world to be. It means not being conformed but transformed so that "culture"—in its fullest sense as what life is in the living of it—has present within it that witness to judgment and to grace by which its norms are judged and called.

This is not some social gospel. It is based, after all, on the reality of personal conversion, which is the crux of all other convertibility towards truth and compassion and joy. But the truly personal conversion never stays with an individual dimension. For, in our Lord's words, it has its incidence in that "wind of the Spirit" everywhere moving "as he lists."

The themes and crises of culture are legion. Much of the Muslim world is caught in a vast sudden influx of wealth, of petro-dollars. One writer has recently written, "The Gulf is an area which has emerged from rags to riches in the space of thirty years. . . . The contrast between a struggling, labor-based survival economy and a wildly wasteful consumer economy fueled by a massive welfare system has been a shattering experience." The situation is complicated by the vast influx of foreigners, until the local population is well-nigh outnumbered. The author concludes,

> The dominant experience of sensitive souls is one of despair, restlessness, transience and futility in work. . . . One gets the feeling that everything is prefabricated, jerry-rigged, and

easily disassembled, from physical structures to the social matrix itself. In the face of this overpowering attack upon the quality of human existence, to what spiritual resources may the people turn?

Other areas face the opposite urgency of drastic poverty, of local population growth far in excess of the capacity to sustain even a deplorable standard of living. What of the struggle for dignity, not to say survival, in a world of such utter crowdedness and fragility? What, as Ezra Pound put it, of "the enormous pathos of the dream in the peasant's bent shoulders"?

There is, clearly, no theme of culture that can be immune to the stress of these and other factors in the human scene where we are looking for conversion. With these, says the apostle, is "our wrestling." What can he mean? Intercession? Truly. But then the God with whom we intercede is liable, as with evangelism, to entrust the issues back again to us, that a man may work for what he prays, but do so in the dimensions his intercession learns. Prayer is certainly not exoneration but involvement.

Ours it is, if we are in Christ, within all cultures, to affirm the sacramental earth, the work of the God who created and meant it unto good, and to witness concretely for that meaning, however partialized it may be by man's waywardness. In so doing we must recruit all the arguable assets that other faiths afford, subduing all these to the criteria that we obey in Christ and him crucified. That means the local churches as caring communities, reaching into the personal needs, the hopes and fears of their neighbors, in an active compassion and a living communication. Such is the will's discipleship in Christ.

Perhaps we can come round full circle and conclude with repentance, where conversion begins. Islam, in its emphasis on *Taubah* (penitence) and on God as *Al-Tawwab* ("cognizant of penitence"), has some kinship here, though its accent is on sin as what we *do* in deeds, rather than on sin as who and how we *are* in character and nature. "The valley of Achor" has to be "a door of hope" (Hos. 2:15). So much of the world is in the valley, without seeing the door. We need to think of penitence in a more vicarious way, as the will to make the evils of society our own, to feel ourselves responsible. This runs against the grain of all societies and cultures. For we all like to think ourselves innocent, to be "justified" even though the "justification" be a false one. Thus even religion, as Albert Camus had it, may be seen as "a great laundering exercise." When it is so, then culture becomes impervious, in its smugness, to a truer quality. Without such accusation, societies decay.

But the only right to press such accusation is in the love that suffers before it can transform. Here is the whole secret of the Cross of Jesus as the Christ and, with it, the whole duty of the Christian in culture.

Part
III. *Culture, Churches, and Ethics*

13. The Church in Culture
—A Dynamic Equivalence Model

by Charles H. Kraft

CHARLES H. KRAFT *is professor of anthropology and African studies, School of World Mission, Fuller Theological Seminary, Pasadena, California. He is author of a new missions textbook,* Christianity in Culture.

WHAT SHOULD THE CHURCH OF JESUS CHRIST look like in relation to the surrounding culture?

I ask this question as one who was involved for several years in church planting in northeastern Nigeria and who now teaches missionaries working largely in nonwestern areas of the world. But each of us, I believe, no matter what part of the world we happen to live in, should be concerned with this issue, as we worship, serve, and witness together as the people of God. We need to discover how to relate our church life most effectively to our cultural environment. In particular, we must ask ourselves what we can learn from the biblical examples concerning how the people of God ought to relate to the cultures in which they live.

TWO INADEQUATE MODELS

During the early years of the modern Protestant missionary movement, most missionaries simply assumed that the churches they founded should be as similar as possible to the churches they had experienced in their home countries. This "traditional" approach is still with us. As one missionary said to me, "We have had two thousand years of experience with Christianity. We know how the church is to be organized and operated." In effect, he felt that it was his task to instruct new believers in the ways of Euroamerican church life.

This approach to church planting not only assumes that western ways are the right ways; it also assumes that the positions advocated by the missionaries' home groups are more correct, in other words, more "biblical," than those of other missionary and denominational groups. These positions are then typically labeled as "the New Testament pattern." Little attention is given to the significance of cultural differences between the missionaries' culture, that of the receiving people, and those of the Scriptures themselves.

No one can doubt the sincerity of the missionaries who have used the traditional approach to church planting. The problem is not that they did not seek to be biblical in their methods. Nor did they knowingly turn to extrabiblical authority. They merely lacked the ability to understand and appreciate the significance of cultural differences. They approached their task from a monocultural, ethnocentric point of view. They saw their ways as superior and "Christian." Whether consciously or unconsciously, they regarded other cultures as inferior to their own home cultures. They set up schools and other training programs common in their home countries to train the receiving people out of their "inferior" ways into so called "Christian" ways, both with respect to the faith and the cultural trappings in which that faith is to be clothed.

Missiologists have long since found this approach inadequate. They see theological naiveness in the assumption that any given denomination, western or otherwise, can see clearly a single scriptural model that is applicable to all peoples in all times and places. Further, they see cultural naiveness in the assumption that models that may serve well in the home country can simply be exported to other cultures without modification.

Even before the turn of the century Henry Venn in England and Rufus Anderson in the United States (and, later, Roland Allen) began to see and to point out the flaws in the paternalistic traditional approach. They then began to advocate another model—one that stresses the need for churches to be "indigenous" in the receiving cultures rather than simply exported from the sending cultures. Their goal for nonwestern churches was expressed in terms of the "three-selfs": self-support, self-government, and self-propagation. Eventually, nearly all mission theorists and field missionaries came to give at least lip service to these principles. Many gave themselves totally to the task of training leaders who would take over the church and mission structures and operate them according to these principles.

This indigenous approach, however, though in theory a considerable advance over the traditional approach, often proved to be no more valid in practice. Indeed, it often devolved into a mere intensification of the training program whereby national leaders were westernized for service in an already westernized church. Though the term "indigenous" points missionaries in the direction of the receptor culture, it fails to get below the surface.

In a landmark article on this subject missionary anthropologist William Smalley presents a telling critique of the "three-selfs" indigenous church model. He strongly points to the need for a deeply *functional* kind of indigeneity in contrast to a merely surface-level approach. On the matter of church government, for instance, he observes,

> It may be very easy to have a self-governing church which is not indigenous. . . . All that is necessary to do is to indoctrinate a few leaders in western patterns of church government, and let them take over. The result will be a church governed in a slavishly foreign manner (although probably modified at points in the direction of local government patterns), but by no stretch of imagination can it be called an indigenous government. ("Cultural Implications of an Indigenous Church," *Practical Anthropology,* 1958, Vol. 5, p. 52)

Clearly, it is not the mere fact of self-government (or self-support or self-propagation) that assures that the church in question is "indigenous." Authentic indigeneity lies in the *manner* in which such selfhood is expressed. Smalley goes on to speak of a church "which is advertised by its founding mission as a great indigenous church, where its pastors are completely supported by the local church members, yet the mission behind the scenes pulls the strings and the church does its bidding like the puppets of the 'independent' iron curtain countries'' (ibid.: p. 54).

We can also find churches where, although the real power is in the hands of national leaders, these leaders are so indoctrinated in foreign ways that the supposed indigeneity is in outward form only. In essence, the meanings and impressions conveyed to the general populace by the mode of existence and operation of the church are all foreign.

AUTHENTIC INDIGENEITY

Strictly speaking, "indigeneity" is not necessarily the most appropriate label for the ideal toward which we strive. A church *totally* indigenous in appearance, function, and meaning would be no different from the rest of the culture. Christianity, because it comes into a culture from the outside, is inevitably intrusive to a certain degree. There is "no such thing as an absolutely indigenous church in any culture," observes Smalley ("What Are Indigenous Churches Like?" *Practical Anthropology,* 1959, Vol. 6, p. 137). Nevertheless, we will employ the term "indigenous church" (as Smalley does) to signify an expression of Christianity that is both culturally authentic and genuinely Christian.

Smalley defines an indigenous church as

a group of believers who live out their life, including their so-cialized Christian activity, in the patterns of the local society, and for whom any transformation of that society comes out of their felt needs under the guidance of the Holy Spirit and the Scriptures. ("Cultural Implications," p. 55)

Such a church will exhibit the kind of autonomy we see in the churches described in the pages of the New Testament. It will express "selfhood" at a far deeper level than can be imposed by any outside organization committed to the three-selfs formula.

Alan Tippett describes this selfhood in terms of six integrally interdependent characteristics (*Verdict Theology in Missionary Theory,* William Carey, 1973, pp. 154-159). An authentically indigenous church will (1) "see itself as *the* church of Jesus Christ in its own local situation, mediating the work, the mind, the word and the ministry of Christ in its own environment"; (2) be made up of interdependent, interacting, yet discreet parts, all functioning together in commitment to and for the good of the whole, and not at the behest of outsiders; (3) make decisions autonomously according to culturally appropriate decision-making patterns; (4) support its own operation and outreach in culturally appropriate ways; (5) hear the Great Commission as directly addressed to itself, and therefore commit itself to indigenous forms of self-propagation; and (6) be self-giving, actively and appropriately serving the wider community as an expression of its Christian self-image.

Smalley highlights five additional considerations. First, since a church is a sociocultural entity, an authentically indigenous church will exhibit patterns of interaction between people consistent with the culture in which the members of the church were brought up. If the patterns of personal interaction of a given church are those of the missionaries from overseas, the church is not truly indigenous.

Second, the transforming presence of the Holy Spirit will be evident, changing both individuals and the group as a whole.

Such transformation occurs differently in different societies, depending on the meaning which people attach to their behavior and the needs which they feel in their lives. . . . An indigenous church is precisely one in which the changes which take place under the guidance of the Holy Spirit meet the needs and fulfill the meanings of that society and not of any outside group. (Smalley, ibid.: p. 56)

Third, when the Holy Spirit prompts changes that are consistent with the culture, it is not uncommon for the missionary community to dislike the results. Even missionaries who consider themselves favorable to indigeneity tend to encourage culture change that makes people more like themselves. Their deeply ingrained reflexes have been conditioned by other cultural patterns, and they most easily recognize the Holy Spirit's work when it is expressed in ways such as experienced in their home countries.

Fourth, a genuinely indigenous church is "planted," not "founded." The "founding" of churches by missionaries, observes Smalley, typically involves the use of organizational procedures familiar to the missionaries from their experience in the home country. This results in the production of such trappings of western life as constitution, doctrinal statement, procedures for the operation of business meetings and elections, disciplinary procedures, and the like. Referring to a case where a constitution was imposed on a supposedly indigenous church, Smalley says,

> To this day no one seems to have sensed the fact that a tribal church *with* a constitution is no more an indigenous church than a tribal church *without* one, as the existence of a constitution is entirely irrelevant to the relation of the church to God and to surrounding human life. (ibid.: p. 61)

In other words, a *planted* (as opposed to a founded) church will adopt indigenous governmental and organizational procedures intact, making whatever modifications need to be made for these procedures to be appropriate to the Christian community. Decisions concerning these procedures, their use and their modification, can best be made by those whose cultural reflexes have been formed by them. Normally, outsiders are not in a good position to make such decisions.

Fifth, genuinely indigenous churches often originate apart from direct mission effort. The most indigenous churches of Africa, for example, are certain of the independent churches. In Southeast Asia an exciting indigenous church among the Meo was planted by a converted Meo shaman (G. Linwood Barney, "The Meo—an Incipient Church," *Practical Anthropology,* 1957, Vol. 4, pp. 31-50).

Smalley sums up the fourth and fifth considerations (above) as follows:

> Our distance from most other cultures is so great, the cultural specialization of the West is so extreme, that there are almost no avenues of approach whereby the work which we do can normally result in anything of an indigenous nature. It is an ironical thing that the West, which is most concerned with the spread of Christianity in the world today, and which

is financially best able to undertake the task of worldwide evangelism, is culturally the least suited for its task because of the way in which it has specialized itself to a point where it is very difficult for it to have an adequate understanding of other peoples. (ibid.: p. 63)

CULTURAL FORMS, FUNCTIONS, AND MEANINGS

The key to the development of a new approach to church planting is to get beneath the surface level to a deeper level of understanding. In anthropological terms, the surface level of cultural phenomena is known as the level of cultural forms. Beneath this level are what may be labeled the level of function and the level of meaning.

The *forms* of a culture are the observable, surface features of that culture. These may be material items such as houses, clothing, pottery, tools, machines, and so forth. More frequently, though, they are non-material elements such as ceremonies, rituals, organizations, language, and the like. A *word* is a fairly simple non-material cultural form. A *wedding ceremony* or a *church* are much more complex cultural forms made up of many subsidiary forms. Cultural institutions such as the family or government, practices such as visiting neighbors or telling stories, customary ways of eating or farming, rituals such as baptism and other initiation rites, and organizations such as clubs and churches, are all cultural forms.

These forms serve a variety of *functions* in a society. Food and rest are basic physical needs, and customs of eating and sleeping have the function of meeting those needs. Cultural forms such as marriage, family structures, educational, political, and economic systems function to meet basic socio-cultural needs. Religious organizations and rituals serve to meet psychological and spiritual needs. Often cultural forms that would seem to serve only certain obvious needs actually perform other functions as well. Eating customs, for example, frequently have ritual or ceremonial significance in addition to meeting people's biological need for food.

The functions that cultural forms serve result in the communication of *meanings* to the people involved. When a family is functioning well it communicates love and security. If it is not functioning well, however, "family" may mean tension, enmity, bitterness, and insecurity to those within it. When a government is functioning well it provides for the greatest good for the greatest number of people and stirs feelings of gratitude, loyalty, and pride. When it is not functioning well, it may become an instrument of exploitation, oppression, and self-interest and therefore stir feelings of fear, insecurity, and anger. When a church is functioning well, it communicates God's care and purpose for his people. When it is not functioning well, other meanings such as foreignness, oppression, insensitivity to people's real needs, may be communicated.

It is essential to recognize that what is signified to receptors by cultural forms is determined *by them,* not by the communicator. Furthermore, when the cultural forms of one culture are employed in another culture, a shift in meaning inevitably occurs. Even when the people of two cultures appear to practice the same custom, we can expect the understood meaning of that custom to differ from group to group.

Two major principles of intercultural interaction thus become evident:

1. When a cultural form (like an axe, word, or the church) is borrowed from one culture to another, there will always be some change in its meaning; and

2. equivalent meanings can only be communicated in another culture if the forms employed are as appropriate for expressing those meanings in the receptor culture as the source forms are in the source culture.

Fortunately, in spite of cultural differences, people are enough alike to understand each other across cultural boundaries if sufficient adjustment is made. Though the receiver of the communication will always have to make some adjustment, the major responsibility for adjustment belongs to the one who seeks to communicate across a cultural barrier. This means, among other things, that the communicator must rely heavily on cultural forms already in use in the receptor culture and employ as few forms as possible from other cultures.

The recognition and employment of these two principles is crucial to an understanding of authentically Christian indigeneity.

For if the cultural form of the church in one culture is simply transplanted to another culture we can be certain that the meaning will be changed. If those in the receiving culture are to understand the church the way that those in the sending culture understand it, the cultural form of the church *must* be changed. What is needed is a kind of "translation" of the meanings of the church from the cultural forms of the source into those forms of the receiving culture that function in such a way that they convey equivalent meanings. Only by changing the forms can the meanings be preserved.

DYNAMIC EQUIVALENCE VERSUS FORMAL CORRESPONDENCE

What I am suggesting is that a truly indigenous church should look in its culture like a good Bible translation looks in its language. In a good Bible translation (1) the original meanings come through clearly, (2) the hearers assume that it is an original work in their language (since they are not forced to learn foreign patterns in order to understand it), and (3) the impact of the message in the receiving language is roughly equivalent to its impact to its original hearers.

Most Bible translators today aim not for "formal correspondence" but for "dynamic equivalence." Translations like the Revised Standard Version (RSV), American Standard Version (ASV), and King James Version (KJV), which are sometimes characterized as literal or word-for-word translations, are more or less products of the formal correspondence approach. They convey a largely non-English (i.e., non-indigenous) flavor because the translators did not carry their task far enough. They did not make sure that the English renderings were as appropriate to the receiving language as the original Hebrew, Aramaic, and Greek expressions were to those languages.

For example, the RSV (one of the better formal correspondence translations) consistently translates *soma* as "body," even though the Greek word covers a somewhat different area of meaning than the English word. If our translations are to be true to the Greek meaning, they should accommodate to English structure (rather than simply transplanting Greek structure) and render *soma* differently, according to the demands of the various contexts.

Thus, in Mark 5:29, an English rendering that would more faithfully convey the Greek meaning would be "herself," rather than "her body"; in Luke 17:37 a more accurate rendering would be "corpse"; in Romans 12:1 it would be "selves"; and in Colossians 2:11 it would be something like "lower nature" (rather than RSV's puzzling "body of flesh," a particularly unhelpful example of formal correspondence). Note a similar ineptness in the RSV's handling of Mark 1:4: "preaching a baptism of repentance for the forgiveness of sins" (intended to mean something like "proclaiming that people should turn away from their sins and be baptized to receive God's forgiveness"); Luke 20:47: "who devour widows' houses" (meaning "who take advantage of widows and rob them of their homes"); or Mark 1:5-10, where the word "and" occurs 12 times (this is poor English style and gives the impression that the original author wrote poorly). A host of additional examples could be cited.

Ministers who preach from these translations frequently have to digress from their main thrust to explain that the words of their text do not have their ordinary English meanings, but, rather, have Greek and Hebrew meanings that only students of the original languages can properly understand and explain. This is because these formal correspondence translations were produced in adherence with a nineteenth-century concept of the nature of language, which saw languages basically as alternative codes, each consisting of a different set of labels for the same reality. Early in this century, however, anthropologists and linguists began to recognize that understandings of reality are structured differently by different cultures and that these differences are strongly reflected in their languages. There is, therefore, no such thing as an exact correspondence between a given word in one language and the most nearly corresponding word in another.

Such translations as Phillips, Good News Bible, New English Bible, and Living Bible are much more in line with contemporary understandings of language and culture. Recognizing the non-equatability of languages, they employ renderings that go beyond mere correspondence of form and thus are more likely to elicit from contemporary readers a response equivalent to that elicited from the original readers of the slangy, communicative Koine Greek (i.e., the common people's Greek).

E. A. Nida and C. R. Taber define a good translation in terms of

> the degree to which the receptors of the message in the receptor language respond to it in substantially the same manner as the receptors in the source language. This response can never be identical, for the cultural and historical settings are too different, but there should be a high degree of equivalence of response, or the translation will have failed to accomplish its purpose. *(The Theory and Practice of Translation,* Brill, 1964, p. 24)

In other words, a dynamic equivalence translation is directed toward equivalence of *response* (based on equivalence of perceived meaning) rather than equivalence of *form*. An important element of this dynamic view is the fact that good translation involves more than simply the conveying of information:

> It would be wrong to think . . . that the response of the receptors in the second language is merely in terms of comprehension of the information, for communication is not merely informative. It must also be expressive and imperative if it is to serve the principal purposes of communications such as those found in the Bible. [It] . . . must present the message in such a way that people can feel its relevance (the expressive element in communication) and can then respond to it in action (the imperative function). (Nida and Taber, ibid.)

This approach shows appreciation for the complexity of language itself and of the process of moving concepts via language from one group of people to another. The biblical writers intended to be understood, not to be merely admired or simply to have their writings so highly thought of that they are transmitted in unintelligible or misleading forms. Faithful translation, therefore, involves doing whatever must be done (including a certain amount of paraphrase) in order to make sure that the message originally phrased in Hebrew and Greek is transmitted in words and idioms that function to produce meanings for the hearers equivalent to those intended by the original authors.

DYNAMIC EQUIVALENCE CHURCHES

All of this is highly suggestive of a new understanding of what churches should look like from culture to culture. For a church is a kind of culture-to-culture "translation." Nida and Taber (ibid.: pp. 3-8) develop seven basic understandings of language required of effective Bible translators. Six of these are equally applicable for the effective planting of indigenous churches.

1. Each language and culture has its own genius, its own distinctiveness, its own special character, its own patterning, its own strengths, weaknesses, and limitations. The effective church planter, like the effective Bible translator, must recognize this distinctiveness.

2. To communicate effectively in another language and culture one must respect and work in terms of this uniqueness. It is the receptor language and culture (with both strengths and weaknesses) that must provide the matrix for the translation and/or the church. Whatever changes in linguistic and cultural forms are demanded by that receiving matrix to assure maximum accurate intelligibility must be acceded to.

3. In general, meanings that are communicable in one language and culture are communicable in another, though in different forms and always with some loss and gain of meaning. Though the correspondence between the original meanings and those received can never be exact, it can be *adequate* if the focus is on the content being transmitted rather than on the mere preservation of the literal forms of the source language and culture. In other words, despite cultural differences, the essential concept of "churchness" is transferrable.

4. "To preserve the content of the message the form must be changed." This principle, applied to church planting, means that the concept and communicational impact of the church is accurately registered in the receptor culture only to the extent that the cultural forms that it employs are as specifically appropriate in the new culture as the forms employed in the source culture were originally. That is, cultural forms of the church will have to differ from culture to culture, as necessary to assure equivalent meanings.

5. We should not regard the languages and cultures of the Bible as too sacred to analyze. Like all other languages and cultures, they show both areas of strength and limitation. Furthermore, as with all languages, the biblical Greek and Hebrew vocabulary, idiom, and grammar participate fully in and have meaning only in terms of the culture in which these languages were used. It is the *message* of the Bible that is sacred, not the human languages and cultures used to convey the message.

As with the relation between the biblical languages and the message of God, so with the biblical cultures and the church of God. The cultures themselves and cultural forms used to convey sacred meanings are not sacred in and of themselves. God's use of them demonstrates his willingness to work in terms of *any* culture, not a desire on his part to perfect and impose any single set of cultural forms.

6. "The writers of the biblical books expected to be understood." Similarly, God expects to be understood through his church. The church is meant to be maximally intelligible to the world around it, conveying meanings equivalent to those conveyed in the biblical era. The faithful churchman will work toward the end of transculturating the church into the appropriate forms of the receptor culture, so that God's message through the church will be understood.

Applying this model to church planting means the eschewing of attempts to produce mere formal correspondence between churches in one culture and those in another. A church in Africa or Asia that is merely a "literal" rendering of an American church in the twentieth century (or even a Greco-Roman church in the first century) should be rejected. Such a church slavishly copies the foreign church that founded it. If the founding church has bishops or presbyters or elders, the younger church will have them too. If the founding church operates according to a written constitution, the younger will as well. If the founding church conducts business meetings according to Roberts' Rules of Order, the younger church will likewise. And so it will be with regard to educational requirements for leadership, times of worship, style of worship, type of music, structures of church buildings, behavioral requirements, the types of educational, medical and benevolent activity, and even the expression of missionary concern. This approach risks utterly disregarding the culturally appropriate functional equivalents and the indigenously understood meanings of all of these things in the culture in which the young church is supposedly functioning and to which it is supposedly witnessing. The impression such churches give to the people of their cultural world is one of foreignness and outside domination, even though the leadership of these churches may be local.

A "dynamic equivalence" church, on the other hand, is the kind of church that produces an impact in its society equivalent to the impact that the original church produced in its cultural environment. To be sure, it will have need of leadership, organization, education, worship, buildings, behavioral standards, and means of expressing Christian love and concern to the people of its own culture who have not yet responded to Christ. But it will look for ways and styles of operating that are appropriate and understandable to the receptors. At the outset, it is possible that the cultural forms available to the church may be only minimally adequate to the tasks at hand. Despite such limitations, however, a dynamic equivalence church will take indigenous forms, possess and adapt them for Christ, and thereby begin the process that will transform them to serve Christian ends and convey Christian meanings to the surrounding society.

According to the above conception, a dynamic equivalence church (1) conveys to its members truly Christian meanings, (2) responds to the felt needs of its society, producing within it an impact for Christ equivalent to that which the first century church produced in its society, and (3) appropriates cultural forms that are as nearly indigenous as possible.

USING THE BIBLICAL DATA

The task of developing a dynamically equivalent church obviously cannot proceed without first ascertaining just what the biblical forms, functions, and meanings are that the church in the receptor culture is expected to reflect. For this information we look primarily to the New Testament (though for many situations culturally closer to Old Testament cultures, the Old Testament offers more easily transferable models). The Acts and Pastoral Epistles provide many insights into matters of organization, leadership, fellowship, witness, and worship. Insights into behavioral matters are likewise found in these books and also in the Corinthian epistles. Certain other epistles focus more on doctrinal matters. Based on these models, contemporary churches are to develop culturally appropriate forms to convey equivalent meanings within contemporary cultural matrices.

Many Euroamerican churches have adopted dynamically equivalent forms in various areas of church life, as for instance in the adoption of democratic principles of church government. But while such forms have proven culturally appropriate in our own setting, they may not be suited overseas where mission organizations have frequently attempted to employ them in cultures where such patterns are quite foreign. This is the case not only in matters of church organization but also with regard to modes of baptism (and the apologetics that accompany them) and observance of the Lord's Supper. It is perhaps most damaging in matters of worship, doctrine, witness, and behavioral standards. Why, for example, should more time be given in Asian and African Bible schools to discussions of the proofs of biblical inspiration and of theories of the atonement (problems which do not seem to be the issues in their contexts that they are in the West) than to dealing with a biblical perspective on evil spirits and ancestor reverence (problems of vital importance within their cultures)?

In attempting to discover a dynamically equivalent form of preaching I once asked a group of Nigerian church leaders how they felt it would be appropriate to present a message such as the Christian message to the village council. They replied,

We would choose the oldest, most respected man in the group and ask him a question. He would discourse, perhaps at length, on the topic and then become silent, whereupon we would ask another question. As the old man talked other old men would comment as well. But eventually he and the others would do less and less of the talking and the leader would do more and more. In this way we would develop our message and it would become the topic for discussion of the whole village.

I asked them why they did not employ this approach in church. "Why, we've been taught that monologue is the Christian way," they replied. "Can this be why no old men come to church?" I asked. "Of course!" they said. "We have alienated them all by not showing them due respect in public meetings." Thus it is that a preaching form that may (or may not) be appropriate in Euroamerican culture may lose its effectivenss and even become counterproductive when exported to another culture.

What we seek is equivalence to the functions and meanings of models found in the Scriptures, not mere imitation of their forms. With regard to leadership, for example, simply because the New Testament churches appointed bishops, elders, and deacons does not mean (as some contend) that churches today must label their leaders by these terms or expect them to lead in the same (rather authoritarian, by American standards) ways that were appropriate for those leaders in their society. In the New Testament we see, in fact, not a single, once-for-all set of leadership forms set down for all time. Rather, we find a variety of culturally appropriate patterns, ranging from a communal approach (Acts 15:4, 6, 22), to the more highly structured patterns reflected in the Pastoral Epistles. We can observe certain organizational differences between the Jewish Jerusalem church and the Greek churches with which Timothy and Titus were connected. And, in the Acts account of the appointment of deacons (Acts 6:1-6), we note the development of a new, culturally appropriate form to meet a need not anticipated at an earlier stage in the life of the Jerusalem church. In each case the organizational form that was adopted responded to felt needs, and was conditioned by the culturally inculcated expectations of the members of the society in which the particular local church operated.

CHURCH LEADERSHIP: A CASE STUDY

In the Pastoral Epistles we find lists of attributes required of leaders in first-century Greco-Roman churches. (Such "ethical lists" were commonly produced in Greek culture to set forth the necessary qualifications of various types of leaders; see B. W. Easton, *The Pastoral Epistles,* SCM, 1948, pp. 197-202.) According to 1 Timothy 3:2 ff. and Titus 1:6 ff. (NEB), such leaders should be unimpeachable or irreproachable in character, which included being "faithful to his one wife, sober, temperate, courteous, hospitable," with proven ability to manage their own households well, and so on. If leaders possessed these attributes they would maintain the proper reputation within and outside of the Christian community in the Greco-Roman culture of the first century.

The quest for dynamic equivalence to this New Testament model will focus not on the specific forms reflected in 1 Timothy and Titus but on the *functions* that lie behind these forms. Indeed, contemporary church leaders need to be just as irreproachable in character as the leaders of the New Testament era. But in order for them to be perceived as beyond reproach they will have to manifest those characteristics regarded as appropriate in *their* societies to convey such a meaning. That is, the precise characteristics (i.e., cultural forms) regarded as proper qualifications for church leaders (i.e., conveying Scriptural meanings) must be those of the receptor culture, and these will not necessarily correspond exactly to the characteristics advocated for church leaders in first-century Greco-Roman culture (or any other culture such as Euroamerican). While there will be basic similarities in leadership criteria, the precise content will vary from culture to culture.

In contemporary American culture, for instance, because of its similarity to Greco-Roman culture, criteria for church leadership include most of the items in the Timothy-Titus lists, with some variation of emphasis. American congregations expect their leaders to be serious, self-controlled, courteous, good teachers (or preachers), not given to drink or violent behavior, not quarrelsome, upright, doctrinally sound. Hospitality, dignity, and not being money-hungry might or might not be specified on such a list, though they would at least be tacitly recognized as desirable.

American congregations, however, are not necessarily so insistent that their leaders be known for their ability to manage a home and family well. In addition to the fact that many American pastors begin their ministerial careers before they have had a chance to establish a family, a majority of congregations want a minister who can offer the vigor of his early and middle years. It appears that American Christians place a higher priority on youth and vigor than on the qualities of seniority which seem to be assumed by the New Testament lists.

The point at which the American and Timothy-Titus lists differ most is probably marital standards. In the Greco-Roman context irreproachability apparently demanded that a person not take a second wife after the death or divorce of his first wife. (See *The International Critical Commentary* and *The Moffatt Commentary* on 1 Tim. 3:2 and Titus 1:6.) American congregations, on the other hand, would not find any problem in a pastor's remarriage if his first wife were to die; most (but not all) would object, however, to remarriage after a divorce and—of course—to divorce itself.

Finally, an American congregation would probably want to add a few elements to the Timothy-Titus lists such as administrative ability, personableness, and (as noted earlier) youth.

If, now, we develop an equivalent list of leadership criteria for a radically different culture such as may be found in Africa (e.g., the Higi culture of northeastern Nigeria), we will find some additions to and substractions from both the American and Greco-Roman lists. Greed, being the cardinal sin of Higiland, will be one of the major proscribed items, while conformance to culturally expected patterns of politeness will be one of the most important prescribed items. Hospitality and its concomitant, generosity, will be highlighted to a much greater degree than would be true for either Greco-Roman or American culture. Soberness, temperance, patience, and the like will appear on the Higi list (more highly valued than in American culture). Higis, in addition, focus on age and on membership in the royalty social class. Furthermore, they strongly emphasize family management—certainly much more strongly than an American congregation would and probably even more strongly than in Greco-Roman churches.

In the link between marital status and family management would lie the most significant formal difference between the Higi ideal and either of the others. For, in order for a Higi leader to effectively maintain the respect of his people, he would not only have to manage his household well but would have to have at least two wives in that household! "How," the Higi person would ask, "can one properly lead if he has not demonstrated his ability by managing well a household with more than one wife in it?" (The Kru of Liberia, with a similar ideal, declare, "You cannot trust a man with only one wife.")

Lining up the lists side by side, with items in approximate

order of priority, we can compare the culturally prescribed requisites for Christian leadership in the three cultures:

Greco-Roman	American	Higi
One wife only	Faithful to spouse	Royal social class
Serious	Self-controlled	Mature age
Self-controlled	Serious	Hospitable
Courteous	Courteous	Generous
Not quarrelsome	Doctrinally sound	Patient
Hospitable	Vigorous	Self-controlled
A good teacher	A good preacher	Serious
Not a money lover	Personable	Courteous
Manage household well	Mature in faith	Manage (polygamous) household well
Mature in faith	Manage household well	A good teacher
Good reputation	A good administrator	

If we were to list the formal characteristics of ideal leaders in the various cultural contexts portrayed in the Old Testament, we would note fewer differences between these criteria and the Higi list. And it would be even clearer that God has chosen throughout history to work in terms of the forms of each culture in order to attain his purposes.

It must be emphasized that at this point we are dealing with the cultural forms with which God is willing to start in order to adequately convey those meanings that are most important at that time. Once he begins to work within the people of a culture a process is started that inevitably leads to the transformation of at least certain of their customs and values. Polygamy, for instance, though accepted and not questioned by God throughout the Bible, ultimately died out in Hebrew culture (it never was present in Greek or Roman cultures). Eventually we may expect Higi churches to change their criteria for leaders at this point (and others) as well. (It may be, too, that the American tendency to value the vigor of youth above the seasoned wisdom and stability of age may be challenged in a healthy way by both Greco-Roman and Higi values.) If, however, outsiders attempt to impose foreign criteria on the Higi chruch, what will be produced will be leadership that corresponds in a formal way to a foreign model but that lacks the dynamic equivalence to biblical models that will adequately convey God's intended meanings in and through the church.

And so it is with each of the elements in the life, doctrine, and worship of churches. The Bible needs to be analyzed culturally to discover the functions served by the forms employed. Then the cultural characteristics of the receptor church should be evaluated to ascertain what forms can be employed to convey the meanings of the Christian faith in ways equivalent to the New Testament models. (See accompanying diagram of this two-fold process.) This will result in the use of cultural forms that differ from those of either first-century Greco-Roman culture or of the culture from which the missionaries come. As with Bible translation, so with the "transculturation" of the church: the extent of the divergence between the forms of the sending and the receiving churches will depend upon the distance between the cultures in question.

In conclusion, I suggest that formal correspondence models of the church result in the same kind of foreign, stilted product that results from formal correspondence approaches to Bible translation. The better approach—the one that enables the church to convey the message of God most faithfully in its surrounding culture—is the dynamic equivalence model.

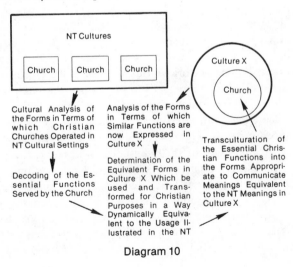

Diagram 10

14. Mission as Inter-Cultural Encounter
—A Sociological Perspective

by Alfred C. Krass

ALFRED C. KRASS *is a former missionary in Ghana and consultant on evangelism for the United Church Board for World Ministries. He is author of* Go . . . and Make Disciples *and* Five Lanterns at Sundown.

"THE PURPOSE OF YOUR MISSION . . . IS TO make known the gospel and plant Christian institutions in that part of Western Central Africa which lies inland from the Portuguese colony of Angola." Thus read the charter given to four American missionaries in 1880, with its explicit two-fold assignment:

1. "make known the gospel."

2. "plant Christian institutions."

The missionaries, and the American Board of Commissioners for Foreign Missions which commissioned them, considered themselves part of a history which traced back to the command of Jesus: "Go therefore and make disciples of all nations, baptizing them in the name of the Father and of the Son and of the Holy Spirit, teaching them to observe all that I have commanded you . . ." (Matt. 28:19, 20). In many ways the four missionaries considered themselves to be quite immediately related to Christ's original commission, to be directly responsive to the Lord who promised "I will be with you always, to the end of the age."

Yet they were part of an intervening history as well, part of a long tradition with many sub-histories and alternative paths and byways. This can be seen when we compare the Board's commissioning statement and Christ's original commission. At no point in his original commission did Christ assign to his disciples the task of "planting Christian institutions." Yet, in 1880 it was assumed right from the beginning that the task of Christian missionaries was not simply to make disciples but also to plant such institutions. In fact, the Board would have found it questionable that disciples in the fullest sense could be made if the institutions were not available to facilitate the transition from the unevangelized state to discipleship.

In fairness, we need to credit the Board with an appreciation for the priority of the Gospel:

> Do not be in a hurry to teach the natives many things until the one thing needful has been learned and received into the heart. Make it your endeavor that the civilization you hope to introduce may not be as varnish laid on the heathen character, rendering it in all likelihood less amenable to the gospel than before, but the growth and outcome of regenerated hearts. Act upon the principle that Christianity must precede civilization if the latter is to be of any value. (American Board of Commissioners for Foreign Missions, Annual Report, 1880.)

Still, notice that it was assumed that the missionaries would hope to "introduce civilization" and that they were missionaries not just of Christ but of "civilization." And there were other assumptions in this statement from the charter—about the character of those who were described as "heathen," and about the nature and process of "regeneration" as it was understood by those particular missionaries at that particular time in American religious history.

How did it come about, then, that in the year 1880 four men were commissioned by this particular mission board with these particular words with the expectation that they would carry out the task in this particular way?

With the benefit of hindsight, we can identify the period during which the four missionaries served in Angola as the "manifest destiny" era of American history. The missionaries represented a stage in the missionary enterprise when evangelism and "spreading Christian civilization" were easily confused with planting English-American religious and cultural institutions.

As a sociologist would look at this, the missionaries were not simply "taking the Gospel" to the Ovimbundu people of "West Central Africa" (now Angola). There was an encounter between the Gospel and the Ovimbundu, to be sure; but in addition there was the encounter of two cultures, that of the Ovimbundu and that of the missionaries and the board which sent them.

All such encounters are sociologically complex affairs. A great deal more is going on than the mere "planting of churches." Above all, it is not a one-way process, with the exponents of "modernization" being the "change-agents" and the people among whom they work being the "changed." Both are affected, first, by their encounter with one another, and second, by the fact that as a result of their encounter they are often knit into a new, larger social body. In other words, the impact of the Gospel, the pros and cons of this or that approach to mission, and the many facets of change that occur among the parties involved, cannot be appreciated without looking at the culture of the missionaries as well as the culture of the people to whom they go.

Each side of this analysis ought to be included in what goes by the name of "missionary social science." What we need is a sociology of intercivilizational process, as applied to Christian mission. Such a study will help us see that the objectivity with which missionaries hope to approach their task is perhaps far less possible than what is commonly supposed. At the same time, it will help us argue—somewhat paradoxically—that missionaries need to operate on a much larger scale than simply the planting of churches if they are to be faithful to the God of the Bible.

Let us trace out these issues by making a case study of the mission to Angola in the 1880s.

THE APPROACH ADOPTED
FOR THE ANGOLA MISSION

The commissioning board, founded in 1810, was the first North American Protestant mission board. By 1880, with headquarters in Boston, it was in effect the Congregational churches' mission board, the mission board through which the biological and spiritual descendants of the Puritans exercised their missionary vocation. (In earlier years, it had functioned as *the* American Protestant board, dispatching missionaries of other denominations as well.) It was not an official agency of the Congregational churches but operated under an independent charter granted by the Commonwealth of Massachusetts, an expression of the principle De Tocqueville and others found pervasive in American life: "voluntaryism."

The four missionaries commissioned to West Central Africa by the Board in 1880 set about their task as follows: They immediately commenced to learn the Umbundu language, and once they had learned it, began with equal dispatch to translate the Bible (and Bunyan's *Pilgrim's Progress)* into it.

Right from the start the missionaries were quite eager to establish good relations not only with the Portuguese (who were then in the process of extending their sway inland from the Angola colony to the Bailundu-Bihé area, where the missionaries settled) but also with the Ovimbundu kings and chiefs, and yet wished to remain somewhat distant from both.

Also, at a very early stage—in most cases after only a few visits—the missionaries sought to obtain, from the kings, land on which to build a house, and then proceeded to build what were intended to be comfortable and permanent dwellings.

In each place they occupied the missionaries took African lads into their homes as paid employees and immediately began to train them. It was from these lads that the first congregations usually started. In fact, the first congregations consisted exclusively of young men and of boys and girls. No attempt seems to have been made to make disciples of mature men and women, or of the chiefs. Preaching services were held for whole villages, or for the kings' or chiefs' households, but there never seems to have been any expectation that such preaching would lead more than a responsive few to baptism and church membership.

The missionaries were in no hurry to baptize anyone—indeed, the contrary may be affirmed: only those who proved themselves over a long period of catechesis to be "of serious endeavor" and ready to "forsake all manner of heathen observance" and polygamy and alcohol, and so forth, and who had mastered the requisite Christian knowledge, were considered fit for baptism. The first congregations were quite small, fourteen or nine or twelve "regenerate souls," no more, baptized on individual confession of faith.

The missionaries never became the pastors of the new congregations but insisted that only natives could be pastors: they chose the one they deemed most fit, gave him special training, and expected the congregation to support him without outside help.

It was expected that wherever a congregation was formed a church building would be erected, but the missionaries expected the members themselves to erect it and offered their good services only as consultants on architecture and engineering, and perhaps to solicit a bell from America.

It was assumed that the proper hymns for the new churches would be American or European hymns, that the proper catechism would be a translated American catechism, that those joining the church would recite a "covenant," and that (according to the Board's 1887 Annual Report) this could be a covenant from a church in Ohio.

The missionaries were from the start active in introducing, either in their homes or in communal projects, physical amenities like bridges, better roads, superior methods of construction, new crops, new tools. Only financial difficulties kept the missionaries from establishing boarding schools and institutions in the early years. In a reference to the Board's work in East Central Africa, the 1891 Annual Report expressed the conviction that the work could progress best if the pupils could be kept more completely separate "from the corrupting influences of their heathen homes."

Two very real concerns for the missionaries were their health and their physical safety (eventually several died and some others had to return to America because of ill health). They were also aware of the Africans' health needs, and very early on began regular medical treatment, and constantly petitioned the Board for missionary doctors, until medical work became a regular part of the mission at every station. In regards to their physical safety, they somewhat welcomed the extension of Portuguese authority to the interior, and availed themselves of official protection when the Ovimbundu kings turned against them.

The missionaries were ethnocentric in many of their perceptions and value-judgments, though with a difference—the Portuguese, being Catholic, and not being noted for their piety ("they seem wholly given up to business and sin," noted a writer in the *Missionary Herald* in 1890), were not quite welcomed as fellow Europeans, and the people of Bailundu and Bihé, though "heathen Africans," were considered to be "vigorous, sturdy and even noble."

To conclude this summary of the missionaries' approach to their work, we include two key observations:

1. There is no record that any of the early missionaries ever questioned that it was God's will that the mission should be carried out; nor did they question their own part in it.

2. Although the missionaries anticipated that great effort would be needed to assure the permanence of the work, in their writings none betrayed the slightest doubt but that West Central Africa would be "won for Christ." All that was needed was time and persistence.

Now that we have seen the characteristics peculiar to the missionary work in West Central Africa in the 1800s, an interesting question may be posed. What if things had been otherwise? For example the missionaries might have—

- decided to function not in Umbundu but in Portuguese, or perhaps even in English.
- cast their lot wholly with either the Portuguese or the Ovimbundu, forsaken their neutrality, and become partisan.
- decided not to obtain land or build dwellings, but merely to accept hospitality offered them or lead an ambulatory existence.
- chosen to work with adults of the villages or to concentrate on the royal families, instead of working with young men and boys and girls.
- decided not to accept individuals on confession of faith, but to look for the baptism of whole social units.
- built large American-style churches for the converts using funds from America.
- restricted their educational endeavors to the training of the

pastor-elect (or they even might have maintained all leadership themselves, bypassing entirely the issue of formal education).

- decided not to translate the Bible, or at least not until a felt need for it arose on the part of the converts.
- encouraged the people to make their own church music and listened to the questions people asked about the faith in order to make a catechism, rather than importing hymns and catechisms.
- introduced no physical improvements and no medical work, or, on the other hand, majored in industrial and medical arts.
- regarded the Ovimbundu as "noble savages" and their own Euro-American cultures as "degenerate," or, on the other hand, they might have regarded the Ovimbundu as of racially inferior stock incapable of civilization.
- and, finally, they might have been very pessimistic about the chances of success for their work.

These possibilities, and others too numerous to mention, are not posed fancifully but seriously. All of them can be documented from the history of Christian missions. Other missionaries at other times have insisted on working only in their own language, baptizing whole villages, building huge churches for the converts, and so on. But the American Board missionaries in the 1880s did not, and our purpose is to ask why.

THE CONTROLLING ROLE OF THE BOARD

The first thing to keep in mind is that these missionaries were not free agents—they were commissioned, given special orders, and were maintained by the Board on the condition that they carried out their orders.

So, if we want to know why the missionaries did what they did in Africa, we have to turn first to America, to Boston, to the *Missionary Herald* magazine, and to the Annual Reports of the ABCFM. These help us understand how the Board secretaries and the Prudential Committee and the Corporation of the ABCFM understood the world and the missionary task. We will look first at (1) how the Board understood the missionary task; and then (2) how the Board understood Africa and non-Christian and non-

"Evangelical" religions, as well as how it understood the conditions it described as "savagery," "barbarism," and "heathenism"; and finally, (3) how the Board understood American and "Evangelical (Protestant) Christianity," and what relation it saw between each of these.

1. How the Board Understood the Missionary Task

In the Annual Report of 1883, we find the work of mission described succinctly:

> Missionary work involves (1) conversion of lost men, (2) organizing them into churches, (3) giving them a competent native ministry, and (4) leading them up to independence and in most cases self-propagation.

A close examination of the above statement reveals that it is a faithful replication of the policies set forth by the Board twenty-seven years earlier. Those policies of 1856 were framed under the pioneering leadership of Rufus Anderson, who dominated the Board. Anderson, in America, and Henry Venn, of the Anglican Church Missionary Society, in England, pioneered what later became known as the "three-self" understanding of Christian missions: missions should lead to self-supporting, self-governing, and self-propagating churches. The work of missions was temporary—it continued only until churches were planted in a given location—and then the task of the missionary was to move on to areas where the Gospel had never been heard. Venn spoke of it as "the euthanasia of missions."

It is worth asking what led up to the principles of the 1856 and 1883 statements, and whether they meant precisely the same thing in the 1880s as they had at mid-century.

The concepts of being "lost" or "saved"—concepts which focused on the spiritual state of individuals and which were foundational to both Anderson and the four missionaries—were products of the eighteenth-century movement known as the Great Awakening. At least the words "saved" and "lost" developed very definite nuances in that century which previously they had not had in America. During Puritan times theologians looked at societies more holistically: the talk was of a "holy commonwealth" or a "righteous empire." The Great Awakening theologian, Jonathan Edwards, was the first to admit that the holy commonwealth no longer existed. Not all members of the commonwealth were, in fact, saved; unless men and women had an "awakening," their faith and salvation could not be unquestioned. They might in fact be "lost."

In the Second Great Awakening (1810), which began under Timothy Dwight, President of Yale College and member of the Board's first Prudential Committee, the attempt to "revive" men continued. The "New Divinity" of Samuel Hopkins (whose grand-nephew, Mark Hopkins, was the President of the Board during our period) and Nathaniel Taylor did for the nineteenth-century revival what Edwards had done for the eighteenth: provided a theological basis for the work of home missions. Distancing themselves from the old-line Calvinists, the New Divinity men at Yale added to the old, once supreme doctrine of the sovereignty of God, a qualified respect for what human beings, responding to God, could do. Thus, they offered a theological justification for the "enthusiasm" of the revival spirit, its tears and outpourings, its uncalvinistic emotion—the "outward signs," the New Divinity men said, of the process of "regeneration"—the lost becoming saved.

In the early years of the nineteenth century, it was this understanding of what it meant to be "saved" that informed the vision of those whose gaze shifted from home missions to foreign missions; and it was this understanding that informed the Anderson formula in 1856 and which was still firmly in place in the minds of the missionaries as they left for Angola in 1880. The universality here was remarkable—the unregenerate were to be found both in "Christendom" and in "heathendom"—very different from the earlier era! Preacher after preacher in the Board's annual meetings in the 1880s repeated the proposition that foreign missions were just the extension abroad of missions at home.

Similarly, the second and third parts of the Board's 1883 definition remained unchanged. Like the 1856 statement, it assumed that the outgrowth of conversions should be the gathering of the newborn into churches. Missions meant church planting. Churches once planted, if they were to be permanent and grow, needed to have a competent, educated ministry as well: the minister was not just an administrator of sacraments but a preacher and teacher. His primary ministry indeed was the ministry of the word.

It is in the last point of the Board's definition that we begin to feel the winds of change. The insertion of the words *in most cases* in the middle of the phrase "leading the churches up to independence and self-propagation" leaves the door open for a shift in emphasis. It was here that the Andersonian principle was experiencing some difficulty. Venn's "euthanasia" of missions might, it seemed, need to be put off:

> In the early days of mission, it was enough to bring men to the acceptance of the great facts of the gospel. . . . Life was simpler in its elements. . . . But in the orderly growth of the work a change comes. A Christian civilization makes its demands. . . . New institutions (literature, schools and colleges) are to be established. . . . To the missionary is given the creation of this social order, and the shaping of institutions to be for the welfare of the millions of his fellow-men. (from the Annual Report of 1880)

From this brief excerpt we can see that the mandate is coming to be understood much more broadly. However, since the Scriptures do not seem, at first sight, to warrant a "civilizing mission," a rationale must be developed for bringing civilization along with the gospel message:

> . . . The inspiring of human hearts with the thought of the living God, the renovation of personal character in the image and spirit of Jesus Christ, the regeneration of the family *and society* according to the power of the Christian faith: this is our great aim, to this end all missionary labor is primarily directed. (Annual Report, 1886; emphasis added)

What has happened? The converts are no longer seen as so many discrete individuals. Missions are directed not just to the regeneration of individuals but to the rebirth of societies as well. There is a synonym we can use: *civilization,* the blessings of which are to be imparted to heathen societies.

In the slip of a tongue, one speaker lets the secret out:

The gospel of Jesus Christ, let us remember, is the power of God unto civilization . . . for civilization is included under salvation. This gospel has proved itself mighty enough to lift the most degraded.

We ourselves have come out of as savage barbarism as now exists in the Bihe and Bailunda. The roll of the centuries has seen barbarous Britain and Scandinavia transformed into England and America. The power which has wrought the transformation has been Christian civilization. (Annual Report, 1880)

In the 1886 Annual Report, Secretary Clark asserts:

When art and science, literature and philosophy, shall lay their tribute at the feet of our risen Lord, and when the social and political, as well as the religious, life of manhood shall bear witness to the transforming power of the gospel of Christ, and the Kingdom of God be set up on the earth. (Annual Report, 1886)

Thereon hangs a tale. H. Richard Niebuhr *(The Kingdom of God in America,* New York, 1937) has demonstrated that the concept of the Kingdom of God has been a powerful motif in American church history, but it has meant at least three different things.

By the Kingdom of God, writes Niebuhr, the Puritans meant the sovereignty of God, as opposed to the sovereignty of human initiative, a continuation of the Reformation emphasis of *sola gratia*. In the Great Awakening, observes Niebuhr, God was seen to be acting in history: "In Jesus Christ he has brought in the great change which has opened to men the kingdom of liberty and love. . . . The reign of Christ was above all a rule of knowledge in the minds of men." It was this concept of the Kingdom which was integrally related to the founding of the American Protestant missionary movement: people everywhere had to *know* the truth of the Gospel.

But the idea which Secretary Clark introduced when he spoke of the Kingdom of God being set up was entirely new. His was a millenarian concept. That is not to say that millennialism was a new thing in Christian history—far from it. It was, however, a product of the kind of "enthusiasm" from which orthodox Roman Catholics and orthodox Protestant types stayed far.

What took place in the nineteenth century in America was that those Protestants who had throughout history eschewed millenarian expectations were converted to them. "Respectable folk" at long last fell prey to what had been the indulgence of Christian outsiders.

The theologian who is credited with having finally given millennialism respectability was Samuel Harris of Yale. Harris outlined how, by the preaching of the word, persons become converted and work for the world's conversion, each working for the triumph of good and the defeat of evil and bringing others to Christ, and the ideas which they espouse becoming incorporated into society, so that they "form public sentiment, determine customs, laws, and institutions, and thus create for themselves an organic force." Then the customs of civilization in turn help the progress of Christ's Kingdom.

Wherever Harris looked around him, he saw the Kingdom growing through the profound activity of "the Christian nations characterized by energy, progressiveness, and "expansiveness." In their face, idolatry was doomed.

Thus, through Harris and others, the idea of the Kingdom on earth was secularized and nationalized. In Richard Niebuhr's words:

> Christianity, democracy, Americanism, the English language and culture, the growth of industry and science, American institutions—these are all confounded and confused. The contemplation of their own righteousness filled Americans with such lofty and enthusiastic sentiments that they readily identified it with the righteousness of God. . . . Henceforth the kingdom of the Lord was a human possession, not a permanent revolution. It is in particular the destiny of the Anglo-Saxon race, which is destined to bring light to the gentiles by means of lamps manufactured in America. Thus institutionalism and imperialism, ecclesiastical and political, go hand in hand.

This brief survey of religious thought in America—from Edwards to Harris—suggests the ethos under which the missionary task in Angola was understood in the 1880s. We have gained a vision of why the casuistries in which the mission leaders engaged were necessary: they had a larger vision of what was possible (and therefore of what must be attempted) than the Scriptures, understood in their proper context, could account for. They had to bend the Scriptures to the cultural mandate which they so strongly felt. Agents of the millennium, they could not limit themselves to the planting of churches. That they did more, that they did not readily accede to the euthanasia of missions, is easily understood. That they did not go to further extremes shows they maintained a certain sense of judgment of the civilization of which they were a part.

2. How the Board and its Missionaries Understood the World in Which They Worked

Missionaries, both then and now, tend to use the same terms their contemporaries do.

The triad "savagery, barbarism, and civilization," so often used by missionaries, was not their own creation but was part of the general currency of the time. Anthropologists such as Lewis Henry Morgan used the terms in a systematic way: savagery was the lowest rung of the ladder of civilization, barbarism a step higher, and civilization the highest rung. Here was a single, unilinear ladder of the development of "culture." (In missionary use "savagery" and "barbarism" were used interchangeably; civilization was thought of as higher than the other two but not necessarily implying the highest stage of human development. The fact that missionary statesmen used the terms in an unsystematic way showed that they had not yet "progressed" from the rather loose anthropology of the eighteenth century to the brave new world of Tylor in England and Morgan in America.)

As the new anthropology taught people to think of "culture" as one "thing"—societies have more or less of "it"—the inference became common that those who had more (i.e., of European culture) were more highly developed and those who had less were "still" undeveloped. This begged the question as to why some peoples of the world should have more and others less. The answer was commonly given, with less and less trepidation (until Boas shattered the myths in the 1920s), "because they have less innate abilities," "their brains are smaller," and so forth.

Missionaries tended not to go this far. To begin with, they were less scientific, and in addition their doctrine forced them to be more charitable. No text seems quoted more often in the meetings of the 1880s than "He hath made of one every nation of men to live on all the face of the earth" (Acts 17:26). The inference drawn from this was that, the world over, "human nature is one." Therefore, there was no place for the compartmentalization of peoples into higher and lower races and classes. Moral judgments there could be ("the cruelties and debasing, bloody superstitions which everywhere prevail among them"), but the categories were in general those applied to moral reprobates at home as well.

Unfortunately, however, the missionaries did begin making judgments about the development or non-development of civilization. Perjorative comparisons abounded; comparisons based upon "civilization" defined ethnocentrically:

> Mohammedan and heathen Africa alike know nothing of domestic purity and peace, and contain within their vast domains scarcely a family ordered after *the natural, which is the Christian, pattern*. The African family is simply a cattle kraal on a slightly elevated scale. (Annual Report, 1880; emphasis added)

Many of the descriptions make embarrassing reading today. The moral righteousness, the lack of self-critical ability, the fawning paternalism, the confusion of the mission of the Gospel with *la mission civilisatrice*—all of these are things missionaries and secular change-agents from the West would like to forget.

And yet, with all of the prejudice, there was a certain openness, which fought, as it were, against the grain, but occasionally broke through to new perceptions and new questioning of the accepted wisdom. In 1883, less than three years after the work in Angola began, reports went back to the Board that "the superior character of the people in kindness, intelligence, and attractiveness is becoming more and more apparent"; "the people disappointed me agreeably . . . .They are really a fine race"; "the word *heathen* . . . would be changed and a new meaning be put into the word, . . . if our Christian people could see the bright, intelligent faces of many of these people."

Lest the missionaries be accused of not even considering to study religions they deemed "heathen," Mr. Currie reported in the *Missionary Herald* in 1890: "These people have a somewhat elaborate system of religion, and a much more methodical form of worship than most people imagine; while both form and system are protected by superstitious beliefs so that neither is likely to change quickly."

One cannot do a revisionist history of nineteenth-century missions which would make the missionaries out to be far better than their contemporaries, or erase their undoubted ethnocentrism. They were, beyond a doubt, people of their times. In the light of a total taxonomy of available missionary methods, it can be maintained that there were alternative possibilities open to them in every aspect of their work; but an analysis of missionary methods in *civilizational perspective* leads us to recognize that the alternatives open to any given set of missionaries at any given time are far fewer than a broad taxonomy might indicate. We ought to judge the missionaries in terms of the alternatives which were actually open to them.

3. How the Board Understood America and Evangelical Christianity, the West, and "Christian Civilization"

There was no crisis of confidence in the America of the 1880s. No matter what the injustices of the times may have been, no matter how many treaties with the Indians might have been broken, no matter what critical appraisals budding socialists might have been offering of the social fabric of the United States, those proud to be at the center of American life—and that certainly included the Congregational establishment—had no doubts that the path of the nation was the correct one—and that its course was upward.

In 1881 Secretary N. G. Clark gave a major address at the Board's annual meeting on the "special trust" which the U.S. had to fulfill in the "economy of Divine Providence." He contrasted America's place with the high place Providence had evidently assigned the British. Say what one might about the role of Britain, "no island could give scope to the divine conceptions of man and his destiny. A virgin soil was required for the grandest development of a higher civilization. A continent was needed."

America, Clark went on, contained "the choicest elements for Protestantism." America had "forgotten race in the larger love of man," and so, as a result, it could offer a vital force made up of "what was best in each nationality, and to blend the various elements into one grand whole . . . to be, not English or Anglo-Saxon, but henceforth and forever AMERICAN."

The key to America's success, Clark felt, was its freedom from "the traditions and conventional usages of the Old World." In America, Christianity was to be organized into a new social life, offering the highest opportunity to all. God intended that America should hold "a great trust for mankind."

It was obvious, Clark felt, as he surveyed the American scene, that America was worthy of the trust:

> The very atmosphere is charged with moral and religious ideas; the common sense of the average American represents an amount of knowledge and moral perception quite unknown to the average man of any other age or country.

Such a nation could not have any lesser mission than to participate in "the spiritual and social regeneration of mankind." To America "preeminently is given the establishment of Christian states and empires around the globe."

Clark was not the only one to speak thus of America in the meetings and annual reports of the Board in the 1880s. Such visions of America's divine destiny dot the pages of the documents the Board produced in those years. The aphorism Secretary Alden quoted in 1886 (which he thought was "a most inspiriting idea") expressed the sense of the Board through those years: "As goes America, so goes the world." The committee reviewing Alden's paper that year felt it only fair to conclude that:

> Our Christian institutions are to be reproduced in other lands. The eyes of the world are upon us. What an impressive thought that America is expected to set the fashion for the world in the transcendent business of building a Christian civilization!

Yet the Board's enthusiasm for America and the western powers was neither boundless nor without qualification. In 1890 a committee of the Board pronounced a gentle but highly significant rebuke to Secretary Smith's enthusiasm about the role of the West:

> . . . let us caution ourselves as to expecting overmuch from the leadership of Christian nations in the world's affairs. Undoubtedly they are becoming more and more the dominant forces in its civilization. But it is not to be forgotten that while they are thus opening the way for the incoming of Christianity among the nations, they are at the same time furnishing the most potent hindrances to its success. Behind the opium traffic is Christian England; and with no excuse whatever save the profits she wrings out of the bodies and souls she helps destroy. Behind the infernal liquor traffic are Christian Germany and Christian America, and with the profits of their rum and gin as their only excuse. . . . let us not fail to pray that these mighty denominators of national destiny may be led to wield their powers in the fear of God and for the furtherance and not the hindrance of his gospel. (Annual Report, 1890)

But in the late 1880s the judgments were few, the praises many. So far as Secretary Smith could see, the powers were serving the Power; not just in a secular way, but, through their secular deeds, they were serving the purposes of the Kingdom: "One and all, they serve his purposes; one and all, dumbly or with articulate speech, they cry, 'Repent! for the kingdom of heaven is at hand!' "

Perhaps that was the ultimate casuistry of the era, to say that the forces of imperialism and colonialism were crying, "Repent!"

SOME TENTATIVE CONCLUSIONS

We began this study with the question as to why the first missionaries carried out their mission in Angola the way they did. In light of our findings, I believe most of the features of their approach are easily explained:

1. The missionaries built permanent homes because, though they continued to mouth Anderson's formulas, they no longer had a conception of mission which would enable them to move quickly on; they were to civilize as well as Christianize, and that would take more than a little time.

2. The missionaries chose to work with young lads rather than adults because their concept of what true Christianity meant was such a total change of life—of socialization as well as of creed—that they doubted whether they could Christianize unless they started with the trees when they were green.

3. The missionaries were in no hurry to baptize anyone, but insisted on tried and proven candidates because (a) they were sure of the ultimate triumph of Christ's cause; and (b) their model of conversion was a total one and not a partial one.

4. The missionaries used American hymns, catechisms, and covenants and offered technical assistance on church architecture and engineering because what was American was not *just* "American" to them, but comprised the new experimental forms, of universal import for the new humanity, merely developed and tested in America.

5. The missionaries were ethnocentric because, with the rise of self-confidence in the West in the nineteenth century, the myth of the "noble savage" was swept away for a century; the noble man was the civilized man, and "civilized men" felt they were not merely cultural types but expressions of "the new manhood," of "universal man."

6. The missionaries had no doubt of the ultimate success of the work because they saw history as pointing clearly in the direction of American development. America—an Evangelical nation —had set the path in which the whole world would walk.

All this seems clear and not hard to envision. Several questions remain, nevertheless.

First, why did the missionaries become such good linguists and translate the Scriptures into Umbundu, if they thought that the Anglo-Saxon nations were leading the way to the future? Would it not have been more logical to "elevate" the natives to the English tongue?

Second, why did the missionaries begin immediately to translate the Bible? Would it not have been sufficient to give the latest, best interpretation of the faith?

Third, why did the missionaries not fall prey to the racism of many of their contemporaries, when they obviously conceived of

America as so far "ahead" and of Africa as in such "darkness"?

Fourth, why did the missionaries accord the respect they did to the indigenous kings and chiefs? Did they not see that the future lay in the hands of the Portuguese?

Fifth, why did the missionaries insist on self-support for the churches and upon an independent native ministry? Their ethnocentrism might have logically led to paternalism.

On these questions the logic seems to break down. Yet it must be remembered that the missionary movement of the 1880s had roots in a remembered and celebrated past. In many ways the past maintained its power over the present.

"Every man a Bible reader," "every man a priest" were two of the dicta of the past which were too powerful to be changed by the present. To hold to this Reformation principle, the Bible *had* to be translated. It was preeminent in Protestant faith and it could not be a secondary introduction.

Similarly, the concept that God had made of one all the races of the earth acted as a check on racism. Human nature was one. Thus Ovimbundus were as fully human as Americans. They had a claim to respect and their language was an expression of who they were. Their system of government, barbaric though it seemed, was part of what made them who they were, and it ought to be (somewhat) respected.

The stress on self-support and an independent, trained African ministry is yet unexplained. Perhaps all that we can say is that Rufus Anderson's missionary policies had come to have an almost scriptural authority for the ABCFM, and they accorded well with the imagery of the American frontier. Even if these principles did not fully "fit the type" encountered in Africa, they could not be done away with. But they could be—and were increasingly—disregarded and postponed. (Note: missionaries exercised pastoral authority in Angola until a few years ago, when independence was achieved.)

APPLICATION TO CONTEMPORARY MISSION

This has been a study of a particular mission to Africa, focusing on the missionaries and their methods rather than on the people to whom the missionaries were sent. The study illustrates, I believe, the difficulty of speaking of "making known the Gospel" and "planting churches" as though these were discrete tasks which missionaries can perform in some completely objective way. In actual fact, the missionaries *and their cultural assumptions are deeply* and subjectively involved.

This difficulty poses a problem for some of the elements of missionary theory and practice associated with the "Church Growth" school. For instance, how feasible is it to plant "dynamic equivalence" churches, given the pervasive cultural presuppositions that attend so much of our missionary labor? "Dynamic equivalence" theory tends to restrict the missionary role to that of catalyst, overlooking the fact that the missionaries themselves are part of the equation. The theory would seem to remove the missionaries too much from the center of focus. Intelligent missionaries, it is assumed, can stand back and look at the situation objectively and decide how they can create a condition in which the proper kind of "New Testament" church will emerge.

The aim—to provide cultural independence for the young church—is proper enough; but is it possible, even given the best of intentions? More is happening in the place where the missionaries do their work than a simple process of church planting. That the missionaries are even present in a given situation is a sign that an intercivilizational encounter is taking place, that the civilization and society from which the missionaries come are in encounter with the civilization and society of the "receptor culture."

The missionaries cannot, for example, tell the people to turn off their transistor radios. They cannot blockade the "receptor culture" against the weekly visits of the van from the Anglo-American Tobacco Company. They cannot keep Bristol-Myers from selling infant formula. They cannot keep Harry Oppenheimer's consortia from recruiting migrant workers. They cannot keep the nation's political parties from calling local people to conventions and seminars. They cannot impede the progress of literacy and planned parenthood campaigns. They cannot forestall fluctuations in world market prices for primary products. They cannot block off the people's vision from jumbo jets flying overhead, nor keep people from knowing about the latest heavyweight championship fight.

Nor will the missionaries stop receiving their weekly copies of *Time* and *Christianity Today,* or cease listening to Voice of America broadcasts. They will notice that their salary payments buy less or more goods at the local market as a result of fluctuations in the value of the dollar and the local currency. They will know that relations between their country and the host country are different under Carter and Andrew Young than they were under Ford and Kissinger. As intelligent beings, they will seek to modify their missionary practice in accordance with the best modern insights into methods of communication and leadership training, of community development and health education.

If the missionaries know how to "read the signs of the times," they will revamp their ideas on the role of women and the function of government, on the nature of racism and the social function of ideology. They will become aware, perhaps painfully, of the ways in which the people with whom they work belong to a directed society and of how they as missionaries come from the director society. They will understand that colonialism has been replaced by neo-colonialism, and that vital decisions about the life of the people to whom they minister are made, not by the people themselves, but by the western world and the country's internal ruling elite—or else by the country's dominant socialist party and its allies in Moscow or Peking. They will see that they are parties to the major drama of our time: the question of power and who will have it, the struggle for domination and liberation.

As they read their Bibles with the people, they will discover that the Bible is not biased toward equilibrium and stasis, but toward change, that the God to whom the Scriptures bear witness is a God of change, who liberates people from their shackles, who overthrows the mighty and exalts the humble and meek, and whose will it is that a new Kingdom should be established, a Kingdom of justice and love, of brotherhood and sisterhood. They will recognize the high role which the Scriptures give to the church, as a sacrament of the salvation God is bringing, the firstfruits of a new creation. They will pray for the new church which is emerging, that, like the church in the Book of Acts, it will turn its local world upside down, exhibiting the dynamism of the Spirit who seeks to create a new Kingdom order.

The danger here, of course, is that mission will fall victim to what has been called a "new Christendom mentality." Certainly, some forms of liberation theology pose this danger. Instead of challenging the world, the world's agenda is merely adopted. God's sovereign independence is compromised, his majesty is reduced. No longer "the opiate of the masses," he becomes their "speed." Utopia is confused with the Kingdom, and ideology with theology.

But the way to avoid this danger is not by retreating into a strict ecclesiastical model of mission, as do those who speak of "dynamic equivalence" churches. Their stage is far more narrow than that of the liberation theologians, their desire more modest. The world they see themselves as working in is much smaller; the task to which they feel called much simpler: to midwife the birth of a church which the local Christians will "feel is an original institution within their own culture," a "church which will possess indigenous forms for Christ, adapting them to Christian ends by fulfilling indigenous functions and conveying Christian meanings through them to the surrounding society." (See Charles Kraft, "Dynamic Equivalence Churches," *Missiology,* Jan. 1973, pp. 39 ff.)

We must, in one real way, welcome this modesty. Through the insights of functionalist anthropology, the advocates of dynamic equivalence are countering the ethnocentrism which has characterized most Christian missions from the West. They offer a biblical way of adopting a certain modicum of legitimate cultural relativism. Their methods are undoubtedly freeing up many African and Asian peoples from cultural imperialism. Missionaries trained by their methods are a new breed, sensitive to cultures, less given to evolutionary racism, full of respect for Third World peoples' desire for selfhood.

But there is a problem, nonetheless. These "liberated" missionaries—and I was one—often run into conflict with the church and people to whom they are ministering. Second- and third-generation Christians accuse them of "syncretism." Educated people accuse them of "romanticism." Politically conscientized people fault them for "irrelevance" and "other-worldliness."

The young people call for technical schools and modern church music; the old people ask for Moody and Sankey and more missionary doctors; and the politically-inclined ask the church to support the national revolution. And the "liberated" missionary does not know what to do about it.

Trained in "Church Growth" missiology, he or she is most likely not suited to discuss questions like migration within the country (except insofar as migration leads to new possibilities for planting churches). The ethics of a migrant economy, the values of a wage-based society, the questions of industrialization and urbanization do not figure into such a missiology. They are part of "secular history," and the missionary supposedly deals only with "sacred history."

I say this by way of confession, not accusation. It has taken me all these years to recognize how unliberated a "liberated" missionary I was, how small the stage was to which I had consigned God's action in history. A missiology which will speak to South Korea in the throes of industrialization, to teeming Lagos and impoverished northeast Brazil, needs to introduce far more parameters than what is usually associated with "church planting" theory. And there—in these highly intercivilizational situations of conflict, injustice, poverty, and burgeoning population (rather than in exotic, isolated places such as typified missions in 1880)—is where the predominant missional challenge of our days is to be found.

Where, then, can we find a missiology which is adequate to cope with today's world and which does not succumb to a new version of the old Christendom mentality? Our starting point must be with the God of the Bible, a God who rules people and nations in accordance with his sovereign will, who can use a leader or a nation as his instrument or dispense with them in sovereign freedom, who is concerned for every sparrow that falls as well as for the whole cosmos, who is actively working to bring in his Kingdom, who forgives sins and raises the dead. He is a God whose concern spans the gamut from the particular to the universal. It is no mythical use of language to say that he is present to every one of his creatures, and no exaggeration to claim that he is Lord of all.

The sovereign God has chosen to be a God of freedom. His creation is plural and he wills that all varieties of individuals and societies and their cultures should be as jewels in his crown. At the same time, his purpose is to "unite all things" in Christ (Eph. 1:10). As the hymn puts it, he is "working his purpose out, as year succeeds to year." In the midst of this complex and confusing world—more characterized by struggle and competition than by solidarity—he is working to bring new unities into being. It is not his will that, at the end of time, each tribe and clan and nation will be isolated in its own cultural cubicle waiting for judgment. Rather, he is the force behind every movement which transcends barriers. The God in whose Son there is "neither slave nor free, Jew nor Greek, male nor female" (Gal. 3:28) is a God who wills that people should now experience new unities across linguistic, racial, sexual, national, and religious boundaries. Under his sovereignty, clans have united into tribes, tribes into nations, and nations have coalesced into civilizations. Today, under that same sovereignty, civilizations and nations are forced to confront the need to construct the world's first planetary society.

The early missionaries to Angola and the Board that sent them knew that, with the coming of the telegraph and the steamboat, a new oneness was in store for the world. They interpreted that oneness in an ethnocentric way, feeling that they were called to make all peoples over in the image of the Anglo-Saxon, and particularly the American, people. They confused the Kingdom of God with "manifest destiny," and missionary responsibility with the "white man's burden." They were far too uncritical of the structures of American and western European capitalism, and far too judgmental of non-western peoples. They assisted in destroying many cultures and established too many "formal correspondence" churches, and they provided a gratuitous apologia for western imperialism and commercial expansion. They contributed to a world in which a "Third World" would produce the primary products that fed a growing "First World" industrial revolution. They contributed to the alienation of land, material resources, and culture from the dark-skinned people of the world. Profiting from the largesse of the commercial entrepreneurs and the colonial governments, they raised their voices all too infrequently at attendant injustice.

But most of them lived according to their own best lights, and it is far too easy for us, with our hindsight, to condemn them for lacks of which they were, largely, unaware. We must at least accord to them the recognition that they differed in many great ways from the colonizers and exploiters. Their efforts led to the birth of churches around the globe, and members of those churches remember them with deep gratitude, for they made

Christ known in places where otherwise his name might not have been heard or his salvation appropriated.

I would like to suggest that, in another important respect, they were closer to the truth than we may have been liable to admit, that is, in terms of their world-historical vision. In a day of minimalism in evangelical mission theory—when we have set our sights on nothing more than planting churches and multiplying cells of believers—we would do well to reorient our mission thinking to the biblical vision of justice, to advocacy of the oppressed, to the spreading of the Good News to the poor; in short, to embrace the agenda of the Kingdom, even while we live as pilgrims in the diaspora of the earth.

Chastened as we are by the taunt of "Missionary, go home," and "Don't export your culture to us," we are all too likely to retreat to the "safe" fortress of "doing only what the Bible tells us"—converting individuals, starting dynamic equivalence churches, and seeking to assume an "objective" position with regard to the affairs of the world. The study of the Angola missionaries should convince us of how difficult this indeed is. To claim that we can be objective may be more arrogant than the frank recognition by the early missionaries that they were seeking to civilize as well as evangelize. The claim to objectivity presumes a dichotomy between subject and object, a dichotomy which has come under question in discipline after discipline in contemporary research. Perhaps the time has come to put it under question in missiology as well.

Missiology is not a "value-free" science. The Gospel we proclaim does not spring full-blown from the forehead of the apostolic age. It has a long history. We have all learned certain ways of understanding the Gospel. We all have our principles of interpretation and modes of application. There can be no such thing as a missionary who enters the mission process only as a catalyst.

The important thing is not to be "value-free" or to pretend to "gospel objectivity," but—in fear and trembling, and with a full faith in the justification of sinners—to be conscious of what our values are, to make them explicit, and to discover as best we can what the values of Scripture are, and to ask how far our values accord with what we perceive those of the Scriptures to be.

The God of the Bible is not a "value-free" God. He has a

bias on behalf of the poor and oppressed. He is engaged in the work of their liberation. The Kingdom of God—and that includes much more than the planting of dynamic equivalence churches— ought to be our guiding star in mission.

If it is true, as Lausanne put it, that God "has been calling out from the world a people for himself" in order that he might "send his people back into the world to be his servants and his witnesses, *for the extension of his kingdom*" (Art. 1, emphasis added), then we will need a missiology which enables us to see that Kingdom in larger than ecclesiastical terms. Among other things, it will include a commitment "to transform and enrich culture for the glory of God" (Art. 10). The "unfinished task of evangelization" will only be finished when the church has brought the Good News of God to bear on the totality of God's fallen creation. As the Covenant puts it (Art. 5), "When people receive Christ they are born again into his kingdom and must seek not only to exhibit but also to spread its righteousness in the midst of an unrighteous world."

Fifty years ago the island of Bali was known around the world by artists, scholars, and tourists for its beauty, rich history, and exotic culture. But its inhabitants knew little of the outside world and virtually nothing of the Gospel of Jesus Christ. For many years, the Dutch colonial government, wishing to preserve Bali as a "living museum" of the Hindu-Bali culture, completely barred Christian missionaries from the island.

In 1931, despite the ban on missionaries, the first Christian community sprang to life—and was ostracized by local Hindu authorities to an inhospitable site on a jungle mountainside at the far end of the island. Though the Christian faith did succeed in spreading slowly, the western orientation of the church rendered the believers vulnerable to charges of being accomplices of the western powers and therefore traitors to their own people.

The present chairman of the Bali Protestant church, I. Wayan Mastra, became a Christian in 1952 at twenty-one years of age, having been raised as a Hindu in a typical village in east Bali. Mastra has capitalized on his Hindu background to highlight the principles of indigenization in evangelism and church life. Under his leadership, the Christian faith has spread through north and east Bali, and the earlier Christian communities in south and west Bali have taken bold steps to affirm their cultural roots and to "contextualize" their Gospel witness through practical social service and through Balinese-style drama, music, and architecture. Several times in the last decade, the village of Blimbingsari—the original Christian community which struggled for survival during the early years of ostracism—has been named by the Indonesian provincial government as "Village of the Year" in recognition of its achievements in educational, medical, and agricultural development and in all-round civic vigor and advancement. Balinese Christians have likewise played a prominent part in the government's transmigration program, designed to relieve the overpopulation of Bali while aiding the development of untamed areas of the Celebes islands.

Mastra's approach to the contextualization of the Bali Protestant Church has been enriched by a close observation of Christian mission in other parts of the world and by studies in the early history of the church and of modern mission history in Indonesia.

15. Contextualization of the Church in Bali
—A Case Study from Indonesia

by I. Wayan Mastra

I. WAYAN MASTRA *is chairman of the* Gereja Kristen Protestan di Bali *(The Bali Protestant Church), Indonesia.*

GOD'S PURPOSE IN CHRIST WAS TO OFFER SALvation not only to the Jews, but also to the entire world. Following their Master's Great Commission, and driven from Jerusalem by persecution, the disciples journeyed to distant lands to bear witness to Christ. To the amazement of the Jewish Christians, Gentiles responded to the Gospel in faith and the Christian community grew significantly.

The disciples soon felt the need to resolve the problem of how to integrate people of different religious traditions into a unified Christianity. The decision of the Jerusalem council was not to trouble Gentile believers with the trappings of Jewish culture and religion (Acts 15:19).

In the second and third centuries, Christian apologists felt the need to defend the faith against the charges and suspicions of the so-called pagan peoples. The most outstanding of these apologists was Justin Martyr. He believed that traces of truth were to be found among the Gentile philosophers since all men shared in the "generative" or "germinative" *Logos;* that is, the *Logos* is to be found in every land as the forerunner of the historical appearance of the *Logos* in the person of Jesus of Nazareth.

Later, Christianity became for a time a self-contained religion in Europe, unchallenged by other religions and cultures; but the advent of Islam with its victorious wars of conquest in North Africa and Spain forced Christianity to conceive of itself in relation to other religions and cultures. A tragic attempt to assert this new self-awareness was the Crusades. When they were ended, Palestine was still occupied by the Muslims and Christianity was still challenged by Islam. But as a result of the cross-fertilization of eastern and western ideas, the Crusades enriched the Christian nations of Europe with culture and science, which became very important factors in the later expansion of the church. The acquisition of new techniques enabled the adventure-loving Christian nations in Europe to engage in new explorations and discoveries, which in turn led to colonial and church expansion. Ultimately, Christianity was found in almost every land; it was no longer confronted by one religion, as with Islam of old, but by all conceivable religions and cultures.

Because of this expansion, Christian theologians began to take great interest in the study of non-Christian religions and cultures. The motive underlying this interest in comparative religion was an apologetic one: to show the superiority of the Christian faith over non-Christian religions.

When the Christian nations of Europe had become world powers and had occupied and were ruling almost all the non-Christian nations of the world, this feeling of cultural and religious superiority had ample opportunity to express itself. But after World War II, when the non-Christian countries became independent and respected nations, Christian theologians began to be more sensitive to a multiplicity of societies, characterized by religious, cultural, and racial pluralism. They encouraged new approaches based upon mutual respect between races, religions, and cultures.

These new approaches showed a tendency to return to the approach of the early Church Fathers. Moreover they recognized that religion is embedded in historical and local features such as custom, language, and art, which are not universal. Thus, understanding non-Christians in both their religious thought and their cultural background has been increasingly recognized as a very important factor in mission work, since it enables us to communicate the Gospel in the thought, language, culture, and feeling of the people.

The recent history of the Bali Protestant Church, in its evangelism, mission, and church life, illustrates an attempt to follow this more respectful approach, while at the same time opening new avenues of witness to the Gospel of the love of Jesus Christ. In this case study, we will look briefly at the land, its history, and culture. Then we shall examine how the Christian message has been related to different cultures throughout history. Finally, in conclusion, we shall see how the Gospel is "contextualized" in Bali.

BALI, ITS LIFE, RELIGION, AND CULTURE

Bali, a two-thousand-square-mile island east of Java, is very small compared with many other Indonesian islands; it is only one hundred miles long and fifty miles wide. But it is perhaps the most famous and unique of all, with epithets such as the "lost paradise," "morning of the world," and "island of many temples."

The mountains that run across Bali from its western to its eastern tip, dividing it into two parts, South and North, play a very important role in the life, religion, and culture of the Balinese. Rivers flow from the mountains south and north, eroding the soft soil of the slopes and creating deep valleys and ridges. Before bridges were built, it was very difficult to have communication between people from one village to the other and to have a strong central authority. During much of its history Bali was divided into eight kingdoms that had great rivalry between them.

Like the mountains, water plays a very important role in the life of Bali. As the rivers flow to the ocean, they give life to the rice in the *sawah* (wet rice paddies) as well as to the people who live on the plains and lowlands. The rivers then continue their journey to the sea, taking with them all the dirt and filth. That is why, according to the Balinese, the gods and goddesses live in the mountains, poeple live on the plains or lowlands, and the dead are in the sea.

Temples and monasteries are built on the slopes of the

mountains, and in each village the main temple faces the mountain. The mountains are symbols of stillness, calm, and peace, the origin of life; the sea is the symbol of roughness and anger, the destination of the dead.

Like other Indonesians, the Balinese belong to the Malay stock. But because of Bali's splendid isolation and the rough sea surrounding it, the people have developed unique traits. The population of 2.5 million is divided into three major religious groups: Bali Hindu, 98 percent; Bali Islam, 1 percent; and Bali Christian, 1 percent (1976 census). The language, a dialect of Malay, has three levels as a result of the caste system of Hinduism. A court action can result if someone uses the wrong level of language, and during one period of the Hindu kingdom people from the superior caste could kill a person of inferior caste if he or she made a mistake in level of language.

In talking about Bali one cannot escape discussing the Hindu Dharma religion which is the source of Balinese culture. Originally the religion was called Bali Hindu, being a mixture of Hinduism and the native Bali religion, and it was exclusively related with the Balinese people. Now they call themselves Hindu Dharma in order to give room for non-Balinese to join (although, in fact, only non-Balinese women can join by marrying Balinese men).

Hinduism was introduced to Bali almost ten centuries ago. A Balinese king married a princess from East Java, and of this marriage a child, Airlangga, was born in A.D. 991. Eventually Airlangga became king of Java and annexed Bali. He sent a Hindu priest from Java to Bali who translated the *pracasti,* or law, from ancient Balinese into Javanese. Airlangga eventually abdicated, became a hermit, and built a Siva Hindu monastery which can still be seen.

After Airlangga's death, Bali became independent again and remained so until A.D. 1343, when it was conquered by Gajah Mada of the kingdom of Majapahit in East Java. He managed to unite under his rule Malaya and all the islands that presently belong to Indonesia. This was the last and the greatest of the Hindu kingdoms in Indonesia. When Majapahit fell in 1478 to Islam, the son of the king of Majapahit fled to Bali. He was followed by his entire court, priests, artists, and intellectuals. They were the most "civilized" in the whole region, the cream of Javanese culture. They transplanted to Bali their art, religion, and philosophy, which have flourished ever since.

During Majapahit's rule a Sivaist Hindu priest, Dang Hyang Nirarta, an expert in ancient Javanese and Sanskrit, came to Bali and diligently went from one village to another teaching Hinduism. It was he who introduced the caste system in Bali.

Archeological evidence indicates that Buddhism also has a long history in Bali. As for the native beliefs in Bali, they are basically animist in nature. The Balinese believed that everything had a soul and that souls were the natural forces that gave life and movement to all things. They worshiped such natural forces as the wind, the sea, volcanoes, springs of water, valleys, jungles, rivers, big trees, and so forth, which they considered to be spirits.

The belief that everything had a soul entailed that man also had a soul, a belief which led the people into ancestor worship. The people considered that the souls of their ancestors were still alive after the death of their bodies and dwelt at the temple of the dead or in the mountains and volcanoes.

When the Buddhists and Hindus came to Bali, they did not change the beliefs of the people, but merely gave new names to the spirits or divine beings in which the people already believed. Since animism, pantheism, and polytheism are very close to nature, there was an easy transition from animism to Buddhism and Hinduism. For example, when the Hindus came to Bali, they gave the name *Brahma* to the spirit of fire, *Vishnu* to the spirit of water, and *Siva* to the spirit of the air or ether. These three main spirits manifest themselves in the sea, in volcanoes, in the jungle, and so forth, and receive a special name in each manifestation. The present generation of Balinese Hindu leaders have formed a doctrine of trinity out of these spirits or deities. When the spirit manifests himself as creator, he is Brahma; as maintainer, he is Vishnu; and as destroyer, he is Siva. They claim that this trinity is monotheistic, Brahma, Vishnu, and Siva being manifestations of the one true God.

Although the process of Hinduization went on for many centuries, the original character of the Balinese remained, as may be seen in various religious practices today. In dealing with the dead, for instance, some leave the corpse on a stone in the cemetery where birds eat the flesh, thus carrying the body to heaven. Also, although the Hindus introduced a new priesthood, the native priest, the *pemangku,* who functions like the shaman or priest-magician among the people of Central Asia and Polynesia, still plays a very important role in village life. Even in the building of Hindu temples the original Balinese tradition and culture can be seen. Bernet Kempers, a Dutch archeologist, believes the temples in Bali—designed as open spaces surrounded by walls—to be in direct line from the old sanctuaries where the spirits of the ancestors as well as the great nature gods were worshiped by the native Indonesians and Polynesians. Inside the wall there was usually the *tachta batu* or throne made of stone where the deities were worshiped. The multiple roofs of Balinese pagodas also suggest the stepped pyramids of the ancient Indonesians and Polynesians.

Thus the Hindu religion has blended with the ancestor worship and animism of the native Balinese to produce the present Balinese religion and culture. Religion is clearly the source of Balinese culture, as evidenced in the dances and ceremonies of the people, and in their paintings, wood carvings, architecture, and music (including the famous *gamelan* orchestra).

Because of the mixture of religions, the people accept the idea that all religions are the same; all are seeking an experience with God, like so many rivers flowing to the sea. This attitude can lead to syncretism and makes it very difficult to proclaim the Gospel which claims that Christ is the way, the truth, and the life.

EARLY CHRISTIAN HISTORY

The very first Christian missionary, the Rev. J. De Vroom of the Netherlands, came to Bali in 1866 (long before the Dutch had conquered the whole island in 1914, introducing western forms of education, administration, and transportation). After much hard work, De Vroom succeeded in winning his first and only convert in 1873. But when this newly converted man returned to his village, he had great difficulty with the other villagers. De Vroom apparently did nothing to console him when they met again, and so the convert killed him in 1881. The convert was subsequently captured and hanged by the Dutch in Jakarta. As a result, for the sake of law and order, Bali becamae a closed area to mission from 1881 to 1931, especially under the Dutch East Indies Company.

But Bali could not be kept closed to Christ. In 1929, when the ban on missionaries was still on, Tsang To Han, a Chinese evangelist of the Christian and Missionary Alliance, received permission from the governor-general to come to Bali to take care of the two Chinese Christians who had arrived from China. He was allowed to work only among the Chinese. His work among them was not successful, but through a Balinese woman who married a Chinese in Denpasar (the capital), he became acquainted with some Balinese mystics who were looking for a new religion. Their leader, a Javanese *guru,* had been linked to the Communist movement in Java and had been removed some years earlier by the Dutch. When Tsang came to Bali to teach the new religion, the villagers thought he was the successor to their previous leader. The Spirit of God worked through him so that on November 11, 1931, the first baptism was administered to a group of eleven believers.

However, Tsang's way of speaking about the Bali Hindu religion aroused feelings of hostility. When a second public baptism took place a year later, it created a sensation in the whole island and even in the central government in Jakarta. The government finally expelled Tsang in 1933. But the church was born; 266 members had been baptized. In spite of many difficulties and ostracism, the church continued to grow, the flame of Christianity spreading very rapidly from one village to the other along family lines which served as "the bridges of God." After a long period of study and negotiation with the colonial government, Hendrik Kraemer of the Dutch Reformed Church obtained permission to shepherd the newly converted people. Thus the people moved from the Christian and Missionary Alliance tradition to the Dutch Reformed tradition. They called themselves the *Gereja Kristen Protestan di Bali* (commonly known as the Bali Church). At present the church has six thousand members who are living in Bali and some twelve thousand people who have migrated to the Celebes.

INDIGENIZATION IN HISTORICAL PERSPECTIVE

The success of the Hindus in winning Balinese for Hinduism was the result of their efforts in introducing Hinduism not in the form of a foreign religious and cultural invasion, but as a seed planted in Balinese soil and growing up in its own way.

This can be compared with the efforts of early Christian missionaries to win Europe for Christ, beginning with the apostle Paul. Paul's success can be credited to his thorough understanding of the non-Christians with whom he dealt. Paul was born in the city of Tarsus, a famous university town and a meeting place for Hellenism and Orientalism. His approach is well exemplified in his mission to the people of Athens. Not wanting to be accused of bringing foreign gods, Paul sought to plant the Gospel inside the minds and hearts of the people by using their own expressions. He capitalized on the existence of an unknown God, to whom the people of Athens had erected an altar (Acts 17:22, 23).

On another occasion, in Corinth, Paul found a problem of division within the church. To counteract this division Paul developed the idea of the church as the "body" (*soma* in Greek) of Christ. This concept came from the Hellenistic fable of the body and its members, which was obviously very familiar to everyone at that time since it was much used for illustrating the various aspects of the corporate life of the community.

The church leaders in Europe later followed Paul's method in adopting and adapting the people's beliefs and worship into the Christian tradition. Thus, according to Hastings' *Encyclopedia of Religion and Ethics,* the cradle of Christ which is used in the Roman Catholic tradition is borrowed from the cult of Adonis (vol. 3, 608 ff.). Similarly, when Boniface (680-754), brought the Gospel from England to Germany, he baptized German cultic practices into a new variety of Christian liturgical tradition. "He replaced the sacrifices to Odin's sacred oak by a fir tree adorned in tribute to the Christ Child" (*Encyclopaedia Britannica,* 1962 edition, vol. 5, 643). Following such an unbroken sequence of repeated usages of the same mission technique, one can see a religious and cultural continuity between pre-Christian and Christianized Europe.

CONTEXTUALIZATION BALI STYLE

The Bali Church has started to take some steps in communicating the Gospel to the people of Bali in the language, culture, and feeling that can be easily understood by them.

1. The Message Must Be Concrete, Visible, and Tangible

Balinese, like many other Asians, are extraordinarily visual. They can understand things after they have seen them. They want everything to become concrete, visible, and tangible. It is important for them to symbolize their faith in action, drama, dance, painting, carving, and architecture.

In the West, where most missionaries come from, religious truth is conceived in abstract terms. Church services are reduced to a verbal proclamation of the Gospel. It appears that the western nations prefer theology which gives intellectual satisfaction; but in the East, people like religious experience in order to make their faith become real and not merely a theoretical conviction.

The verbal proclamation of the Gospel can also give a feeling of superiority of the Christian religion and culture over non-Christian religion and culture. In the past missionaries and early Balinese Christians used to say their new religion and culture were superior to their traditional religion and culture. As a result, Christianity, as herald of a new culture, was generally labeled as a foreign religion with a foreign God and Savior. During the struggle for national independence from 1945-1949, many Christians suffered persecution at the hands of the revolutionaries because they were considered collaborators of the Dutch.

After the revolution in which the country obtained its independence, the Balinese Christians suddenly found themselves in a totally new situation to which they were forced to adjust. They were confronted with two major problems: (a) they had to struggle hard to be accepted as part of the Balinese community, and (b) they had to prove the validity of their faith, that is, that Jesus was really Lord of the world, of all nations, and above all, of the Balinese as well.

That is why the Balinese Christians take the attitude that because they love their own people and culture, they try to adapt as much as may be permissible for the church. At the same time, they know that the Gospel transforms people into a new creation. The New Testament describes the process in terms of both birth and death. To have faith means to be born again into a new religion and also to die to one's old religion.

Once when I was preaching the Gospel, I found a lady who was not happy because her husband and children had become

Christians. When I talked to her, she expressed her anxieties. I discovered that she was unhappy because she was afraid that her ancestors and deities would punish her husband and children because they no longer brought offerings to the family temples. I then told her that the Christians had already made their offering at mount Golgotha in Palestine once and for all in the person of Jesus Christ, God himself who became man for our sakes. Hence Christians do not have to bring offerings and shed blood any more because the offering of Jesus Christ was enough. Christians, however, do bring offerings to church in the form of money out of a spirit of dedication and love, for the continuation of God's saving act in the world. The woman accepted my explanation and wanted to become a Christian. She is now one of the most active Christians in Bali.

Following this example, we should not condemn or attack the non-Christian religions and cultures, because that only excites a hostile reaction and hate, emotions that may eventually endanger Christians themselves as well as the mission of the church. How then are we to understand the problem of the continuity and discontinuity between religions? As a convert from Hinduism to Christianity, I find that there is both continuity and discontinuity between religions. Since I was raised in the Hindu-Balinese religion, I initially understood Christianity from the point of view of that religion. Even though new converts formulate their faith and understanding of the Gospel of salvation in Christ from the religious perceptions that they already have, through the guidance of the Holy Spirit they grow and become more mature in their faith and knowledge concerning the essence of the Gospel of Christ.

When we respect non-Christian religions and cultures, it does not mean that we abandon the mission of the church. Nor does this approach lead to syncretism or defeatism in our missionary endeavors. We do not approach other religious *systems,* but rather we approach *people* of other faiths. Hence, we do not need to compare one religious statement of truth with another statement of religious truth, nor do we need to challenge one claim with another.

Religion, being very personal, must relate to personal religious experience in faith. That is why in Bali—where people are still strong believers in the role of the spirits of the ancestors—

when a person dies, and relatives try to console the spirits through mediums, we stress the need and the important role of prayer. People have religious experiences when they encounter Christ directly in their prayers and find him answering their prayers. Prayers are very important in order to dramatize our faith that Christ is the same yesterday, today, and forever (Heb. 13:8). If Jesus could cure a person in the past, as we read in the Gospels, surely he will be able to do so at this time, because he is the same. In Bali we have at least two congregations which were started because people felt they had met Christ personally in answer to their prayers. Their faith became real and they were able to overcome many temptations and persecutions. With a strong faith, they will also follow Christ's commandment, so that they will have a high ethical life and deep social concerns. Thus the religious experience dramatizes Christ's presence, and it helps to meet the needs of the people who want everything to become concrete, visible, and tangible.

Moreover, we need to demonstrate lives which are ruled by Christ by bringing forth the fruits of the Spirit as they can be seen in our high ethical conduct in following Jesus' steps. The people also want to see the sign of Jesus' sincere concern for people who are in need and trouble. That is why we have to be involved in social action in order to dramatize Christ's love and concern.

It is in this light that the Balinese Christians see their efforts to bring the Gospel to the Balinese. We avoid communication in verbal abstractions that the people find too difficult to understand. We also avoid preaching too much on sin and punishment, but rather demonstrate Christ's love and concern. People do not know the Christian concept of sin, until they read and know the Bible. But it is quite different with love, because they are oppressed by the ruling class, so that Christ's invitation: "Come to me, all who labor and are heavy laden, and I will give you rest" (Matt. 11:28) really is attractive to them, and many are converted.

2. Some Focal Points in Indigenization

As we have seen, church leaders in Europe through time have baptized or Christianized pagan, religious, and national practices together with art and legend, and this has become part of western Christian culture. Thus the Gospel has been planted and grows in each section of Europe, having become indigenous and unique in its own area. But when Christianity was introduced in Bali, the missionaries identified the culture and religion as demonic and urged their destruction. To correct this situation, the Bali church has become conscious of the fact that if it wants to win the people for Christ, it should take some steps to bring the culture as much as possible to the church.

These efforts have not always been welcomed by all Christians, particularly the older generation—those baptized in the 1930s. They said: "Why should we try to use these cultural practices that we have left behind?" Once I talked with an older minister who wanted to build a new church building for the congregation. I suggested building the church in Balinese style by using Balinese artistic expression and philosophy. But the minister wanted it to "look like a church," so he built it like a garage, since that was the kind of churches first built in Bali. But a western-style building, completely closed in, is too hot in Bali, and the construction too expensive. Some of the materials have to be imported and the village carpenters do not know how to make them.

But if we look at the village temple, it is beautiful from the artistic point of view; it fits the tropical climate; it is cheap because local materials can be used; and the village artists have a chance to glorify their deities through their artistic talents. Why does not the church give a chance to the newly converted people to glorify their God through their artistic talents which have been inherited from their ancestors?

Fortunately, the younger generation has been making a reappraisal of the church's relationship to Balinese culture. A Bali Cultural and Training Center was completed and dedicated with the name *Dhyana Pura* ("meditation center") May 21, 1977. The theme for the Dhyana Pura is taken from Isaiah 6:1-8. When Isaiah was in trouble, he went to the temple to meditate. He was purified and then heard the Word of God. As a result he became sensitive to the needs of his people and offered himself by saying, "Here am I, Lord! Send me!" That is the purpose of *Dhyana Pura*.

The Bali church is also busy rebuilding and remodeling church buildings by introducing traditional Balinese art and architecture as well as inserting Balinese symbols and philosophy in the light of Christ. Balinese traditional decorations have been used in the church for church festivals. In order to meet the need of the people's lively imagination, the church encourages the people to paint the biblical stories in the Balinese traditional way of painting. The church building is also decorated with reliefs telling biblical stories in traditional Balinese carving.

The Balinese love of dramatic symbols has been incorporated by using dances, where all the beautiful movements symbolically present the faith. In the same manner, the Balinese *tembang* (opera) and *gamelan* orchestra have been used in connection with presentations of the Gospel to the people. Hence the people feel closer to the Gospel. They do not think of Christianity as a foreign religion any more when they can see and hear that the Gospel has been given Balinese clothes. Gospel performances in Balinese dance and drama are always crowded. On the other hand, if we were to bring moving pictures or slides about the life of Christ, we would not have many hearers, because these media are strange to them.

Color also plays an important role in the life of the people and has symbolic meaning. The traditional black robe of the ministers has been replaced by a white robe since white is related to good spirits and black is related to evil spirits or demons.

In addition, the Bali church seeks to go beyond verbal abstractions in preaching the love of Christ. That is why the Bali church is active in social action, in improving the people's condition by building schools, dormitories, a hospital, an experimental farm, a chicken farm, and a fish pond as a demonstration of our love as well as a model for improving the people's condition. We try to make the people aware of our presence among them in witnessing and bringing Christ's love to them. We hope that they will come longing to drink of the living water and make a decision to follow him.

As we carry out our mission, we must remember that the Gospel is not related to a particular nation and must not be related to any nationalistic movement. The Gospel is universal. Jesus is the light of the world, and God is the God of all nations. This is the answer to those who feel that converting people to Christianity is wrong. Such people ignore the principle of religious freedom, the right of people to embrace a religion as well as to leave it.

Although it is right to relate to the traditional culture of a people, we must also remember that no culture is static. As cultures encounter one another, they are constantly changing. It certainly must not become the goal of the church to preserve a particular culture or civilization. In the process of change, indigenization or contextualization is a tool for communicating the Gospel so that the Gospel message becomes relevant. This gives some flexibility and serves the church as a strategy of mission, enabling Christianity to root itself in the soul of the society. In this way Christians will not be foreigners in their own country, and Christ can be truly felt by the people as the Savior of all nations.

Finally, we must remember that our efforts to establish an indigenous church will mean nothing for the strategy of mission if the Christians do not have a real concern and a deep love for the people. As Paul said:

> If I speak in the tongues of men and of angels but have not love, I am a noisy gong or a clanging cymbal. And if I have prophetic powers, and understand all mysteries and all knowledge, and if I have all faith, so as to remove mountains, but have not love, I am nothing. If I deliver my body to be burned, but have not love, I gain nothing.
>
> (1 Corinthians 13:1-3)

16. The Christian Life-style

by Gottfried Osei-Mensah

GOTTFRIED OSEI-MENSAH, *a former pastor in Niarobi, Kenya, is executive secretary of the Lausanne Committee for World Evangelization.*

TO A KEEN OBSERVER OF THE WORLD SCENE, IT is apparent that there is a growing multi-racial, multi-cultural, international "tribe" which can be found in the cities and urban centers of our rapidly shrinking world (the global village). From time to time this process of growing together produces its backlash in the crisis of identity and the quest for "roots." This process can be expected to go on with the increasing mobility and intermingling among the nations. For example, the urban congregation to which I ministered for five years included seven hundred young people from some fifteen different nations—including North Americans, Europeans, British, Asians, as well as African peoples. This leads us to ask: What normative biblical principles apply when we consider the Christian life-style in the context of such cultural diversity?

In seeking an answer to this basic question we will begin by briefly reviewing the principles of discipleship which are the foundation of Christian life-style. These principles were variously stated by the Lord Jesus Christ himself. As the Lord, he claimed first place in his disciples' lives, loyalty, love, affection, and obedience (Luke 14:26). His disciples must renounce all their personal rights, and hand over the control of everything they have to him (Luke 14:33; Mark 10:28). Furthermore, they must submit to him and to his authoritative teaching in a life of daily, costly obedience and service (Luke 9:23; John 12:26).

If the terms of discipleship are demanding, what the Lord promised in compensation for his disciples' total commitment and costly obedience are even more astounding: "Anyone who leaves home or brothers or sisters or mother or father or children or fields for me, and for the gospel, will receive much more in this present age . . . and in the age to come he will receive eternal life" (Mark 10:29, 30, TEV).

The Lord Jesus taught his disciples that "a man's life does not consist in the abundance of his possessions." Rather, the true self-realization and fulfillment which men and women vainly search for in possessions, pleasures, and personal relationships is to be found in a whole-hearted commitment to Christ as the Lord. "For whoever would save his life will lose it; and whoever loses his life for my sake, he will save it" (Luke 9:24, 25, RSV).

SERVANTS AND STEWARDS

If these principles are to work out effectively in the daily lives of committed Christians, it is essential that they see themselves in the two-fold role of servants and stewards.

Discipleship is inseparably linked with servanthood (Luke 17:7-10). The disciple is committed to follow, obey, and serve his Master, as well as learn from him. By his teaching and especially by his example the Lord oriented the disciples' minds from a "master" mentality to servanthood:

You know that the rulers of the Gentiles lord it over them, and their great men exercise authority over them. It shall not be so among you; but whoever would be great among you must be your servant, and whoever would be first among you must be your slave; even as the Son of man came not to be served but to serve, and to give his life a ransom for many. (Matt. 29:25-28, RSV; cf. John 13:13-16)

To call Jesus Christ "Lord," then, involves a submission not only to obey and serve him, but also to serve other people for his sake (2 Cor. 4:5).

When a disciple renounces his rights and hands over the control of everything he has to the Lord Jesus, he becomes a steward of a far greater trust than the privileges and possessions he surrendered. Usually, of course, he receives back from the Lord his possessions, only now no longer as his own but on trust, to be used as the Lord directs. He becomes also a steward of the gifts, special abilities, and skills (both natural and spiritual) with which he is endowed. The new motivation of his life is to develop all these resources and potentials to the fullest for the service of the Lord and his people. It is the controlling love of Christ and the solemn sense of accountability to him which leads the Christian to resolve no longer to live for himself but only for the Lord who died and was raised to life for his sake (2 Cor. 5:10, 14, 15). It follows, then, that a deficient sense of stewardship in a Christian community signifies an inadequate grasp both of what Christ in love has done for his people, and of the reality of the day of reckoning.

In his teachings the Lord Jesus described the qualities he expected of his stewards (Luke 12:42-48). First and foremost, stewards must be faithful to the Master and share the Master's concern, purpose, and goal. They must be trustworthy and honest with their Master's goods (Luke 16:10-12) and must use these resources in the most effective way to achieve the Master's objectives. Christ's stewards must be caring and outgoing towards people. People matter (at least to Christ) more than things! His entire mission was people-oriented, and so must ours be if we share his objectives.

Our perennial temptation is to squander our Master's resources in creating unprofitable structures which glorify man rather than God. But a far worse abuse of our stewardship is to appropriate our trust for our own selfish pleasure. This is tantamount to robbery and oppression of the needy, who are our responsibility, and courts our Master's hot displeasure (Luke 12:45, 46).

Christ's stewards must also be wise and industrious in cultivating and developing their gifts and potentials (Matt. 25:14-30; Luke 19:11-27). The Lord commends diligence in this respect as a measure of his servants' love and loyalty, but condemns slothfulness as a wicked sabotage of his interests. Under normal circumstances, hard work combined with modesty in providing for our own needs (and those of our household) will result in increased resources. Our natural temptation is to upgrade our standard of living accordingly, or worse, to become dependent on (or preoccupied with) our growing bank balance.

The proper course of action is to seek the Lord's help in continued faithfulness to our enlarged responsibility. The warning of Scripture is, "If your riches increase, don't depend on them" (Ps. 62:10). "The man to whom much is given, of him much is required; the man to whom more is given, of him much more is required" (Luke 12:48, TEV; cf. 1 Tim. 6:17, 18).

SURVIVAL AND DIGNITY

Two major considerations which determine the style of life in every culture are survival and dignity.

Every society of people must come to terms with the forces (benevolent or malevolent) that bear on its survival. The necessity to develop adequate supplies of the vital resources of water, food, energy, to provide security for life and property, to protect against want, illness, redundancy, and so forth, is a factor which unites people together in communities. For example, the Ashanti nation (in Ghana) had a highly organized system of clans for the purpose of defense against external aggression and for community development. Social welfare was organized at the level of the extended families within the clans. The still smaller units of a compound, each consisting of a husband (the headman) with his several wives, children, and dependents, provided the immediate sense of security and belonging. All this made good sense in a tropical, rural, agricultural society with a rather high mortality rate.

The advantage of such closely knit societies is that they tend to give direct expression to the principle that people matter. On the whole, individuals receive within such structures the care and attention they need as human beings. It used to be said there were no "lonely individuals" *(ankonam)* in Ashanti, only members of the families of the nation *(omanfo)*. The security which people find in proper interpersonal and community relationships is an effective check on the self-seeking instinct. Consequently material possessions are shared more freely and evenly. It is an observable fact that people who live in such societies are usually very generous.

Industrialization, on the other hand, tends to shift values from people to things. Gradually people become mere cogs in the wheels of good production. A man's value in an industrialized society is inevitably reckoned in economic terms. The organization of industrial production disrupts normal community and social life; and even the so-called nuclear family comes under considerable strain.

The resulting loneliness of individualism leads people to seek security in the acquisition of material goods. Anxiety, worry, selfishness, and indifference to the needs and interests of others are the symptoms of individualism in industrialized nations. The insatiable urge to acquire more and better possessions is the underlying cause of the rat race in such societies. Paul calls it a trap: "Those who want to get rich fall into temptation and are caught in the trap of many foolish and harmful desires, which pull men down to ruin and destruction" (1 Tim. 6:9, TEV). Preoccupation with mammon misses out on the real values (i.e., wholesome human relationships and a vital faith in God) and must inevitably lead to frustration and disappointment. Paul went on to say, "Some have been so eager to have it that they have wandered away from the faith and have broken their hearts with many sorrows" (v. 10).

Before we consider Christ's response to the question of survival, we must note the other factor, namely, the quest for dignity.

No people are content merely to exist. The human urge is to live—in dignity. Every human society has its ideals, values, customs, and procedures which it considers to be proper. The measure of dignity in that society is the degree to which its members approximate those accepted ideals. The outward expressions of dignity and self-respect usually include the quality of clothes and ornaments worn, foods served, and dwellings lived in. It may also include a man's estate, material possessions, and the size of his family and dependents.

Egalitarian tribal societies are not necessarily classless. However, many organized tribes have built-in safeguards against excesses and ostentation on the part of individual members of the community. Among the Ashantis, for example, certain items of clothing, ornaments, and furniture could only be used by chiefs and heads of clans. So even if an ordinary member of the clan could afford those things, he was not permitted to use them. This policy contributed to sharing and an even distribution of material possessions within the extended families and clans.

In our modern industrialized consumer societies there is no limit to what an individual may legitimately acquire, provided he can afford it. The media and advertising business exploit to the full the acquisitive instinct which is part of our human weakness. Those who can afford to do so surround themselves with all the status symbols of our age, while those who cannot, admire or envy them!

Christ's answer to the disciples' perfectly human quest for survival and dignity may be expounded from Matthew 6:24-34. Men and women everywhere look for survival and dignity in terms of material possessions. The Gross National Product is virtually worshiped as the economic deity of modern society to which all other values must be sacrificed! It is against the background of a similar travesty that the Lord Jesus warned the disciples: "You cannot serve both God and money" (v. 24). He proceeded to show them the way to adequacy in God, who claims their exclusive devotion and loyalty. We can summarize the Lord's teaching by remembering that: (1) We have a Father God who cares. (2) Having such a Father should make all the difference between our attitude to questions of survival and dignity and that of the pagans in our society. (3) The primary concern and commitment of God's people should be the extension of his kingly reign and the spreading of his righteous requirements.

The Lord's argument is unanswerable. God has done the greater in creating our bodies and giving us life. We can at least trust him to do the lesser—to care for our survival and fulfillment (v. 25). Here are two telling illustrations from nature.

The birds do not have to worry about survival. If any creatures should worry, it is surely they! They have not the capacity to sow, harvest, and store away, but we have! And the God who takes care of these lesser creatures of his is our Father in heaven (whose resources are limitless). The Lord has a sense of humor: "Can any of you live a bit longer by worrying about it?" (v. 27). Anxiety and worry, we know, are always counterproductive. To worry about living longer is the surest way to die younger!

Also, the wild flowers do not have to worry about beautiful and dignified clothes. Could any other creature be more helpless in this respect? They cannot even move about, let alone work and make clothes for themselves, but we can! And the God who takes such astonishing care of ephemeral things like grass and wild flowers is our Father! Moreover, he knows that we need food and clothes. So then we must trust him for our needs and not worry about them. Rather, our preoccupation should be with our personal submission to his kingly reign, and with our commitment to live out and spread its righteous requirements in society everywhere.

Christ commands and exhorts his followers not to worry about the necessities of life. Over-anxiety is therefore sinful. It is disobedience as well as unbelief. When we worry, we distrust our Father's wisdom, love, and ability to keep his promise to provide for his people.

But suppose we argue: We have seen many go without; and wisdom dictates we must lay up for the future against such eventualities. Could it be, perhaps, that many are having to go without the necessities of life because others, entrusted with more than they need, are hoarding? What about the greed of God's stewards who live wastefully on his resources? God's stewards must function as channels through which his adequate supplies can reach all, not as buckets to hold all our anticipated needs for the unforeseeable future!

ATTITUDES AND BEHAVIOR

An attempt must now be made to answer a number of specific questions relevant to our discussion of the Christian life-style: Can godliness and holiness of life in Christ demand in a given culture attitudes and behavior that in another culture are not required? Is true discipleship compatible with acquiescence in values that weaken and even hinder full obedience to Christ? Are there aspects of a Christian life-style that may be regarded as normative for the worldwide Church?

The Lausanne Covenant rightly states that "the Gospel does not presuppose the superiority of any culture to another, but evaluates all cultures according to its own criteria of truth and righteousness, and insists on moral absolutes in every culture'' (Para. 10: Evangelism and Culture). Accordingly, we affirm that discipleship to Christ demands certain basic principles of attitude and behavior which apply to all cultures. Nevertheless, the issues may vary from culture to culture. For example, to take a personal stand for Christ costs far more in a Muslim or Communist society than in a free western society. But a personal stand for Christ is required of every disciple. The issue of stewardship of possessions may be quite simple to Christians living in more or less individualistic societies. It is not so simple for those living in closely knit communities and extended family systems. Their possessions are really not theirs personally to dispose of as they wish. They are held in trust for the whole extended family.

It would seem, then, that the church in every culture has the responsibility to pray, reflect, and work out the implications of obedience to the Lord in the light of biblical teaching and in the context of her cultural situation. In this ongoing exercise, the shared experience of churches in other cultures will be helpful; but it should never become a substitute for local reflection and decision making.

But the question may be asked: If the church in every culture sufficiently succeeded in reflecting her distinctive cultural situation, how would the universal, supra-cultural nature of Christianity appear? Could a Christian brother from the United States feel a sense of belonging and welcome in the congregation of a typical African church on the Ivory Coast? Undoubtedly there will be some feeling of strangeness at first, in addition to the obvious problem of language and communication. But the universal mark of the Church of Christ is his discernible presence among his people everywhere through the Holy Spirit, and the sense of reverence, love, purity, peace, and joy experienced in the fellowship of real believers (Rom. 14:17; Gal. 5:22, 23). Moreover, the Spirit-generated desire among Christians to share Christ beyond their own cultural boundaries inevitably exposes many to other cultures. Through the ministry of such international Christians, the universal nature of the Christian Church is manifested and affirmed.

THE PRESSURE TO CONFORM

Christians live in a world in revolt against God and his Christ (Psalm 2). The Bible teaches that behind man's rebellion against God, and consequent slavery to sin, stands a sinister spiritual personality—Satan. He has hosts of other wicked spirits at his command, by the aid of which he exercises a usurped dominion of darkness over man and his world (Eph. 6:11, 12). He labors unceasingly to ensure that the very structures, values, attitudes, and life-style of the world are all organized in opposition to Christ and his Kingdom. Christians must expect to face this opposition as they seek to live out their obedience and loyalty to the Lord Jesus Christ in human society.

In every society there is usually a small group of the elite who wield ideological power over the rest. Their main interest may be social, political, economic, or religious. Someone has defined an ideology as a system of ideas and attitudes, with pretensions of objectivity and universality, which conceal the interests of a group, a class, or a nation. Since the interest of the elite group or class is best protected by the acceptance of (or at least acquiescence in) the particular system by the entire society, every dissent or proposal of an option becomes a threat. If the Christians' witness and way of life becomes identified with the protest against the particular ideology, they can expect to experience a variety of pressures to conform.

For instance, national leaders with ideological interests have been known to try to silence the church's prophetic voice, first of all, through flattery and bribery of her leadership. When this has failed, they have used ridicule and blackmail, followed by threats and active persecution. The worst that active persecution can do to a committed people of God is to drive them to operate underground. But there is no future for a church which trims its message and compromises its obedience to Christ in order to become acceptable and respectable in society.

And there is a far worse state into which the spirit of compromise may lead the church. This is when the people of God become the religious advocates of the popular ideology, and thereby sanction sectional interests in the name of Christ.

The Basel Letter, issued by a World Evangelical Fellowship

Consultation on Church and Nationhood (1976), has some relevant words to say on this matter. It recognizes the desperate situation developing in many countries today:

> Some churches are growing rapidly but are finding the civil authorities eager to use them to further political objectives. Other churches are tiny minorities in vast pagan populations. Frequently they are oppressed by secular powers and, on occasion, dismissed with savage contempt. Still others are being enticed to abandon their distinct Christian identity and reduce their mission to mere political activity.

The Letter counsels a clear-cut stand on a number of issues, including the following:

1. Christians should resist pressure on churches to make them mere religious tools of the State. At the same time, our churches should not be permitted to enlist the State as their political tool. We should not tolerate an intermingling of the Gospel with any political, economic, cultural, or nationalistic ideology in such a way as to compromise the Gospel; nor should we yield to the temptation of making our people or nation or our nation's institutions the object of near-religious loyalty. The loyalty of Christians to the one worldwide Body of Christ should transcend loyalty to tribe, class, race, or nation.

2. Our Christian concern for the community of mankind created by God in his likeness should enable us to stand firmly against all forms of legislated discrimination based on race or color.

3. Churches are called upon to exercise their prophetic role in society. They should summon civil authorities to their God-appointed task of promoting justice in society. The cost of such a prophetic ministry in terms of the Christians' call to participatory suffering is fully recognized.

4. The prevailing moral decay, economic injustice, and political oppression makes urgent the church's role as salt of the earth and light of the world. Crucial to this role is its corporate life, as the sign of Christ's Kingdom, in a visible community that exhibits the righteousness, peace, and love of his reign.

NORMATIVE LIFE-STYLE?

Can we really speak of a normative Christian life-style in spite of the obvious diversity of our social, political, racial, and cultural backgrounds? I believe we can, provided we mean something much deeper than what these superficial differences imply. The rationale behind the distinctively Christian style of life urged on us everywhere in Scripture is the new (divine) nature we now share in common with our risen Lord and Savior Jesus Christ (Rom. 7:4-6). This is the glorious result of our new birth into God's family by God's Spirit with God's Word (John 1:12, 13; 3:5; James 1:18; 1 Pet. 1:23; Gal. 3:26).

The Spirit of Christ has written God's law deep on our hearts and minds as the new principle of life (2 Cor. 3:2, 3). He has taken up residence in us as our indwelling source of moral and spiritual strength to live the life worthy of our Lord and pleasing to him in everything (Rom. 8:2, 9). Submission to the sanctifying and renewing work of the Holy Spirit with God's Word produces in every Christian (from whatever cultural background) the same fruit of the Spirit.

Essentially, then, a normative Christian life-style may be described as a life habitually fed and led by God's truth (the Scriptures), which results in a progressive reflection of God's holiness (Christlikeness) in personal character, and God's love and righteousness in personal relationships.

The Bible contains numerous descriptions of this life and its essential qualities. For example, the fruit of the Spirit is love, joy, peace, patience, kindness, goodness, faithfulness, gentleness, self-control (Gal. 5:22, 23; cf. 1 Cor. 13:4-7).

Since the inner force of the distinctive Christian life manifests itself in terms of truth, holiness, and love, the particular cultural dress which these qualities may wear from place to place is of secondary importance. "Here there cannot be Greek and Jew, circumcised and uncircumcised, barbarian, Scythian, slave, free man, but Christ is all, and in all" (Col. 3:11). The most outstanding things about any Christian, therefore, should not be the externals of culture—hairstyle, jewelry, clothes, and so on—but the "true inner self, the ageless beauty of a gentle and quiet spirit, which is of the greatest value in God's sight" (1 Pet. 3:4). It must be so, for it reflects the beauty of His Son who invites us to learn from Him because He is gentle and humble in spirit (Matt. 11:29). By the same token the Christian's true inner beauty will inevitably manifest itself in modest tastes and choices in clothes, food, dwellings, or furniture, always having an eye to the needs of others as well as to his or her own needs (1 Tim. 2:9, 10).

LIFE-STYLE AND MISSION

The Lausanne Covenant calls for sacrificial living and sacrificial giving with a purpose—namely, in order to contribute more generously to both relief and evangelism. The basis of the call is the urgency of the evanglistic task: the spiritual needs of the more than two-thirds of mankind who have yet to be evangelized. Then there are the poor, starving millions of humanity—victims of socio-economic injustice or natural disaster or both—for whom God's people have inescapable Christian responsibility. That is the task from a global perspective.

From the point of view of Christians' immediate contact and involvement with their fellow men, their life-style affects (for better or for worse) both the credibility and the communication of their message. Speaking on Christian service and witness at the Pan-African Christian Leadership Assembly, John Mbiti gave the following challenge to the church in Africa:

> The Christian Faith is not just a private bank account which the depositor uses secretly or privately. It is public property which has to be shared through service and proclaimed through evangelism. It is at the very heart of what our Lord Himself did: He went about preaching the Gospel, healing the sick, raising the dead, feeding the hungry . . .
>
> African Church Life must reflect and incarnate this work of our Lord, within the context of the peoples of Africa. There are many who are ready to listen to the Gospel—but they must hear it in their own languages and life situations. There are many who are sick; the Gospel must bring them hope, healing and newness of life. There are many who are spiritually and morally dead, politically oppressed, economically exploited, socially ostracized. The Gospel and the Church must bring healing to them all. There are many who are

hungry—physically starving, eating only the crumbs that fall from their master's table, babies suffering from malnutrition, thousands crying out for the food of love, the food of justice, the food of care. . . . the Gospel and the Church must feed them first. Unless they have enough to eat and drink, unless they are touched by the grain of love, they will be too concerned about their stomachs to hear the Gospel; and unless they are socially and economically given to eat (set free), they will not understand what the Gospel is all about. The center of the hungry man is his stomach, and not his heart. The center of the oppressed man is the chains that bind his legs and hands, and not his head. The center of the destitute is not his soul but his basic rights and his craving for love. African Church life should address itself to these centers of human life.

This is the language of self-sacrificing, caring love which is understood in every culture of man. Every Christian's life-style, regardless of his or her own culture, should reflect this love.

17. Contextualization of the Gospel in Fiji
—A Case Study from Oceania

by Alan R. Tippett

ALAN R. TIPPETT *is an Honorary Research Fellow, St. Mark's Library, Canberra, A.C.T. Australia. He is author of* People-Movements of Southern Polynesia, Solomon Islands Christianity, *and* God, Man and Church Growth.

THE GOSPEL CAME TO THE FIJI ISLANDERS IN 1835. In the subsequent century and a half, the Fijian church faced fundamental shifts in its cultural environment as the islands passed from pre-colonial into colonial and finally post-colonial history.

Because of these cultural shifts, and because of the rich and innovative dynamics of indigenous Fijian life, we have in the Fijian church an ideal focus for the study of the contextualization of the Gospel—contextualization being defined as the process of making evangelism and the Christian life-style relevant to the specifics of time and place.

From an anthropological perspective the introduction of the Gospel in a non-Christian society is a study in "directed change." Culture change, if it is to be relevant and permanent, must take into account the basic social functions performed by indigenous institutions. The advocates of change will weigh carefully whether these institutions should be maintained, expurgated, or expanded. This applies no less in the case of the messengers of the Gospel. If the Good News of Jesus Christ is to be successfully contextualized, there must be a sensitive interaction with the current indigenous culture. And beyond that, the agents of change must reckon with the flow of history.

Fiji graphically illustrates both the cultural and historical dimensions of contextualization. In the pre-colonial period the focus is on the pioneering efforts of the missionaries and their Fijian colleagues, with special attention to traditional (yet mobile) Fijian institutions. In the colonial and post-colonial periods, what is highlighted is the Fijian church's response to the social changes wrought by internal and external historical forces. At any point in the process of evangelization and development of a Christian lifestyle, the church can fail the test of contextualization. On the one hand, the structures and values of the believing community can appear "foreign" due to unwarranted cultural imports via cross-cultural missionaries; or, on the other hand, a church may persist in archaic patterns long after the inevitable impact of history has called for change.

In Fiji, certain cultural continuities run through the three periods of history. We will therefore consider these first, and then take up the unique elements that characterize each period. Against the flow of the cultural continuities and the historical changes we will be able to see just how indigenous the Fijian church has been since its founding.

BASIC CONTINUITIES

Three notions in the Fijian way of thinking and operating were accepted from the beginning of the Fijian mission. Their ramifications run throughout the history of the Fijian church and can be detected to this day. Without incorporating them, the church could not have been indigenous. They are: multi-individual people movements as the form of culture change; the role of herald, or go-between, in community ceremonial; and provision for cultural change via approved persons and mechanisms.

1. Multi-individual people movements: The mission to Fiji came from the British Wesleyans, with the pioneering missionaries,

Cross and Cargill, landing in Lakeba in 1835. Both had served a short term in Tonga, where they witnessed the Great Awakening, a people movement that spread throughout Tonga in a couple of years. The importance of this was that the Fiji mission began with the acceptance of the notion of large people movements from paganism to Christ. What happened in Fiji in the 1840s and 1850s was exactly what the missionaries expected. They understood the multi-individual character of decision-making and group action.

2. *The go-between in community ceremonial:* During their Tongan experience, Cross and Cargill were introduced to aspects of the Fijian context, as there was considerable trade and social intercourse between Fiji and Tonga. A Fijian chief, who initially came to Tonga to teach the Fijian war dances, had been converted in the Great Awakening and became an active evangelical Christian. This man, whose Christian name was Josua Mateinaniu, served the Gospel's cause by playing the all-important role of "herald."

The herald, or go-between, is the cog in the whole Fijian system. His is a sacred and protected position—serving as a mediator between two enemies, two chiefs, or two families, between chiefs and commoners, between two occupation groups, and so on. He interprets, he negotiates, he argues, he pleads, he welcomes, he farewells. The missionaries did not impose this role on the Fijian society, they found it already there.

When Cross and Cargill came to Fiji, Josua Mateinaniu returned with them. He taught them the rudiments of Fijian and guided them through the maze of Fijian ceremonials of introduction and request, which secured the formal acceptance of missionary residence in Lakeba. Through Mateinaniu's good services, the missionaries went everywhere in the correct manner, they approached the right people and performed the right courtesies. They leaned heavily on Mateinaniu for all kinds of decision-making, and especially for thrusts into new regions of Fiji. (He had enough chiefly status to command a hearing, but not too much so as to be politically suspect.)

Many missions in the Pacific failed at this point. Without a knowledge of correct procedure, they ran into all kinds of obstructions. But in Fiji, where customary procedure is as complicated as anywhere, the missionaries had little trouble because they had a good herald.

3. Provision for social change: In spite of persecution in some places, Fiji was ripe for the Gospel. The principle has been established by anthropologists that people change when and if they want to do so. Though advocates of innovations may "sell" their ideas, the real innovators are the acceptors. They alone bring about change.

A popular myth is to dichotomize human societies as either tribal and static, or innovative and progressive. Nothing could be more unfair to tribal societies. The possibility of social and/or religious change is built into every society. Every village assembly, every meeting of the gerontocracy, every family council implies some topic for discussion, some decision to be debated before action, some potential change to be made. As with the legal system in western societies, tribal tradition and custom provide reasonable social stability; but there is no human society so rigid that it will not consider innovation.

In hundreds of ways Fiji was already intensely innovative, even before the missionaries arrived. This is obvious in Fijian poetry, chanting, and art. Customs like cannibalism and widow-strangling, which had a social and religious underpinning, were very much on the decline before the Fijians became Christian. Sexual songs were being cast aside and a new type was emerging. Fijian warriors and cannibals were using Tongan-made weapons of war, and Fijian craftsmen were copying them, thus illustrating the Fijian readiness to borrow from outsiders. In some places the technology of carving war clubs and spears was being channeled into the manufacture of more peaceful artifacts.

Once the missionaries arrived, Fijian craftsmen readily adopted western technology in the burning of lime and crushing juice from sugar cane. Gardens began to appear and missionary wives taught the Fijian women to knit and crochet—the latter being one of the most highly developed Fijian skills today, and an interesting case of a western skill which became utterly indigenized.

Fiji, at the time of the missionaries' arrival, was divided between seven kingdoms, none powerful enough to subdue the rest or unify the whole. Western arms and ammunition, alcohol, venereal disease, and cannibalistic wars were reducing the population at a tremendous rate. Although Fiji was looking for a military unifier, she was open even to a non-military message.

Without doubt the Gospel came to Fiji in a day of dramatic social change, to a people who were ready to consider the claims of new forms of prayer and worship. The whole religious system was open for change.

Literacy was one of the most strategic changes advocated by the missionaries. Within twelve years the New Testament had been reduced to Fijian writing, and every Fijian convert learned to read and write. It was the Fijian New Testament which gave Fiji a lingua franca and, except for two mountain tribes, unified Fiji.

The structuring of Fijian society encouraged innovation. In most of the commonplace things of life, Fijians were their own decision-makers. The craftsmen, hunters, fishermen, agriculturalists, potters, and so on, were free within the confines of their occupations. Except for communal social responsibilities, all were free to go and come in their own pursuits.

Priests were remarkably free to innovate. Often they took the initiative in rejecting the old religion and turning first to the Gospel. (Normally they were either the first or the last to be converted, the prime acceptors or the prime objectors.) Any individual could reject his personal religion, domestic "gods," or cast out his sacred paraphernalia. However, the family gods were a family matter, and the tribal gods were a tribal matter. These called for group action after discussion. Sometimes several meetings were held before a consensus was reached. There are even cases on record of the group giving permission to a sub-group to convert. In such cases, the remainder usually followed a month or so later.

On the level of the kingdom, the people hesitated to convert without the king's approval. However, when the famous cannibal king Cakobau found that the Christians (or those who wanted to become Christian) were his most loyal supporters, he granted them the freedom of choice in the matter of religion. Several whole islands immediately became Christian.

In summary, let me reiterate: there is no doubt whatever about the freedom to innovate in a tribal society. The matter of deeper concern is to pay due respect to the in-built social mechanisms for such change. The missionary advocates can win or lose all in this matter of how converts go about separating themselves from their old ways and joining the Christian community.

THE PRE-COLONIAL PERIOD

As we turn to examine in more detail the pagan/Christian encounter in the Fijian context in the pre-colonial period I want to differentiate between what may be called *direct* and *indirect* encounter. The former involved cultural institutions founded on false values or beliefs. In Fiji there were areas of belief and practice that were manifestly incompatible with the Gospel, which were obstructions to conversion and which had to be replaced by Christian values and beliefs. Both the pioneering envangelists and the pagan Fijians knew this, and so face-to-face conflict was inevitable. There could be no "dynamic equivalence" here, no Christian functional substitutes because the basic values were anti-Christian. The best examples of such encounter in Fiji were pagan warfare, cannibalism, widow-strangling, and patricide.

Indirect types of encounter relate to customary procedures and to the meeting of felt-needs; these call for a deeper appreciation of function. Sometimes, while such items in the Fijian context presented no obstruction to conversion, they nevertheless could create moral problems for believers later on. These indirect encounters were not so clear-cut and raised a different set of questions. What should be preserved? What should be discarded? What should be modified? Examples of such subtle encounters concerned social structure, kinship loyalties, rites of passage, aesthetics, agriculture, economics, and technology. We will briefly consider examples of both types.

Warfare: When the Gospel first came to Fiji, the island societies were completely involved in war. In spite of the fact that the people were psychologically ready for religious change, the missionaries' first contextual confrontation was with war itself. They found that war hindered both the acceptance and the spread of the Gospel.

There were two kinds of warfare in old Fiji: petty skirmishing on the local level, which related to social functions like training youth for war, cannibalism, and low-level rivalries; and the large-scale "war of the chiefs" between tribes. At one time in the early period of missionary contact seven major wars were being fought at the same time. In this situation, a lone Christian convert (i.e., a pacifist) could hardly survive within a pagan village. He might detach himself from the village and remove to a Christian village, or join a mixed group of Christian refugees who had settled near some mission station; but in any case he was extremely vulnerable.

When a village turned Christian its very existence was precarious for a period of time. Scores of such villages were completely wiped out by pagan war parties. Such massacres were initiated either by the warriors for the sake of plunder or by local priests who felt threatened by the spread of Christianity. The justification for all such massacres was that it was appropriate to the tribal disloyalty of the victims.

Yet in spite of this, Christianity spread because of the fearless faith of its converts. The greatest Fijian peacemaker was Ilaija Varani, the Viwa war lord and righthand man of Cakobau. The heathen, astonished at his conversion, organized a plot to humiliate him and force him into an act of military retaliation. His Christian reaction convinced everyone of the genuineness of his conversion, and thereafter he traveled fearlessly from one warring state to another as a Christian peacemaker, a ministry which eventually cost him his life.

The social value which the pagan Fijian felt was threatened by Christianity was the notion that skill and victory in war was the only way of safeguarding the perpetuity of the tribe. The Christian converts ultimately demonstrated this to be a false assumption, but many lost their lives doing so.

Cannibalism: The first missionaries to Fiji found themselves in a world of institutionalized cannibalism, although this was passing through a rapid transition at the time. Originally, cannibalism was a ritualized mechanism for correcting social wrongs, prosecuting feuds, and relieving feelings of hate. As with many other inhumane customs, it was religiously ritualistic and hedged with taboos. It was confined to certain persons and to specific situations, and was completely barred from women and children.

The breakdown of cannabilism began in the first decade of the nineteenth century, when sandalwood traders and escaped convicts began bringing western arms and ammunition to Fiji and participating in Fijian wars. As a result of the upset of the balance of power, cannabilism was running out of control. With a surplus of cannibal flesh for the ovens, women began to partake of the feasting, and they rubbed the flesh on the lips of their infants to cultivate their taste for it. By the time the missionaries arrived, the system had been completely secularized. Many chiefs, displeased with the changes, felt that cannibalism had run its course and should be disposed of; some rejected it of their own volition by the end of the 1850s.

In areas of Christian influence cannibalism declined even before the people were converted. Before long the practice survived only in hard-core pagan areas where it was perceived as a kind of anti-Christian resistance symbol. In any case, Christianity stood in direct encounter with cannibalism. There was no middle course, and both Christian and pagan knew it.

Widow-strangling: Widows were strangled for burial with their deceased husbands, especially in the case of great chiefs and warriors. For a regional paramount chief a body guard of warriors and a few slaves might also be strangled. This was considered an honorable death, and it was shameful for a widow to attempt escape. In Christian times when the custom declined, many widows cried out bitterly for it, and some even committed suicide.

The custom had a theological, eschatological motivation. A big chief or warrior, upon his death, would be deified, normally as a war divinity with a particular interest in his own clan or tribe. Those who had fought and lived under his authority would begin to worship him and depend on him for the perpetuity of the group. To dishonor the dead would bring tribal disaster, and the clearest form of dishonor was to dispatch him into the afterlife without wives and servants, so that he arrived there an insignificant person.

The only counter for this complex of belief and custom was a Christian eschatology, and this was a matter of instruction after conversion. The missionaries, supported by their converts, battled against this custom and used all the ceremonial procedures of courtesy and respectful request in their attempt to persuade the leaders of the funerary rites to spare the lives of the widows. These appeals throughout were correctly done according to Fijian custom and the pleaders were given a respectful hearing. Because of this mutual respect, the missionaries were partly successful, but not until the people became Christian and learned a new Christian eschatology was widow-strangling fully brought under control.

We have here an important anthropological point: when the

locus of encounter between Christian and pagan values has an ultimate theological underpinning nothing less than a theological change can dispose of it. In this case, the compromise of sparing some widows but not all shows that the pagans had not conceded anything at the level of the belief system. They compromised out of respect for appeals correctly made, and no more. Furthermore, the widows who were spared were left without any social mechanism for their comfort and protection. Such widows had no alternative but to become Christian with or without spiritual conviction; some preferred suicide.

Patricide: Another custom the early missionaries encountered was the killing of the aged. This was either by strangling or by live burial. The aged might be strangled or buried for any one of several reasons. Care of the aged was always a social burden in a society subject to sudden enemy attack. When age or sickness rendered a person incapable of caring for himself, he might be ceremonially strangled with all due pomp and ceremony by his eldest son and heir. This was to give him honor and avoid the possibility of his being left behind to be clubbed by the enemy and possibly eaten, a shameful death that demanded retaliation.

A great chief or warrior might become aware that "his hand had lost its cunning" and know that in the interest of tribal security his son should take over his office. He might find his son preparing his funerary rites even while he was yet alive. Then, with all due decorum he would find himself in the grave, with his son stamping down the earth on the mat above him with the ceremonial words, "Sir, your sun has set!" The old man himself would consider his death a merciful act, as he believed that the body passed on into the afterlife in the state it was at death. It was therefore bad to become aged or decrepit, another example of a custom with faulty eschatology, which nothing could correct but conversion followed by education in the doctrine of Christian hope.

We now turn to moral problems in more subtle areas which arose in the Fijian context after conversion.

Social structure: We have already discussed several aspects of Fijian social organization, such as the system of mediation through the person of the herald, and the group decision-making process by which, after long discussion, consensus was achieved that permitted corporate action. The Fijian church adopted these social mechanisms without fear of compromise to the faith. In fact, the emerging church manifested remarkable structural similarities with the political organization of Fiji itself. For example, the idea of the assembly *(bose)* of the group for discussion *(veivosaki)* and decision-making *(lewā)*, which ran through every level of social life from the household to the nation, was closely paralleled in the various levels of the church courts.

Furthermore, the growing Christian community was recognized as a religious group because it was recognizably so: it used the prayer/worship/sacrifice/chant vocabulary of the Fijian religious life and reached out to the Power beyond man. The church took over the system of presentation of offerings that came from the pre-Christian way of life. There is nothing western about the *soli vakamisoneri* even today. The annual offerings for the support of the church ministry reflected in style and procedure a pre-Christian presentation of war resources at a military review *(taqa)* or a ceremonial presentation of craft work and food for the rebuilding of a heathen temple. The first western missionaries accepted this as meaningful to the Lord. As a result many of these indigenous forms survive to the present day.

Thus, the transition from the pagan to the Christian lifestyle in social organization raised no moral problems. There were some social issues, however, as in marriage, the dance and chanting, that did raise moral questions for the convert.

Marriage: Polygamous converts were free to worship in the congregation and join in the prayer meetings, but they did not achieve full member status until after baptism, and this implied a greater degree of instruction and maturity in their Christian experience. Most who turned from paganism to Christianity wanted to go the whole way and became monogamous, which was a condition for baptism. The time of training for baptism varied from a few months to a number of years. More often than not it was the polygamy issue which occasioned the longer waiting.

Fijian society was not universally polygamous. The multiplicity of wives was limited to the upper classes, who also had concubines. There were two undergirding supports of the system. The first of these was the need for perpetuity of the lineage, and a belief that power passed from the chief through blood to his offspring. A second support for polygamy was the use of the institution for political purposes, such as a military alliance. A union along these lines was often held together fairly loosely and could be terminated when the political expediency had passed. This made it possible for a chief who became Christian to send his wives home without dishonoring the marriage and without repercussion, provided he did it with the appropriate formal ceremonies.

Adult men on a lower level had no wives at all; this was especially so with the warriors who lived in male communal houses. They were "rewarded" sexually by the enslavement and abuse of women captured in war.

Life for the men in the communal houses was grim. These men were quickly attracted to the Christian idea of each man having his own wife and home, however humble. As the wars came to an end, and men were no longer rewarded with captive women, the Christian requirement became more popular among the rank and file. (In fact, the Fijian family as we know it today is a Christian innovation.)

The dance and the chant: People express their emotions and subliminal wants in aesthetic forms, which become psychologically central in their value system. The pre-Christian Fijian expressed these deep feelings in the dance and chant (as indeed Fijians still do today).

We have numerous descriptions of pagan dancing and chanting. War dances glorified war and cannibalism, and mocked at the sexual impotence of captured heroes about to go to the ovens. The victors, on the other hand, were glorified in terms of sexual power, and given honorific titles which implied they were also "lords of sex." Naturally enough, the missionaries recoiled from these demonstrations.

Not all Fijian chants and dances, however, were sexual or vulgar. Some were extremely beautiful and pleasant to the ear. Some recounted early tribal migrations; some explained the origin of tribal customs; others featured nature parables or offered praise for the beauty of nature; still others were historical dirges about epidemics, hurricanes, and floods, or honorific dirges upon the death of some great man, or for the commemoration of some technological achievement like the building of a temple, the construction of a canal, or the launching of a giant double canoe.

The dance and chant were so basic for the expression of Fijian feeling that they were one of the first focal points for moral issues faced by the Christian converts. (Fortunately, this area was dealt with in the 1840s and 1850s, rather than in the 1880s and 1890s when the missionaries were more children of the later Victorian Age.) Of course, the early missionaries and their Fijian advisors determined that the sexual performances had to go. The two most vulgar dances, which featured both war and sex, and which were tied up with the ancestral religion, disappeared altogether; today even the words have dropped from the Fijian vocabulary and memory.

But the parables, the nature songs, the historical dirges, tribal migration songs, and honorific dirges, these may still be found today in chant and dance in Christian assemblies. They still speak deeply to the Fijian soul, so much so that new ones are created for specifically Christian use. The dedication of a Christian church building frequently features a Fijian chant and/or dance. The chant of the *Yabaki Drau* (a historical catalogue of the events of the first Christian century) is used all over Fiji in Christian worship. I myself once composed a historical Christian chant for an accompanying dance. Three or four preachers reported to me that the performance produced a response on the level of Fijian Christian tradition which penetrated to their subliminal feelings. We have here a case of a pagan cultural institution being transformed and remaining functionally creative in its new Christian context.

One might also point out that as the Fijian form of Christianity took shape it revealed many affinities with the Hebrew religion of the Old Testament. Indeed, many of the lyrical passages of Scripture were so aesthetic to the Fijians that scores of them were simply taken over into the Fijian worship service and liturgy. Stories of the acts of God, like the Creation; for dedication commemorations, the building of Solomon's temple, or the description of the New Jerusalem; the more formal code recitals like the Ten Commandments (for liturgical use); the praise passages, like many of the Psalms; and the Old Testament dirges—any of these one may hear in a Christian worship service or an outdoor church assembly.

The pre-Christian complex of the dance and chant in Fiji has thus been taken over by the young church (a case of *maintenance);* purged of sex, cannibalism, and war *(expurgation);* and adapted for purposes of Christian worship and evangelism *(expansion)*. Here we have the full range of the church's response to its indigenous context—notable examples of contextualization being carried out with vigor and sensitivity.

Theological conceptualization: Before closing this section I would like to add some observations about the potential for transforming indigenous thought forms into the service of Christian theology. Not all early missionaries to the Pacific were persuaded that such a potential existed, and therefore they became advocates of the "civilize in order to evangelize" approach. They thus overlooked whole conceptual areas in the Fijian context that lent themselves to Christian "dynamic equivalence." Consider these brief examples:

1. When the westerner, who is deficient in his understanding of sacrificial systems in the first place, begins to expound the Scriptures, he finds the biblical world of sacrifice too diversified for his western vocabulary. But when the first missionaries began translating the Scriptures they found a sacrificial vocabulary in Fiji more diversified even than that of Scripture. The Fijian convert thus had a capacity for a theology of sacrifice very much superior to that of the average westerner. One of the prized items in my collection of Fijian memorabilia is a sermon outline of a century ago, prepared by a Fijian preacher, dealing with Christ's sacrifice as a propitiation for our sins. The sermon reviews the character of a pre-Christian sacrifice for sin in old Fiji. The preacher uses the significant points as a typology which brings him to the superior sacrifice of Christ. It is a treatment worthy of the Letter to the Hebrews and must have spoken to the Fijian congregation just as the New Testament letter did to its Hebrew Christian audience.

2. The Old Testament Day of Atonement, the role of the scapegoat, and the use of the cities of refuge had their counterparts in Fijian life. There was, for example, a certain mountain village in Viti Levu where an offender might run and find protection by climbing upon a great rock. Here the avenger would shake his club in vain. "You know you are guilty," he would say. "You know you are saved only because you have stood on the rock of refuge." People with social mechanisms like that will have no trouble wrestling with a theology of salvation, even though the Great Rock is now a Person.

3. Neither will a people who use a system of heralds or go-betweens have any trouble with a theology of mediation. The Christian notion of the Father sending forth his Son to declare him is a totally Fijian way of thinking. Neither is there difficulty with the theology of the Son and the Father being one. A Fijian son not only mediates, he represents his father. He is the substitute of the father and acts with the latter's authority. In Fiji when a high authority sends a substitute, the latter does not go in his own authority but in that of the sending authority. With very little instruction the Fijian converts were able to grasp this world of Christian doctrine.

4. The first battle for conversion was a power encounter with the old gods, the spirits, and deified ancestors. It was conceptualized in the thought-world of *mana*. This is the thought-world of Joshua at Shechem (Josh. 24) and Elijah at Carmel (1 Kings 18); it is reminiscent of Jesus confronting the evil spirits and the Ephesian episode in Acts 19:13-20. By the use of *mana, kalou, masu,* and many other such power terms, the Christian religion was born in Fiji. Never did the Fijian deny the reality of the evil powers, but he certainly discovered the Power above all powers. Every one of these power terms required a theological transition, but by the Spirit's help it was achieved.

THE COLONIAL PERIOD

The pre-colonial period of mission in Fiji lasted for about four decades. By this time all the coastal Fijians were Christian and only two pagan tribes remained in the interior. (A decade later they, too, were becoming Christian, evangelized by the coastal believers.) These coastal Fijians were mostly second-generation Christians. The church was being carried along by the momentum of forty triumphant years. But with the introduction of colonial rule (the islands were ceded by Fijian chiefs to Britain in 1874), dramatic changes came, bringing in their wake new sets of problems and moral confrontations.

Under the new colonial government a great army of white adventurers and land speculators came to Fiji. This was followed by a long series of social, economic, and political changes.

Particularly tragic was the measles epidemic which immediately followed Cession; it carried off over forty thousand Fijians and so physically weakened the race that there followed a long series of other epidemics—whooping cough, influenza, and so forth. By the end of the century it was widely speculated that the Fijians would die out and the (European) planters would be left without labor. This led to the importation of indentured laborers from India. As a result the population balance of the country was upset, and in time the Indians became the largest racial group. The indenture system continued for nearly four decades, in spite of the Fijian outcry against it, leaving the Fijians with a set of social problems not of their own making.

The colonial government supported large vested interests rather than small plantations. This transformed the economy of the colony and changed the balance of power. Relations between the government and the people were also complicated by the appointment of "government chiefs"—Fijians who had no "birth" by traditional criteria, and who were therefore unqualified for positions of authority. This produced much confusion which the church had not experienced in prior years.

The missionaries themselves were more paternalistic and Victorian than the first generation of missionaries. And the Christian mission to the Indian population was completely different from what the Fijians had known; its patterns came from India and its missionary values were colonial rather than traditional. This created many obstructions which had to be removed before the two churches could move together.

The colonial period lasted for nearly a century (the islands were returned to Fijian sovereignty in 1970). The fact that the Fijian church was able to retain its indigenous character against paternalism, colonialism, and the various forces of acculturation, speaks worlds for its early strength. Its evangelizing spirit and missionary concern for the islands beyond the horizon has been one of the Fiji church's strong continuities. After World War II, the church was ready for and moving toward independence before the colony itself.

Let us briefly mention two of the challenges and problems of the colonial period.

Evangelization of the Fiji Indians: The colonial period was one of missionary expansion—to New Britain and New Ireland, to

Papua, to the Solomons, to North Australia and eventually to the New Guinea Highlands—yet Fiji's witness to the Indian migrants was slight. The first Indian indentured laborers reached Fiji in 1879 and the "trade" continued until 1916. Hitherto, labor had come from the other Pacific islands, and the Fijian churches had ministered to it. The Indian, therefore, was thought to be "just another kind of islander," and the first pastoral care was supplied by a Fijian missionary just returned from New Britian. But the experiment failed. A subsequent appeal for a full-time worker from the Wesleyan home board for the Indian community went unanswered. In the 1890s the Fijian Synod negotiated with the Synod in Calcutta and obtained the services of an Indian catechist from the same region as the migrants. But his English was very poor, and neither his missionary superintendent nor the Fijian chairman of the project knew Hindustani. With another unsuccessful appeal for a full-time missionary, two decades of opportunity were lost.

After the turn of the century a layman, a minister, and a missionary sister were established in the Indian work. They were unable to handle their program within the Fijian structures and insisted on being constituted as a separate Synod of their own. Thus were the Fijian and Indian programs recognized as ethnically and socially different, and each proceeded thereafter along its own lines, one retaining its traditional pre-colonial values, and the other using models derived from India, including a highly institutionalized educational base, a colonial mission structure, and western life-style complete with hilltop mission houses maintained by servants. The saddest thing about the division of the Indian and Fijian mission was that it relieved the Fijian churches of a sense of responsibility for the Indian population.

When I came to Fiji in the early 1940s, the polarity between the two missions shocked me. Finally, a change in attitude could be noted. A new constitution, drawn up in the mid-1940s, introduced major structural changes. The European missionary structure was deprived of its entity and authority; the missionaries were absorbed into their respective Fijian or Indian Synods, and there outnumbered; and a representative united synod was created to develop the unity of the church at large. When I left Fiji in 1960, Hindustani was being taught to the Fijian theological students by an Indian minister; the concern for evangelization of the Indians had been rekindled! Thus the Fijian church marked the end of the period of paternalism and prepared the way for the full independence of the colony.

Coming of age: Male and female initiation rites, featuring circumcision and tatooing, disappeared from Fijian life with the coming of Christianity. These rites, being associated with the pre-Christian religion, were not seen by the missionaries at the time to have any basic functional value. On the contrary, these rites of young manhood and womanhood were very important, serving among other things as the occasion for imparting a new understanding of life and education on the facts of life. In the missionaries' view, it seemed that a harmless visit to the hospital for the operation of circumcision, and the holding of a simple feast of entry into manhood back in the village upon their return, was all that was needed and was more "Christian." But there were problems for subsequent generations.

The members of the younger generation were now left to pick up their knowledge as best they could by sharing stories with equally uneducated peers. There was never a formal substitute for sex education, and the second generation was thereby exposed to unsavory boy/girl speculations or to the temptation to experiment. This is a typical example of the danger of the disposal of ritual without due regard to its true function, and thereby creating the occasion for a new type of moral problem.

As with sex education, so too with the nature of courtship. In the pre-colonial days a Fijian marriage was arranged by the two families by correct approaches and responses, the presentation of mutual gifts, and the giving and accepting of assurances. Not just two people but two families were brought together, families who would hold the marriage together through all kinds of marital stress. Folk normally courted and married within certain cultural boundaries. The missionaries were happy to leave this aspect of the new Christian way to the Fijian native ministers, and for a century things ran smoothly.

But in the later colonial period, various forces disrupted this pattern. First there emerged the new itinerant professions—school teachers, magistrates, ministers of religion, and others—who were stationed in different parts of the colony and did not locate in their homelands. They mixed with government and mission leaders—

foreigners who married according to their taste and status. These became the first Fijians to marry by individual choice. When this philosophy hit the theological students at Davuilevu in the 1950s, for the first time Christian young people began seeking the counsel of their white missionary leaders rather than their own senior Fijian ministers.

The most threatening factor to Fijian marriage in the later colonial period was the increasing migration to the city. There, a Fijian clerk and typist, say, whose families were far removed and did not even know of each other, would enter into the Hollywood version of marriage. Here was a marriage utterly without security of any kind, with no tribal support, and no social mechanisms to hold it together under stress, and no financial undergirdings.

The colonial period is also known for the inhumane aspects of the indenture system; the social inequities caused by economic upheavals; disordering adjustments in education and political life; and various social evils introduced by white travelers, sailors, and settlers.

THE POST-COLONIAL PERIOD

The contours of the post-colonial structures were already manifest in the closing two decades of the colonial period which saw a renaissance of Fijian indigenous enthusiasm.

The colonial period had seen remarkably few evidences of nationalism. The years of Fijian anomie which followed the measles epidemic and the establishment of colonial rule were marked by a continual decline in Fijian population, a decline which continued until 1920. It was not until the end of World War II, when it became known that the Indian population had surpassed the Fijian, that new expressions of Fijian nationalism began to appear.

It was at this time that the Fijian and Indian missions reorganized with a new constitution, which enhanced the renaissance of indigenous Fijian Christianity. The New Constitution gave the Fijians a majority vote on everything, including the stationing of missionaries. Missionaries going on furlough could not return unless invited by the Fijian Synod. The aim of the constitution was to transform the mission into a church, dispose of western paternalism by eliminating the European Synod altogether, substituting a representative one that would bring Indian and Fujian together.

A Bible school was established to raise the level of candidates for the ministry and to prepare Fijian laymen for church service. Among their extracurricular activities they presented biblical dramas in the larger Fijian villages as congregational education.

At the theological institution, where Fijian ministers and a few Indians were trained, a transitional two-track curriculum was introduced and ran for ten years. One was a rural church syllabus which trained men who would safeguard against too rapid a cut-off from traditional Fiji. The other was an academic syllabus which trained others for urban and industrial conditions and gave them a foundation for any subsequent degree work they might want to do. The youth department was handed over to a dynamic Fijian and suddenly experienced a burst of new life. Youth camps were held around the islands. Young people began to appear on church committees; church music was charged with innovations. A new day was being born.

The Fijian church, passing through a series of centenaries from 1947 onward, rediscovered the history of her pioneering period. Historical plays were presented across the country by the Bible school and other groups. The church paper, which had been largely used as an instrument for printing Sunday school lessons, became more truly a Christian newspaper. This was accompanied by a period of increased vernacular publication and many of the articles in the paper were reprinted as tracts for free distribution.

When I left Fiji the movement towards full church independence was approaching its goal. The new constitution and its years of practical application provided the leadership required. In 1964 independence came in the church, six years ahead of national independence. Indeed, it was partly the effectiveness of the church independence which convinced the Fijian political leaders that the country itself would be better off as an independent power than as a Crown Colony.

THE CONTEMPORARY SCENE

The Fijian Church has now completed more than a decade of independence, the Dominion a little less. In 1977 I had the opportunity of returning and assessing the results.

The country seems far better off as an independent dominion. Development has been considerable. New networks of roads
reach inland and large tracts of land have been opened up. Rice
fields have replaced the cane in the Rewa delta. Many small indus-
tries have come into being, and the local products in the stores
(now supermarkets) show a greater diversification of industry. Fijian canned tuna stands on the shelves beside the imported cans
and is much cheaper. There are more banks and they have many
more branches. I surveyed the personnel in the largest central
bank where I remembered an entirely white staff; it is now completely Fijian, Indian, and Chinese.

Next to the complete localization of industry and the end of
the old paternalism, the greatest change is probably the suburban-
ization of Suva and its environs. A university has been established
and a number of other academic institutions in the same area have
changed the south side of the peninsula.

I remember the day when folk migrating into Suva from the
rural areas would seek out the area where their fellow tribesmen
were squatting and build themselves an unapproved shanty. This
has all gone and proper buildings have taken their place. They still
often have their ethnic character but many now have cement
houses and automobiles. They have good jobs, better salaries, and
are buying city homes rather than thinking of returning in old age
to the village. The suburb is a new element in the Fijian context,
reflecting, I believe, a shift from subsistence farming to wage-earn-
ing.

I used to go across the river from Davuilevu to preach to
forty or fifty persons at Nausori meeting in an old, dilapidated
church, with very little enthusiasm. During my recent visit I
preached there in a new building, ornamented with Fijian motifs.
There were two choirs and four hundred people crowded into the
building.

Many of the activities that accompany the new suburban developments have a strong awareness of selfhood. In the Nausori
area, for instance, where a strong women's group draws participants from various quarters, the women wear dresses which indicate their congregational affiliation. Thus while they meet in the
unity of a common faith they also are reminded of the diversity of
their representation. In all the places I visited I felt that the church
people had a grip on the ever-changing situation. They were part

of the context itself. But it was no melting pot of cultures. They were the Fijian component, but they recognized other components and reached out to them. I also noted that the church has elected an Indian as their President though the majority vote is with the Fijians.

Another feature of the contemporary scene is the interinsular cooperation, which began in the 1950s when Tonga, Samoa, and Fiji moved towards each other in the programs relating to theological training and youth work. The World Council of Churches sponsored a conference in Samoa and the WCC Theological Education Fund a consultation on theological education in the Pacific. The fruit of these programs was the establishment of the Pacific Theological College, which takes graduates from the various denominational island training institutions and offers them a bachelor's degree in divinity. This institution began with the support of sixteen missionary bodies in the islands. Unfortunately the curriculum has turned out to be more western than intended, but the recent appointment of a national president may improve things.

Fiji has participated in numerous conferences, including the 1974 Lausanne Congress on World Evangelization. Thus the country is aware of the religious world beyond her shores. She has expressed herself vigorously on public issues which touch the Pacific—as, for example, the French atomic bombings. The island church of Fiji fully understands that the world is "one world" and she cannot live in isolation.

The church is exploring new fields of university and industrial evangelism. I found the Fijian evangelist of today quite experimental—for example, running weekly question-time evangelism during the lunch hour in an industrial workshop.

In such a study as this, we cannot lose sight of the fact that cultures are not static. The context in which our grandfathers worked is not the same as ours even though we speak virtually the same language and have the same culture. This is why I treated the Fijian church in three time periods, for the historical aspect of a contextual analysis is as important as the cultural. In one's own specific mission, one needs to identify two things: the cultural context, and the point in time in the cultural history. Only thus can the contextualization of the Gospel meet all the demands of time and place.

Conclusion:
The Willowbank Report

Report on a Consultation on GOSPEL AND
CULTURE held at Willowbank, Somerset Bridge,
Bermuda from 6th to 13th January 1978 Sponsored
by the Lausanne Theology and Education Group

Copyright © 1978 Lausanne Committee for World Evangelization, P.O.
Box 1100, Wheaton, IL 60187, U.S.A.

*In encouraging the publication and study of this paper, the Lausanne
Committee for World Evangelization does not necessarily endorse every
viewpoint expressed in it.*

Contents

INTRODUCTION

The process of communicating the gospel cannot be isolated from the human culture from which it comes, or from that in which it is to be proclaimed. This fact constituted one of the preoccupations of the Lausanne Congress on World Evangelization in July 1974. So the Lausanne Committee's Theology and Education Group convened a consultation on this topic to meet in January 1978. It brought 33 theologians, anthropologists, linguists, missionaries and pastors together from all six continents to study "Gospel and Culture." Co-sponsored by the Lausanne Committee's Strategy Working Group, it had four goals:

1. To develop our understanding of the interrelation of the gospel and culture with special reference to God's revelation, to our interpretation and communication of it, and to the response of the hearers in their conversion, their churches and their life style.

2. To reflect critically on the implications of the communication of the gospel cross-culturally.

3. To identify the tools required for more adequate communication of the gospel.

4. To share the fruits of the consultation with Christian leaders in Church and mission.

This Report reflects the content of 17 written papers circulated in advance, summaries of them and reactions to them made during the Consultation, and many viewpoints expressed in plenary and group discussions.

Our programme for six days was very full, and we worked at high pressure. In consequence, basic methodological questions about the presuppositions and procedures of theology and the social sciences, and about the proper way to relate them to each other, could not be explored; and there were points at which our discussions clearly reflected this fact. Also, many questions which were raised had to be left on one side, and many particular debates had to be foreclosed as we went along. We are conscious, therefore, that what we say is to some extent provisional, and may need to be sharpened and deepened at various points in the light of future work. In addition, we resort to a number of generalizations; more case-studies are needed to see how these relate to specific situations.

Before the Consultation ended, we spent time together working through the draft report and revising it. The final document is a Report, not a Statement or Declaration; so none of us has signed it. But we send it out as a summary of what took place at Willowbank, and we commend it to our fellow Christians throughout the world for study and appropriate action.

1. The Biblical Basis of Culture

"Because man is God's creature, some of his culture is rich in beauty and goodness. Because he is fallen, all of it is tainted with sin and some of it is demonic." (Lausanne Covenant, para. 10)

God created mankind male and female in his own likeness by endowing them with distinctive human faculties--rational, moral, social, creative and spiritual. He also told them to have children, to fill the earth and to subdue it (Gen. 1:26-28). These divine commands are the origin of human culture. For basic to culture are our control of nature (that is, of our environment) and our development of forms of social organisation. Insofar as we use our creative powers to obey God's commands, we glorify God, serve others and fulfill an important part of our destiny on earth.

Now however, we are fallen. All our work is accompanied by sweat and struggle (Gen. 3:17-19), and is disfigured by selfishness. So none of our culture is perfect in truth, beauty or goodness. At the heart of every culture-- whether we identify this heart as religion or world-view--is an element of self-centredness, of man's worship of himself. Therefore a culture cannot be brought under the Lordship of Christ without a radical change of allegiance.

For all that, the affirmation that we are made in God's image still stands (Gen. 9:6; James 3:9), though the divine likeness has been distorted by sin. And still God expects us to exercise stewardship of the earth and of its creatures (Gen. 9:1-3, 7), and in his common grace makes all persons inventive, resourceful and fruitful in their endeavors. Thus, although Genesis 3 records the fall of humanity, and Genesis 4 Cain's murder of Abel, it is Cain's descendants who are described as the cultural innovators, building cities, breeding livestock, and making musical instruments and metal tools (Gen. 4:17-22).

Many of us evangelical Christians have in the past been too negative towards culture. We do not forget the human fallenness and lostness which call for salvation in Christ. Yet we wish to begin this Report with a positive affirmation of human dignity and human cultural achievement. Wherever human beings develop their social organisation, art and science, agriculture and technology, their creativity reflects that of their Creator.

2. A Definition of Culture

Culture is a term which is not easily susceptible of definition. In the broadest sense, it means simply the patterned way in which people do things together. If there is to be any common life and corporate action, there must be agreement, spoken or unspoken, about a great many things. But the term "culture" is not generally used unless the unit concerned is larger than the family, unitary or extended.

Culture implies a measure of homogeneity. But, if the unit is larger than the clan or small tribe, a culture will include within itself a number of subcultures, and subcultures of subcultures, within which a wide variety and diversity is possible. If the variations go beyond a certain limit, a counterculture will have come into being, and this may prove a destructive process.

Culture holds people together over a span of time. It is received from the past, but not by any process of natural inheritance. It has to be learned afresh by each generation. This takes place broadly by a process of absorption from the social environment, especially in the home. In many societies certain elements of the culture are communicated directly in rites of initiation, and by many other forms of deliberate instruction. Action in accordance with the culture is generally at the subconscious level.

This means that an accepted culture covers everything in human life.

At its centre is a world-view, that is, a general understanding of the nature of the universe and of one's place in it. This may be "religious" (concerning God, or gods and spirits, and of our relation to them), or it may express a "secular" concept of reality, as in a Marxist society.

From this basic world-view flow both standards of judgement or values (of what is good in the sense of desirable, of what is acceptable as in accordance with the general will of the community, and of the contraries) and standards of conduct (concerning relations between individuals, between the sexes and the generations, with the community and with those outside the community).

Culture is closely bound up with language, and is expressed in proverbs, myths, folk tales, and various art forms, which become part of the mental furniture of all members of the group. It governs actions undertaken in community--acts of worship or of general welfare; laws and the administration of law; social activities such as dances and games; smaller units of action such as clubs and societies, associations for an immense variety of common purposes.

Cultures are never static; there is a continuous process of change. But this should be so gradual as to take place within the accepted norms; otherwise the culture is disrupted. The worst penalty that can be inflicted on the rebel is exclusion from the culturally defined social community.

Men and women need a unified existence. Participation in a culture is one of the factors which provide them with a sense of belonging. It gives a sense of security, of identity, of dignity, of being part of a larger whole, and of sharing both in the life of past generations and in the expectancy of society for its own future.

Biblical clues to the understanding of the human culture are found in the threefold dimension of people, land, and history, on which the Old Testament focuses attention. The ethnic, the territorial, and the historical (who, where and whence we are) appear there as the triple source of economic, ecological, social and artistic forms of human life in Israel, of the forms of labour and production, and so of wealth and well-being. This model provides a perspective for interpreting all cultures.

Perhaps we may try to condense these various meanings as follows: Culture is an integrated system of beliefs (about God or reality or ultimate meaning), of values (about what is true, good, beautiful and normative), of customs (how to behave, relate to others, talk, pray, dress, work, play, trade, farm, eat, etc.), and of institutions which express these beliefs, values and customs (government, law courts, temples or churches, family, schools, hospitals, factories, shops, unions, clubs, etc.), which binds a society together and gives it a sense of identity, dignity, security, and continuity.

3. Culture in the Biblical Revelation

God's personal self-disclosure in the Bible was given in terms of the hearers' own culture. So we have asked ourselves what light it throws on our task of cross-cultural communication today.

The biblical writers made critical use of whatever cultural material was available to them for the expression of their message. For example, the Old Testament refers several times to the Babylonian sea monster named "Leviathan," while the form of God's "covenant" with his people resembles the ancient Hittite Suzerain's "treaty" with his vassals. The writers also made incidental use of the conceptual imagery of the "three-tiered" universe, though they did not thereby affirm a a pre-Copernican cosmology. We do something similar when we talk about the sun "rising" and "setting."

Similarly, New Testament language and thought-forms are steeped in both Jewish and Hellenistic cultures, and Paul seems to have drawn from the vocabulary of Greek philosophy. But the process by which the biblical authors borrowed words and images from their cultural milieu, and used them creatively, was controlled by the Holy Spirit so that they purged them of false or evil implications and thus transformed them into vehicles of truth and goodness.

These undoubted facts raise a number of questions with which we have wrestled. We mention five:

(a) *The nature of biblical inspiration.*

Is the biblical author's use of the words and ideas of their own culture incompatible with divine inspiration? No. We have taken note of the different literary genres of Scripture, and of the different forms of the process of inspiration which they imply. For instance, there is a broad distinction in form between the work of the prophets, receiving visions and words of the Lord, and historians and writers of letters. Yet the same Spirit uniquely inspired them all. God used the knowledge, experience and cultural background of the authors (though his revelation constantly transcended these), and in each case the result was the same, namely God's word through human words.

(b) *Form and meaning.*

Every communication has both a meaning (what we want to say) and a form (how we say it). The two--form and meaning-- always belong together, in the Bible as well as in other books and utterances. How then should a message be translated from one language into another?

A literal translation of the form ("formal correspondence") may conceal or distort the meaning. In such cases, the better way is to find in the other language an expression which makes an equivalent impact on the hearers now as did the original. This may involve changing the form in order to preserve the meaning. This is called "dynamic equivalence." Consider, for example, the RSV translation of Rom. 1:17, which states that in the gospel "the righteousness of God is revealed through faith for faith." This gives a word-for-word rendering of the original Greek, that is, a "formal correspondence" translation. But it leaves the meaning of the Greek words "righteousness" and "from faith to faith" unclear. A translation such as TEV--"the gospel reveals how God puts people right with himself: it is through faith from beginning to end"--abandons the principle of one-to-one correspondence between Greek and English words; but it expresses the meaning of the original sentence more adequately. The attempt to produce such a "dynamic equivalence" translation may well bring the translator to a deeper understanding of Scripture, as well as make the text more meaningful to people of another language.

Some of the biblical forms (words, images, metaphors) should be retained, however, because they are important recurring symbols in Scripture (e.g., cross, lamb, or cup). While retaining the form, the translators will try to bring out the meaning. For example, in the TEV rendering of Mark 14:36-- "take this cup of suffering away from me"--the form (i.e., the "cup" image) is retained, but the words "of suffering" are added to clarify the meaning.

Writing in Greek, the New Testament authors used words that had a long history in the secular world, but they invested them with Christian meanings, as when John referred to Jesus as "the Logos." It was a perilous procedure, because "logos" had a wide variety of meanings in Greek literature and philosophy, and non-Christian associations doubtlessly clung to the word. So John set the title within a teaching context, affirming that the

Logos was in the beginning, was with God, was God, was the agent of creation, was the light and life of men, and became a human being (John 1:1-14). Similarly, some Indian Christians have taken the risk of borrowing the Sanskrit word "avatar" (descent), used in Hinduism for the so-called "incarnations" of Vishnu, and applied it, with careful explanatory safeguards, to the unique incarnation of God in Jesus Christ. But others have refused to do so, on the ground that no safeguards are adequate to prevent misinterpretation.

(c) The normative nature of Scripture.

The Lausanne Covenant declares that Scripture is "without error in all that it affirms" (para. 2). This lays upon us the serious exegetical task of discerning exactly what Scripture is affirming. The essential meaning of the biblical message must at all costs be retained. Though some of the original forms in which this meaning was expressed may be changed for the sake of cross-cultural communication, we believe that they too have a certain normative quality. For God himself chose them as wholly appropriate vehicles of his revelation. So each fresh formulation and explanation in every generation and culture must be checked for faithfulness by referring back to the original.

(d) The cultural conditioning of Scripture.

We have not been able to devote as much time as we would have liked to the problem of the cultural conditioning of Scripture. We are agreed that some biblical commands (e.g., regarding the veiling of women in public and washing one another's feet) refer to cultural customs now obsolete in many parts of the world. Faced by such texts, we believe the right response is neither a slavishly literal obedience nor an irresponsible disregard, but rather first a critical discernment of the text's inner meaning and then a translation of it into our own culture. For example, the inner meaning of the command to wash each other's feet is that mutual love must express itself in humble service. So in some cultures we may clean each other's shoes instead. We are clear that the purpose of such "cultural transposition" is not to avoid obedience but rather to make it contemporary and authentic.

The controversial question of the status of women was not debated at our Consultation. But we acknowledge the need to search for an understanding which attempts with integrity to do justice to all the biblical teaching, and which sees the relations between men and women as being both rooted in the created order and at the same time wonderfully transformed by the new order which Jesus introduced.

(e) The continuing work of the Holy Spirit.

Does our emphasis on the finality and permanent normativeness of Scripture mean that we think the Holy Spirit has now ceased to operate? No, indeed not. But the nature of his teaching ministry has changed. We believe that his work of "inspiration" is done, in the sense that the canon of Scripture is closed, but that his work of "illumination" continues both in every conversion (e.g., 2 Cor. 4:6) and in the life of the Christian and the church. So we need constantly to pray that he will enlighten the eyes of our hearts so that we may know the fulness of God's purpose for us (Eph. 1:17ff) and may be not timorous but courageous in making decisions and undertaking fresh tasks today.

We have been made aware that the experience of the Holy Spirit revealing the application of God's truth to personal and church life is often less vivid than it should be; we all need a more sensitive openness at this point.

Questions for Discussion

1. The commands of Genesis 1:26-28 are sometimes referred to as "the cultural mandate" which God gave to mankind. How responsibly is it being fulfilled today?
2. In the light of the definition of culture in Section 2, what are the main distinctive elements of your own culture?
3. If you know two languages, make up a sentence in one and then try to find a "dynamic equivalence" translation of it into the other.
4. Give other examples of "cultural transposition" (see 3d), which preserve the biblical text's "inner meaning" but transpose it into your own culture.

4. Understanding God's Word Today

The cultural factor is present not only in God's self-revelation in Scripture, but also in our interpretation of it. To this subject we now turn. All Christians are concerned to understand God's word, but there are different ways of trying to do so.

(a) Traditional approaches

The commonest way is to come straight to the words of the biblical text, and to study them without any awareness that the writer's cultural context differs from the reader's. The reader interprets the text as if it had been written in his own language, culture and time.

We recognize that much Scripture can be read and understood in this way, especially if the translation is good. For God intended his word for ordinary people; it is not to be regarded as the preserve of scholars; the central truths of salvation are plain for all to see; Scripture is "useful for teaching the truth, rebuking error, correcting faults, and giving instruction for right living" (2 Tim. 3:16, TEV); and the Holy Spirit has been given to be our teacher.

The weakness of this "popular" approach, however, is that it does not seek first to understand the text in its original context; and, therefore, it runs the risk of missing the real meaning God intends and of substituting another.

A second approach takes with due seriousness the original historical and cultural context. It seeks also to discover what the text meant in its original language, and how it relates to the rest of Scripture. All this is an essential discipline because God spoke his word to a particular people in a particular context and time. So our understanding of God's message will grow when we probe deeply into these matters.

The weakness of this "historical" approach, however, is that it fails to consider what Scripture may be saying to the contemporary reader. It stops short at the meaning of the Bible in its own time and culture. It is thus liable to analyse the text without applying it, and to acquire academic knowledge without obedience. The interpreter may also tend to exaggerate the possibility of complete objectivity and ignore his or her own cultural presuppositions.

(b) The contextual approach

A third approach begins by combining the positive elements of both the "popular" and the "historical" approaches. From the "historical" it takes the necessity of studying the original context and language, and from the "popular" the necessity of listening to God's word and obeying it. But it goes further than this. It takes seriously the cultural context of the contemporary readers as well as of the biblical text, and recognizes that a dialogue must develop between the two.

It is the need for this dynamic interplay between text and interpreters which we wish to emphasize. Today's readers cannot come to the text in a personal vacuum, and should not try to. Instead, they should come with an awareness of concerns stemming from their cultural background, personal situation, and responsibility to others. These concerns will influence the questions which are put to the Scriptures. What is received back, however, will not be answers only, but more questions. As we address Scripture, Scripture addresses us. We find that our culturally conditioned presuppositions are being challenged and our questions corrected. In fact, we are compelled to reformulate our previous questions and to ask fresh ones. So the living interaction proceeds.

In this process of interaction our knowledge of God and our response to his will are continuously being deepened. The more we come to know him, the greater our responsibility becomes to obey him in our own situation, and the more we respond obediently, the more he makes himself known.

It is this continous growth in knowledge, love and obedience which is the purpose and profit of the "contextual" approach. Out of the context in which his word was originally given, we hear God speaking to us in our contemporary context, and we find it a transforming experience. This process is a kind of upward spiral in which Scripture remains always central and normative.

(c) The learning community

We wish to emphasize that the task of understanding the Scriptures belongs not just to individuals but to the whole Christian community, seen as both a contemporary and a historical fellowship.

There are many ways in which the local or regional church can come to discern God's will in its own culture today. Christ still appoints pastors and teachers in his church. And in answer to expectant prayer he speaks to his people, especially through the preaching of his word in the context of worship. In addition, there is a place for "teaching and admonishing one another" (Col. 3:16) both in group Bible studies and in consulting sister churches, as well as for the quiet listening to the voice of God in the Scriptures, which is an indispensable element in the believer's Christian life.

The church is also a historical fellowship and has received from the past a rich inheritance of Christian theology, liturgy and devotion. No group of believers can disregard this heritage without risking spiritual impoverishment. At the same time, this tradition must not be received uncritically, whether it comes in the form of a set of denominational distinctives or in any other way, but rather be tested by the Scripture it claims to expound. Nor must it be imposed on any church, but rather be made available to those who can use it as a valuable resource material, as a counterbalance to the spirit of independence, and as a link with the universal church.

Thus the Holy Spirit instructs his people through a variety of teachers of both the past and the present. We need each other. It is only "with all the saints" that we can begin to comprehend the full dimensions of God's love (Eph. 3:18,19). The Spirit "illumines the minds of God's people in every culture to perceive its (that is, the Scripture's) truth freshly through their own eyes and thus discloses to the whole church ever more of the many-coloured wisdom of God" (Lausanne Covenant, para. 2, echoing Eph. 3:10).

(d) The silences of Scripture

We have also considered the problem of Scripture silences, that is, those areas of doctrine and ethics on which the Bible has nothing explicit to say. Written in the ancient Jewish and Graeco-Roman world, Scripture does not address itself directly, for example, to Hinduism, Buddhism, or Islam today, or to Marxist socio-economic theory, or modern technology. Nevertheless, we believe it is right for the church guided by the Holy Spirit to search the Scriptures for precedents and principles which will enable it to develop the mind of the Lord Christ and so be able to make authentically Christian decisions. This process will go on most fruitfully within the believing community as it worships God and engages in active obedience in the world. We repeat that Christian obedience is as much a prelude to understanding as a consequence of it.

Questions for Discussion

1. Can you recall any examples of how either of the two "traditional approaches" to Bible reading had led you astray?
2. Choose a well-known text like Matthew 6:24-34 (anxiety and ambition) or Luke 10:25-38 (the Good Samaritan) and use the "contextual approach" in studying it. Let a dialogue develop between you and the text, as you question it and it questions you. Write down the stages of the interaction.
3. Read Sections 3e and 4c, and then discuss practical ways of seeking the guidance of the Holy Spirit today.

5. The Content and Communication of the Gospel

Having thought about God's communication of the gospel to us in Scripture, we now come to the very heart of our concern, our responsibility to communicate it to others, that is, to evangelize. But before we consider the communication of the gospel, we have to consider the content of the gospel which is to be communicated. For "to evangelize is to spread the good news--" (Lausanne Covenant, para. 4). Therefore there can be no evangelism without the evangel.

(a) The Bible and the gospel

The gospel is to be found in the Bible. In fact, there is a sense in which the whole Bible is gospel, from Genesis to Revelation. For its overriding purpose throughout is to bear witness to Christ, to proclaim the good news that he is lifegiver and Lord, and to persuade people to trust in him (e.g., John 5:39,40; 20:31; 2 Tim. 3:15).

The Bible proclaims the gospel story in many forms. The gospel is like a multi-faceted diamond, with different aspects that appeal to different people in different cultures. It has depths we have not fathomed. It defies every attempt to reduce it to a neat formulation.

(b) The heart of the gospel

Nevertheless, it is important to identify what is at the heart of the gospel. We recognize as central the themes of God as Creator, the universality of sin, Jesus Christ as Son of God, Lord of all, and Saviour through his atoning death and risen life, the necessity of conversion, the coming of the Holy Spirit and his transforming power, the fellowship and mission of the Christian church, and the hope of Christ's return.

While these are basic elements of the gospel, it is necessary to add that no theological statement is culture-free. Therefore, all theological formulations must be judged by the Bible itself, which stands above them all. Their value must be judged by their faithfulness to it as well as by the relevance with which they apply its message to their own culture.

In our desire to communicate the gospel effectively, we are often made aware of those elements in it which people dislike. For example, the cross has always been both an offense to the proud and folly to the wise. But Paul did not on that account eliminate it from his message. On the contrary, he continued to proclaim it, with faithfulness and at the risk of persecution, confident that Christ crucified is the wisdom and the power of God. We too, although concerned to contextualize our message and remove from it all unnecessary offense, must resist the temptation to accommodate it to human pride or prejudice. It has been given to us. Our responsibility is not to edit it but to proclaim it.

(c) Cultural barriers to the communication of the gospel

No Christian witness can hope to communicate the gospel if he or she ignores the cultural factor. This is particularly true in the case of missionaries. For they are themselves the product of one culture and go to people who are the products of another. So inevitably they are involved in cross-cultural communication, with all its exciting challenge and exacting demand. Two main problems face them.

Sometimes people resist the gospel not because they think it false but because they perceive it as a threat to their culture, especially the fabric of their society, and their national or tribal solidarity. To some extent this cannot be avoided. Jesus Christ is a disturber as well as a peacemaker. He is Lord, and demands our total allegiance. Thus, some first-century Jews saw the gospel as undermining Judaism and accused Paul of "teaching men everywhere against the people, the law, and this place," i.e., the temple (Acts 21:28). Similarly, some first-century Romans feared for the stability of the state, since in their view the Christian missionaries, by saying that "there is another King, Jesus," were being disloyal to Caesar and advocating customs which it was not lawful for Romans to practise (Acts 16:21; 17:7). Still today Jesus challenges many of the cherished beliefs and customs of every culture and society.

At the same time, there are features of every culture which are not incompatible with the lordship of Christ, and which therefore need not be threatened or discarded, but rather preserved and transformed. Messengers of the gospel need to develop a deep understanding of the local culture, and a genuine appreciation of it. Only then will they be able to perceive whether the resistance is to some unavoidable challenge of Jesus Christ or to some threat to the culture which, whether imaginary or real, is not necessary.

The other problem is that the gospel is often presented to people in alien cultural forms. Then the missionaries are resented and their message rejected because their work is seen not as an attempt to evangelize but as an attempt to impose their own customs and way of life. Where missionaries bring with them foreign ways of thinking and behaving, or attitudes of racial superiority, paternalism, or preoccupation with material things, effective communication will be precluded.

Sometimes these two cultural blunders are committed together, and messengers of the gospel are guilty of a cultural imperialism which both undermines the local culture unnecessarily and seeks to impose an alien culture instead. Some of the missionaries who accompanied the Catholic *conquistadores* of Latin America and the Protestant colonizers of Africa and Asia are historical examples of this double mistake. By contrast, the apostle Paul remains the supreme example of one whom Jesus Christ first stripped of pride in his own cultural privileges (Phil. 3:4-9) and then taught to adapt to the cultures of others, making himself their slave and becoming "all things to all men" in order by all means to save some (1 Cor. 9:19-23).

(d) Cultural sensitivity in communicating the gospel

Sensitive cross-cultural witnesses will not arrive at their sphere of service with a pre-packaged gospel. They must have a clear grasp of the "given" truth of the gospel. But they will fail to communicate successfully if they try to impose this on people without reference to their own cultural situation and that of the people to whom they go. It is only by active, loving engagement with the local people, thinking in their thought patterns, understanding their world-view, listening to their questions, and feeling their burdens, that the whole believing community (of which the missionary is a part) will be able to respond to their need. By common prayer, thought and heart-searching, in dependence on the Holy Spirit, expatriate and local believers may learn together how to present Christ and contextualize the gospel with an equal degree of faithfulness and relevance. We are not claiming that it will be easy, although some Third World cultures have a natural affinity to biblical culture. But we believe that fresh creative understandings do emerge when the Spirit-led believing community is listening and reacting sensitively to both the truth of Scripture and the needs of the world.

(e) Christian witness in the Islamic world

Concern was expressed that insufficient attention had been given at our Consultation to the distinctive problems of the Christian mission in the Islamic world, though there are approximately 600 million Muslims today. On the one hand, a resurgence of Islamic faith and mission is taking place in many lands; on the other hand, there is a new openness to the Gospel in a number of communities which are weakening their ties to traditional Islamic culture.

There is a need to recognize the distinctive features of Islam which provide a unique opportunity for Christian witness. Although there are in Islam elements which are incompatible with the gospel, there are also elements with a degree of what has been called "convertibility." For instance, our Christian understanding of God, expressed in Luther's great cry related to justification, "Let God be God," might well serve as an inclusive definition of Islam. The Islamic faith in divine unity, the emphasis on man's obligation to render God a right worship, and the utter rejection of idolatry could also be regarded as being in line with God's purpose for human life as revealed in Jesus Christ. Contemporary Christian witnesses should learn humbly and expectantly to identify, appreciate and illuminate these and other values. They should also wrestle for the transformation—and, where possible, integration—of all that is relevant in Islamic worship, prayer, fasting, art, architecture, and calligraphy.

All this proceeds only within a realistic appreciation of the present situation of the Islamic countries characterized by technological development and secularization. The social liabilities of new wealth and traditional poverty, the tensions of political independence, and the tragic Palestinian dispersion and frustration--all of these afford areas of relevant Christian witness. The last has given birth to much passionate poetry, one note in which is the paradigm of the suffering Jesus. These and other elements call for a new Christian sensitivity and a real awareness of the habits of introversion under which the church has for so long laboured in the Middle East. Elsewhere, not least in sub-Sahara Africa, attitudes are more flexible and possibilities more fluid.

In order to fulfill more adequately the missionary challenge, fresh attempts are needed to develop ways of association of believers and seekers, if need be outside the traditional church forms. The crux of a lively, evangelizing sense of responsibility towards Muslims will always be the quality of Christian personal and corporate discipleship and the constraining love of Christ.

(f) An expectation of results

Messengers of the gospel who have proved in their own experience that it is "the power of God for salvation" (Rom. 1:16) rightly expect it to be so in the experience of others also. We confess that sometimes, just as a Gentile centurion's faith put to shame the unbelief of Israel in Jesus' day (Matt. 8:10), so today the believing expectancy of Christians in other cultures sometimes shows up the missionary's lack of faith. So we remind ourselves of God's promises through Abraham's posterity to bless all the families of the earth and through the gospel to save those who believe (Gen. 12:1-4; 1 Cor. 1:21). It is on the basis of these and many other promises that we remind all messengers of the gospel, including ourselves, to look to God to save people and to build his church.

At the same time, we do not forget our Lord's warnings of opposition and suffering. Human hearts are hard. People do not always embrace the gospel, even when the communication is blameless in technique and the communicator in character. Our Lord himself was fully at home in the culture in which he preached, yet he and his message were despised and rejected, and his Parable of the Sower seems to warn us that most of the good seed we sow will not bear fruit. There is a mystery here we cannot fathom. "The Spirit blows where he wills" (John 3:8). While seeking to communicate the gospel with care, faithfulness and zeal, we leave the results to God in humility.

Questions for Discussion

1. In Section 5 a and b the Report refuses to give a "neat formulation" of the gospel, but identifies its "heart." Would you want to add to these "central themes," or subtract from them, or amplify them?

2. Clarify the "two cultural blunders" of 5 c. Can you think of examples? How can such mistakes be avoided?

3. Think of the cultural situation of the people you are wanting to win for Christ. What would "cultural sensitivity" mean in your case?

6. Wanted: Humble Messengers of the Gospel!

We believe that the principal key to persuasive Christian communication is to be found in the communicators themselves and what kind of people they are. It should go without saying that they need to be people of Christian faith, love, and holiness. That is, they must have a personal and growing experience of the transforming power of the Holy Spirit, so that the image of Jesus Christ is ever more clearly seen in their character and attitudes.

Above all else we desire to see in them, and specially in ourselves, "the meekness and gentleness of Christ" (2 Cor. 10:1), in other words, the humble sensitivity of Christ's love. So important do we believe this to be that we are devoting the whole of this section of our Report to it. Moreover, since, we have no wish to point the finger at anybody but ourselves, we shall use the first person plural throughout. First, we give an analysis of Christian humility in a missionary situation, and secondly, we turn to the Incarnation of God in Jesus Christ as the model we desire by his grace to follow.

(a) An analysis of missionary humility

First, there is the humility to acknowledge the problem which culture presents, and not to avoid or over-simplify it. As we have seen, different cultures have strongly influenced the biblical revelation, ourselves, and the people to whom we go. As a result, we have several personal limitations in communicating the gospel. For we are prisoners (consciously or unconsciously) of our own culture, and our grasp of the cultures both of the Bible and of the country in which we serve is very imperfect. It is the interaction between all these cultures which constitutes the problem of communication; it humbles all who wrestle with it.

Secondly, there is the humility to take the trouble to understand and appreciate the culture of those to whom we go. It is this desire which leads naturally into that true dialogue "whose purpose is to listen sensitively in order to understand" (Lausanne Covenant, para. 4). We repent of the ignorance which assumes that we have all the answers and that our only role is to teach. We have very much to learn. We repent also of judgemental attitudes. We know we should never condemn or despise another culture, but rather respect it. We advocate neither the arrogance which imposes our culture on others, nor the syncretism which mixes the gospel with cultural elements incompatible with it, but rather a humble sharing of the good news—made possible by the mutal respect of a genuine friendship.

Thirdly, there is the humility to begin our communication where people actually are and not where we would like them to be. This is what we see Jesus doing, and we desire to follow his example. Too often we have ignored people's fears and frustrations, their pains and preoccupations, and their hunger, poverty, deprivation or oppression, in fact their "felt needs," and have been too slow to rejoice or to weep with them. We acknowledge that these "felt needs" may sometimes be symptoms of deeper needs which are not immediately felt or recognized by the people. A doctor does not necessarily accept a patient's self-diagnosis. Nevertheless, we see the need to begin where people are, but not to stop there. We accept our responsibility gently and patiently to lead them on to see themselves, as we see ourselves, as rebels to whom the gospel directly speaks with a message of pardon and hope. To begin where people are not is to share an irrelevant message; to stay where people are and never lead them on to the fulness of God's good news, is to share a truncated gospel. The humble sensitivity of love will avoid both errors.

Fourthly, there is the humility to recognize that even the most gifted, dedicated and experienced missionary can seldom communicate the gospel in another language or culture as effectively as a trained local Christian. This 'fact has been acknowledged in recent years by the Bible Societies, whose policy has changed from publishing translations by missionaries (with help from local people) to training mother-tongue specialists to do the translating. Only local Christians can answer the questions, "God, how would you say this in our language?" and "God, what will obedience to you mean in our culture?" Therefore, whether we are translating the Bible or communicating the gospel, local Christians are indispensable. It is they who must assume the responsibility to contextualize the gospel in their own languages and cultures. Would-be cross-cultural witnesses are not on that account necessarily superfluous; but we shall be welcome only if we are humble enough to see good communication as a team enterprise, in which all believers collaborate as partners.

Fifthly, there is the humility to trust in the Holy Spirit of God, who is always the chief communicator, who alone opens the eyes of the blind and brings people to new birth. "Without his witness, ours is futile" (Lausanne Covenant, para. 14).

(b) The Incarnation as a model for Christian witness

We have met for our Consultation within a few days of Christmas, which might be called the most spectacular instance of cultural identification in the history of mankind, since by his Incarnation the Son became a first-century Galilean Jew.

We have also remembered that Jesus intended his people's mission in the world to be modelled on his own. "As the Father has sent me, even so I send you," he said (John 20:21; cf. 17:18). We have asked ourselves, therefore, about the implications of the Incarnation for all of us. The question is of special concern to cross-cultural witnesses, whatever country they go to, although we have thought particularly of those from the West who serve in the Third World.

Meditating on Philippians 2, we have seen that the self-humbling of Christ began in his mind: "he did not count equality with God a thing to be grasped." So we are commanded to let his mind be in us, and in humility of mind to "count" others better or more important than ourselves. This "mind" or "perspective" of Christ is a recognition of the infinite worth of human beings and of the privilege it is to serve them. Those witnesses who have the mind of Christ will have a profound respect for the people they serve, and for their cultures.

Two verbs then indicate the action to which the mind of Christ led him: "he emptied himself...he humbled himself..." The first speaks of sacrifice (what he renounced) and the second of service, even slavery (how he identified himself with us and put himself at our disposal). We have tried to think what these two actions meant for him, and might mean for cross-cultural witnesses.

We began with his *renunciation*. First, the renunciation of status. "Mild he laid his glory by," we have been singing at Christmas. Because we cannot conceive what his eternal glory was like, it is impossible to grasp the greatness of his self-emptying. But certainly he surrendered the rights, privileges, and powers which he enjoyed as God's Son. "Status" and "status symbols" mean much in the modern world, but are incongruous in missionaries. We believe that wherever missionaries are they should not be in control or work alone, but always with—and preferably under—local Christians who can advise and even direct them. And whatever the missionaries' responsibility may be they should express attitudes "not of domination but of service" (Lausanne Covenant, para. 11).

Next the renunciation of independence. We have looked at Jesus--asking a Samaritan woman for water, living in other people's homes and on other people's money because he had none of his own, being lent a boat, a donkey, an upper room, and even being buried in a borrowed tomb. Similarly, cross-cultural messengers, especially during their first years of service, need to learn dependence on others.

Thirdly, the renunciation of immunity. Jesus exposed himself to temptation, sorrow, limitation, economic need, and pain. So the missionary should expect to become vulnerable to new temptations, dangers and diseases, a strange climate, an unaccustomed loneliness, and possibly death.

Turning from the theme of renunciation to that of *identification,* we have marvelled afresh at the completeness of our Saviour's identification with us, particularly as this is taught in the Letter to the Hebrews. He shared our "flesh and blood," was tempted as we are, learned obedience through his sufferings and tasted death for us (Heb. 2:14-18; 4:15; 5:8). During his public ministry Jesus befriended the poor and the powerless, healed the sick, fed the hungry, touched untouchables, and risked his reputation by associating with those whom society rejected.

The extent to which we identify ourselves with the people to whom we go is a matter of controversy. Certainly it must include mastering their language, immersing ourselves in their culture, learning to think as they think, feel as they feel, do as they do. At the socio-economic level we do not believe that we should "go native," principally because a foreigner's attempt to do this may not be seen as authentic but as play-acting. But neither do we think there should be a conspicuous disparity between our life style and that of the people around us. In between these extremes, we see the possibility of developing a standard of living which expresses the kind of love which cares and shares, and which finds it natural to exchange hospitality with others on a basis of reciprocity, without embarassment. A searching test of identification is how far we feel that we belong to the people, and—still more—how far they feel that we belong to them. Do we participate naturally in days of national or tribal thanksgiving or sorrow? Do we groan with them in the oppression which they suffer and join them in their quest for justice and freedom? If the country is struck by earthquake or engulfed in civil war, is our instinct to stay and suffer with the people we love, or to fly home?

Although Jesus identified himself completely with us, he did not lose his own identity. He remained himself. "He came down from heaven...and was made man" (Nicene Creed); yet in becoming one of us he did not cease to be God. Just so, "Christ's evangelists must humbly seek to empty themselves of all but their personal authenticity" (Lausanne Covenant, para. 10). The Incarnation teaches identification without loss of identity. We believe that true self-sacrifice leads to true self-discovery. In humble service there is abundant joy.

Questions for Discussion

1. If the main key to communication lies in the communicators, what sort of people should they be?

2. Give your own analysis of the humility which all Christian witnesses should have. Where would you put your emphasis?

3. Since the Incarnation involved both "renunciation" and "identification," it was obviously very costly for Jesus. What would be the cost of "incarnation evangelism" today?

7. Conversion and Culture

We have thought of the relations between conversion and culture in two ways. First, what effect does conversion have on the cultural situation of converts, the ways they think and act, and their attitudes to their social environment? Secondly, what effect has our culture had on our own understanding of conversion? Both questions are important. But we want to say at once that elements in our traditional evangelical view of conversion are more cultural than biblical and need to be challenged. Too often we have thought of conversion as a crisis, instead of as a process as well; or we have viewed conversion as a largely private experience, forgetting its consequent public and social responsibilities.

(a) The radical nature of conversion

We are convinced that the radical nature of conversion to Jesus Christ needs to be reaffirmed in the contemporary church. For we are always in danger of trivializing it, as if it were no more than a surface change, and a self-reformation at that. But the New Testament authors write of it as the outward expression of a regeneration or new birth by God's Spirit, a re-creation, and resurrection from spiritual death. The concept of resurrection seems to be particularly important. For the resurrection of Jesus Christ from the dead was the beginning of the new creation of God, and by God's grace through union with Christ we have shared in this resurrection. We have therefore entered the new age and have already tasted its powers and its joys. This is the eschatological dimension of Christian conversion. Conversion is an integral part of the Great Renewal which God has begun, and which will be brought to a triumphant climax when Christ comes in his glory.

Conversion involves as well a break with the past so complete that it is spoken of in terms of death. We have been crucified with Christ. Through his cross we have died to the godless world, its outlook, and its standards. We have also "put off" like a soiled garment the old Adam, our former and fallen humanity. And Jesus warned us that this turning away from the past may involve painful sacrifices, even the loss of family and possessions (e.g., Lk. 14:25ff).

It is vital to keep together these negative and positive aspects of conversion, the death and the resurrection, the putting off of the old and the putting on of the new. For we who died are alive again, but alive now with a new life lived in, for, and under Christ.

(b) The lordship of Jesus Christ

We are clear that the fundamental meaning of conversion is a change of allegiance. Other gods and lords--idolatries every one--previously ruled over us. But now Jesus Christ is Lord. The governing principle of the converted life is that it is lived under the lordship of Christ or (for it comes to the same thing) in the Kingdom of God. His authority over us is total. So this new and liberating allegiance leads inevitably to a reappraisal of every aspect of our lives and in particular of our world-view, our behaviour, and our relationships.

First, our world-view. We are agreed that the heart of every culture is a "religion" of some kind, even if it is an irreligious religion like Marxism.

"Culture is religion made visible" (J.H. Bavinck). And "religion" is a whole cluster of basic beliefs and values, which is the reason why for our purposes we are using "world-view" as an equivalent expression. True conversion to Christ is bound, therefore, to strike at the heart of our cultural inheritance. Jesus Christ insists on dislodging from the centre of our world whatever idol previously reigned there, and occupying the throne himself. This is the radical change of allegiance which constitutes conversion, or at least its beginning. Then once Christ has taken his rightful place, everything else starts shifting. The shock waves flow from the centre to the circumference. The convert has to rethink his or her fundamental convictions. This is *metanoia,* "repentance" viewed as a change of mind, the replacement of "the mind of the flesh" by "the mind of Christ." Of course, the development of an integrated Christian world-view may take a lifetime, but it is there in essence from the start. If it does grow, the explosive consequences cannot be predicted.

Secondly, our behaviour. The lordship of Jesus challenges our moral standards and whole ethical life style. Strictly speaking, this is not "repentance" but rather the "fruit that befits repentance" (Matt. 3:8), the change of conduct which issues from a change of outlook. Both our minds and our wills must submit to the obedience of Christ (cf. 2 Cor. 10:5; Matt. 11:29,30; John 13:13).

Listening to case-studies of conversion we have been impressed by the primacy of love in the new convert's experience. Conversion delivers both from the inversion which is too preoccupied with self to bother about other people and from the fatalism which considers it impossible to help them. Conversion is spurious if it does not liberate us to love.

Thirdly, our relationships. Although the convert should do his utmost to avoid a break with nation, tribe and family, sometimes painful conflicts arise. It is clear also that conversion involves a transfer from one community to another, that is, from fallen humanity to God's new humanity. It happened from the very beginning on the Day of Pentecost: "Save yourselves from this crooked generation," Peter appealed. So those who received his message were baptized into the new society, devoted themselves to the new fellowship, and found that the Lord continued to add to their numbers daily (Acts 2:40-47). At the same time, their "transfer" from one group to another meant rather that they were spiritually distinct than that they were socially segregated. They did not abandon the world. On the contrary, they gained a new commitment to it, and went out into it to witness and to serve.

All of us should cherish great expectations of such radical conversions in our day, involving converts in a new mind, a new way of life, a new community, and a new mission, all under the lordship of Christ. Yet now we feel the need to make several qualifications.

(c) The convert and his culture

Conversion should not "de-culturize" a convert. True, as we have seen, the Lord Jesus now holds his or her allegiance, and everything in the cultural context must come under his Lord's scrutiny. This applies to every culture, not just to those of Hindu, Buddhist, Muslim, or animistic cultures but also to the increasingly materialistic culture of the West. The critique may lead to a collision, as elements of the culture come under the judgement of Christ and have to be rejected. At this point, on the rebound, the convert may try to adopt the evangelist's culture instead; the attempt should be firmly but gently resisted.

The convert should be encouraged to see his or her relation to the past as a combination of rupture and continuity. However much new converts feel they need to renounce for the sake of Christ, they are still the same people with the same heritage and the same family. "Conversion does not unmake; it remakes." It is always tragic, though in some situations it is unavoidable, when a person's conversion to Christ is interpreted by others as treachery to his or her own cultural origins. If possible, in spite of the conflicts with their own culture, new converts should seek to identify with their culture's joys, hopes, pains, and struggles.

Case histories show that converts often pass through three stages: (1) "rejection" (when they see themselves as "new persons in Christ" and repudiate everything associated with their past); (2) "accommodation" (when they discover their ethnic and cultural heritage, with the temptation to compromise the new-found Christian faith in relation to their heritage); and (3) "the re-establishment of identity" (when either the rejection of the past or the accommodation to it may increase, or preferably, they may grow into a balanced self-awareness in Christ and in culture).

(d) The power encounter

"Jesus is Lord" means more than that he is Lord of the individual convert's world-view, standards and relationships, and more even than that he is Lord of culture. It means that he is Lord of the powers, having been exalted by the Father to universal sovereignty, principalities and powers having been made subject to him (1 Peter. 3:22). A number of us, especially those from Asia, Africa, and Latin America, have spoken both of the reality of evil powers and of the necessity to demonstrate the supremacy of Jesus over them. For conversion involves a power encounter. People give their allegiance to Christ when they see that his power is superior to magic and voodoo, the curses and blessings of witch doctors, and the malevolence of evil spirits, and that his salvation is a real liberation from the power of evil and death.

Of course, some are questioning today whether a belief in spirits is compatible with our modern scientific understanding of the universe. We wish to affirm, therefore, against the mechanistic myth on which the typical western world-view rests, the reality of demonic intelligences which are concerned by all means, overt and covert, to discredit Jesus Christ and keep people from coming to him. We think it vital in evangelism in all cultures to teach the reality and hostility of demonic powers, and to proclaim that God has exalted Christ as Lord of all and that Christ, who really does possess all power, however we may fail to acknowledge this, can (as we proclaim him) break through any world-view in any mind to make his lordship known and bring about a radical change of heart and outlook.

We wish to emphasize that the power belongs to Christ. Power in human hands is always dangerous. We have called to mind the recurring theme of Paul's two letters to the Corinthians—that God's power, which is clearly seen in the cross of Christ, operates through human weakness (e.g., 1 Cor. 1:18-2:5; 2 Cor. 4:7; 12:9,10). Worldly people worship power; Christians who have it know its perils. It is better to be weak, for then we are strong. We specially honour the Christian martyrs of recent days (e.g., in East Africa) who have renounced the way of power, and followed the way of the cross.

(e) Individual and group conversions

Conversion should not be conceived as being invariably and only an individual experience, although that has been the pattern of western expectation for many years. On the contrary, the covenant theme of the Old Testament and the household baptisms of the New should lead us to desire, work for, and expect both family and group conversions. Much important research has been undertaken in recent years into "people movements" from both theological and sociological perspectives. Theologically, we recognize the biblical emphasis on the solidarity of each *ethnos*, i.e., nation or people. Sociologically, we recognize that each society is composed of a variety of subgroups, subcultures or homogeneous units. It is evident that people receive the gospel most readily when it is presented to them in a manner which is appropriate—and not alien—to their culture, and when they can respond to it with and among their own people. Different societies have different procedures for making group decisions, e.g., by consensus, by the head of the family, or by a group of elders. We recognize the validity of the corporate dimension of conversion as part of the total process, as well as the necessity for each member of the group ultimately to share in it personally.

(f) Is conversion sudden or gradual?

Conversion is often more gradual than traditional evangelical teaching has allowed. True, this may be only a dispute about words. Justification and regeneration, the one conveying a new status and the other a new life, are works of God and instantaneous, although we are not necessarily aware when they take place. Conversion, on the other hand, is our own action (moved by God's grace) of turning to God in penitence and faith. Although it may include a conscious crisis, it is often slow and sometimes laborious. Seen against the background of the Hebrew and Greek vocabulary, conversion is in essence a turning to God, which continues as all areas of life are brought in increasingly radical ways under the lordship of Christ. Conversion involves the Christian's complete transformation and total renewal in mind and character according to the likeness of Christ (Rom. 12:1,2).

This progress does not always take place, however. We have given some thought to the sad phenomena called "backsliding" (a quiet slipping away from Christ) and "apostasy" (an open repudiation of him). These have a variety of causes. Some people turn away from Christ when they become disenchanted with the church; others capitulate to the pressures of secularism or of their former culture. These facts challenge us both to proclaim a full gospel and to be more conscientious in nurturing converts in the faith and in training them for service.

One member of our Consultation has described his experience in terms of turning first to Christ (receiving his salvation and acknowledging his lordship), secondly to culture (rediscovering his natural origins and identity), and thirdly to the world (accepting the mission on which Christ sends him). We agree that conversion is often a complex experience, and that the biblical language of "turning" is used in different ways and contexts. At the same time, we all emphasize that personal commitment to Jesus Christ is foundational. In him alone we find salvation, new life, and personal identity. Conversion must also result in new attitudes and relationships, and lead to a responsible involvement in our church, our culture, and our world. Finally, conversion is a journey, a pilgrimage, with ever-new challenges, decisions, and returnings to the Lord as the constant point of reference, until he comes.

Questions for Discussion

1. Distinguish between "regeneration" and "conversion" according to the New Testament.
2. "Jesus is Lord." What does this mean for you in your own culture? See Section 7 b and d. What are the elements of your cultural heritage which you feel (a) you must, and (b) you need not, renounce for the sake of Christ?
3. What is sudden and what is (or may be) gradual in Christian conversion?

8. Church and Culture

In the process of church formation, as in the communication and reception of the gospel, the question of culture is vital. If the gospel must be contextualized, so must the church. Indeed, the sub-title of our Consultation has been "the contextualization of Word and Church in a missionary situation."

(a) Older, traditional approaches

During the missionary expansion of the early part of the 19th century, it was generally assumed that churches "on the mission field" would be modelled on churches "at home." The tendency was to produce almost exact replicas. Gothic architecture, prayer book liturgies, clerical dress, musical instruments, hymns and tunes, decision-making processes, synods and committees, superintendents and archdeacons--all were exported and unimaginatively introduced into the new mission-founded churches. It should be added that these patterns were also eagerly adopted by the new Christians, determined not to be at any point behind their western friends, whose habits and ways of worship they had been attentively watching. But all this was based on the false assumptions that the Bible gave specific instructions about such matters and that the home churches' pattern of government, worship, ministry, and life were themselves exemplary.

In reaction to this monocultural export system, pioneer missionary thinkers like Henry Venn and Rufus Anderson in the middle of the last century and Roland Allen earlier in this century popularized the concept of "indigenous" churches, which would be "self-governing, self-supporting and self-propagating." They argued their case well. They pointed out that the policy of the apostle Paul was to plant churches, not to found mission stations. They also added pragmatic arguments to biblical ones, namely that indigeneity was indispensable to the church's growth in maturity and mission. Henry Venn confidently looked forward to the day when missions would hand over all responsibility to national churches, and then what he called "the euthanasia of the mission" would take place. These views gained wide acceptance and were immensely influential.

In our day, however, they are being criticized, not because of the ideal itself, but because of the way it has often been applied. Some missions, for example, have accepted the need for indigenous leadership and have then gone on to recruit and train local leaders, indoctrinating them (the word is harsh but not unfair) in western ways of thought and procedure. These westernized local leaders have then preserved a very western-looking church, and the foreign orientation has persisted, only lightly cloaked by the appearance of indigeneity.

Now, therefore, a more radical concept of indigenous church life needs to be developed, by which each church may discover and express its selfhood as the body of Christ within its own culture.

(b) The dynamic equivalence model

Using the distinctions between "form" and "meaning," and between "formal correspondence" and "dynamic equivalence," which have been developed in translation theory and on which we have commented in Section 3, it is being suggested that an analogy may be drawn between Bible translation and church formation. "Formal correspondence" speaks of a slavish imitation, whether in translating a word into another language or exporting a church model to another culture. Just as a "dynamic equivalence" translation, however, seeks to convey to contemporary readers meanings equivalent to those conveyed to the original readers, by using appropriate cultural forms, so would a "dynamic equivalence" church. It would look in its culture as a good Bible translation looks in its language. It would preserve the essential meanings and functions which the New Testament predicated of the church, but would seek to express these in forms equivalent to the originals but appropriate to the local culture.

We have all found this model helpful and suggestive, and we strongly affirm the ideals it seeks to express. It rightly rejects foreign imports and imitations, and rigid structures. It rightly looks to the New Testament for the principles of church formation, rather than to either tradition or culture, and it equally rightly looks to the local culture for the appropriate forms in which these principles should be expressed. All of us (even those who see limitations in the model) share the vision which it is trying to describe.

Thus, the New Testament indicates that the church is always a worshipping community, "a holy priesthood to offer spiritual sacrifices to God through Jesus Christ" (1 Pet. 2:5), but forms of worship (including the presence or absence of different kinds of liturgy, ceremony, music, colour, drama, etc.) will be developed by the church in keeping with indigenous culture. Similarly, the church is always a witnessing and a serving community, but its methods of evangelism and its programme of social involvement will vary. Again, God desires all churches to have pastoral oversight *(episkopē)*, but forms of government and ministry may differ widely, and the selection, training, ordination, service, dress, payment, and accountability of pastors will be determined by the church to accord with biblical principles and to suit the local culture.

The questions which are being asked about the "dynamic equivalence" model are whether by itself it is large enough and dynamic enough to provide all the guidance which is needed. The analogy between Bible translation and church formation is not exact. In the former the translator controls the work, and when the task is complete it is possible to make a comparison of the two texts. In the latter, however, the original to which an equivalent is being sought is not a detailed text but a series of glimpses of the early church in operation, making the comparison more difficult, and instead of a controlling translator the whole community of faith must be involved. Further, a translator aims at personal objectivity, but when the local church is seeking to relate itself appropriately to the local culture, it finds objectivity almost impossible. In many situations it is caught in "an encounter between two civilizations" (that of its own society and that of the missionaries'). Furthermore, it may have great difficulty in responding to the conflicting voices of the local community. Some clamor for change (in terms of literacy, education, technology, modern medicine, industrialization, etc.), while others insist on the conservation of the old culture and resist the arrival of a new day. It is asked whether the "dynamic equivalence" model is dynamic enough to face this kind of challenge.

The test of this or any other model for helping churches develop appropriately, is whether it can enable God's people to capture in their hearts and minds the grand design of which their church is to be the local expression. Every model presents only a partial picture. Local churches need to rely ultimately on the dynamic pressure of the Living Lord of history. For it is he who will guide his people in every age to develop their church life in such a way as both to obey the instructions he has given in Scripture and to reflect the good elements of their local culture.

(c) The freedom of the church

If each church is to develop creatively in such a way as to find and express itself, it must be free to do so. This is its inalienable right. For each church is God's church. United to Christ, it is a dwelling place of God through his Spirit (Eph. 2:22). Some missions and missionaries have been slow to recognize this, and to accept its implications in the direction of indigenous forms and an every-member ministry. This is one of the many causes which have led to the formation of Independent Churches, notably in Africa, which are seeking new ways of self-expression in terms of local culture.

Although local church leaders have also sometimes impeded indigenous development, the chief blame lies elsewhere. It would not be fair to generalize. The situation has always been diverse. In earlier generations there were missions which never manifested a spirit of domination. In this century some churches have sprung up which have never been under missionary control, having enjoyed self-government from the start. In other cases missions have entirely surrendered their former power, so that some mission-founded churches are now fully autonomous, and many missions now work in genuine partnership with churches.

Yet this is not the whole picture. Other churches are still almost completely inhibited from developing their own identity and programme by policies laid down from afar, by the introduction and continuation of foreign traditions, by the use of expatriate leadership, by alien decision-making processes, and especially by the manipulative use of money. Those who maintain such control may be genuinely unaware of the way in which their actions are regarded and experienced at the other end. They may be felt by the churches concerned to be a tyranny. The fact that this is neither intended nor realized illustrates perfectly how all of us (whether we know it or not) are involved in the culture which has made us what we are. We strongly oppose such "foreignness," wherever it exists, as a serious obstacle to maturity and mission, and a quenching of the Holy Spirit of God.

It was in protest against the continuance of foreign control that a few years ago the call was made to withdraw all missionaries. In this debate some of us want to avoid the word "moratorium" because it has become an emotive term and sometimes betrays a resentment against the very concept of "missionaries." Others of us wish to retain the word in order to emphasize the truth it expresses. To us it means not a rejection of missionary personnel and money in themselves, but only of their misuse in such a way as to suffocate local initiative. We all agree with the statement of the Lausanne Covenant that "a reduction of foreign missionaries and money...may sometimes be necessary to facilitate the national church's growth in self-reliance..." (para. 9).

(d) Power structures and mission

What we have just written is part of a much wider problem, which we have not felt able to ignore. The contemporary world does not consist of isolated atomic societies, but is an interrelated global system of economic, political, technological, and ideological macro-structures, which undoubtedly results in much exploitation and oppression.

What has this got to do with mission? And why do we raise it here? Partly because it is the context within which the gospel must be preached to all nations today. Partly also because nearly all of us either belong to the Third World, or live and work there, or have done so, or have visited some countries in it. So we have seen with our own eyes the poverty of the masses, we feel for them and with them, and we have some understanding that their plight is due in part to an economic system which is controlled mostly by the North Atlantic countries (although others are now also involved). Those of us who are citizens of North American or European countries cannot avoid some feeling of embarrassment and shame, by reason of the oppression in which our countries in various degrees have been involved. Of course, we know that there is oppression in many countries today, and we oppose it everywhere. But now we are talking about ourselves, our own countries, and our responsibility as Christians. Most of the world's missionaries and missionary money come from these countries, often at great personal sacrifice. Yet we have to confess that some missionaries themselves reflect a neo-colonial attitude and even defend it, together with outposts of western power and exploitation such as Southern Africa.

So what should we do? The only honest response is to say that we do not know. Armchair criticism smacks of hypocrisy. We have no ready-made solutions to offer to this worldwide problem. Indeed, we feel victims of the system ourselves. And yet we are also part of it. So we feel able to make only these comments.

First, Jesus himself constantly identified with the poor and weak. We accept the obligation to follow in his footsteps in this matter as in all others. At least by the love which prays and gives we mean to strengthen our solidarity with them.

Jesus did more than identify, however. In his teaching and that of the apostles the corollary of good news to the oppressed was a word of judgement to the oppressor (e.g., Luke 6:24-26; Jas. 5:1-6). We confess that in complex economic situations it is not easy to identify oppressors in order to denounce them without resorting to a shrill rhetoric which neither costs nor accomplishes anything. Nevertheless, we accept that there will be occasions when it is our Christian duty to speak out against injustice in the name of the Lord who is the God of justice as well as of justification. We shall seek from him the courage and wisdom to do so.

Thirdly, this Consultation has expressed its concern about syncretism in Third World churches. But we have not forgotten that western churches fall prey to the same sin. Indeed, perhaps the most insidious form of syncretism in the world today is the attempt to mix a privatized gospel of personal forgiveness with a worldly (even demonic) attitude to wealth and power. We are not guiltless in this matter ourselves. Yet we desire to be integrated Christians for whom Jesus is truly Lord of all. So we who belong to, or come from, the West will examine ourselves and seek to purge ourselves of western-style syncretism. We agree that "the salvation we claim should be transforming us in the totality of our personal and social responsibilities. Faith without works is dead" (Lausanne Covenant, para. 5).

(e) The danger of provincialism

We have emphasized that the church must be allowed to indigenize itself, and to "celebrate, sing and dance" the gospel in its own cultural medium. At the same time, we wish to be alert to the dangers of this process. Some churches in all six continents go beyond a joyful and thankful discovery of their local cultural heritage, and either become boastful and assertive about it (a form of chauvinism) or even absolutize it (a form of idolatry). More common than either of these extremes, however, is "provincialism," that is, such a retreat into their own culture as cuts them adrift from the rest of the church and from the wider world. This is a frequent stance in western churches as well as in the Third World. It denies the God of creation and redemption. It is to proclaim one's freedom, only to enter another bondage. We draw attention to the three major reasons why we think this attitude should be avoided.

First, each church is part of the universal church. The people of God are by his grace a unique multi-racial, multi-national, multi-cultural community. This community is God's new creation, his new humanity, in which Christ has abolished all barriers (see Ephesians 2 and 3). There is therefore no room for racism in the Christian society, or for tribalism—whether in its African form, or in the form of European social classes, or of the Indian caste system. Despite the church's failures, this vision of a supra-ethnic community of love is not a romantic ideal, but a command of the Lord. Therefore, while rejoicing in our cultural inheritance and developing our own indigenous forms, we must always remember that our primary identity as Christians is not in our particular culture but in the one Lord and his one body (Eph. 4:3-6).

Secondly, each church worships the living God of cultural diversity. If we thank him for our cultural heritage, we should thank him for others' also. Our church should never become so culture-bound that visitors from another culture do not feel welcome. Indeed, we believe it is enriching for Christians, if they have the opportunity, to develop a bi-cultural and even a multi-cultural existence, like the apostle Paul who was both a Hebrew of the Hebrews, a master of the Greek language, and a Roman citizen.

Thirdly, each church should enter into a "partnership...in giving and receiving" (Phil. 4:15). No church is, or should try to become, self-sufficient. So churches should develop with each other relationships of prayer, fellowship, interchange of ministry and cooperation. Provided that we share the same central truths (including the supreme lordship of Christ, the authority of the Scriptures, the necessity of conversion, confidence in the power of the Holy Spirit, and the obligations of holiness and witness), we should be outgoing and not timid in seeking fellowship; and we should share our spiritual gifts and ministries, knowledge, skills, experience, and financial resources. The same principle applies to cultures. A church must be free to reject alien cultural forms and develop its own; it should also feel free to borrow from others. This way lies maturity.

One example of this concerns theology. Cross-cultural witnesses must not attempt to impose a ready-made theological tradition on the church in which they serve, either by personal teaching or by literature or by controlling seminary and Bible college curricula. For every theological tradition both contains elements which are biblically questionable and have been ecclesiastically divisive and omits elements which, while they might be of no great consequence in the country where it originated, may be of immense importance in other contexts. At the same time, although missionaries ought not to impose their own tradition on others, they also ought not to deny them access to it (in the form of books, confessions, catechism, liturgies and hymns), since it doubtless represents a rich heritage of faith. Moreover, although the theological controversies of the older churches should not be exported to the younger churches, yet an understanding of the issues, and of the work of the Holy Spirit in the unfolding history of Christian doctrine, should help to protect them from unprofitable repetition of the same battles.

Thus we should seek with equal care to avoid theological imperialism or theological provincialism. A church's theology should be developed by the community of faith out of the Scripture in interaction with other theologies of the past and present, and with the local culture and its needs.

(f) The danger of syncretism

As the church seeks to express its life in local cultural forms, it soon has to face the problem of cultural elements which either are evil or have evil associations. How should the church react to these? Elements which are intrinsically false or evil clearly cannot be assimilated into Christianity without a lapse into syncretism. This is a danger for all churches in all cultures. If the evil is in the association only, however, we believe it is right to seek to "baptize" it into Christ. It is the principle on which William Booth operated when he set Christian words to popular music, asking why the devil should have all the best tunes. Thus many African churches now use drums to summon people to worship, although previously they were unacceptable, as being associated with war dances and mediumistic rites.

Yet this principle raises problems. In a proper reaction against foreigners, an improper flirtation with the demonic element of local culture sometimes takes place. So the church, being first and foremost a servant of Jesus Christ, must learn to scrutinize all culture, both foreign and local, in the light of his lordship and God's revelation. By what guidelines, therefore, does a church accept or reject culture traits in the process of contextualization? How does it prevent or detect and eliminate heresy (wrong teaching) and syncretism (harmful carry-overs from the old way of life)? How does it protect itself from becoming a "folk church" in which church and society are virtually synonymous?

One particular model we have studied is that of the church in Bali, Indonesia, which is now about 40 years old. Its experience has provided the following guidelines:

The believing community first searched the Scriptures and learned from them many important biblical truths. They then observed that other churches (e.g., round the Mediterranean) used architecture to symbolize Christian truth. This was important because the Balinese are very "visual" people and value visible signs. So it was decided, for example, to express their affirmation of faith in the Trinity in a Balinese-style three-tiered roof for their church buildings. The symbol was first considered by the council of elders who, after studying both biblical and cultural factors, recommended it to local congregations.

The detection and elimination of heresy followed a similar pattern. When believers suspected an error in life or teaching, they would report it to an elder, who would take it to the council of elders. Having considered the matter, they in their turn passed their recommendations to the local churches who had the final word.

What was the most important safeguard of the church? To this question the answer was: "we believe that Jesus Christ is Lord and Master of all powers." By preaching his power, "the same yesterday and today and forever," by insisting at all times on the normative nature of the Scriptures, by entrusting elders with the obligation to reflect on Scripture and culture, by breaking down all barriers to fellowship, and by building into structures, catechism, art forms, drama, etc., constant reminders of the exalted position of Jesus Christ, his church has been preserved in truth and holiness.

Sometimes, in different parts of the world, a cultural element may be adopted which deeply disturbs oversensitive consciences, especially those of new converts. This is the problem of the "weaker brother" of whom Paul writes in connection with idol-meats. Since idols were nothing, Paul himself had liberty of conscience to eat these meats. But for the sake of "weaker" Christians with a less well-educated conscience, who would be offended to see him eat, he refrained, at least in specific situations in which such offence might be caused. The principle still applies today. Scripture takes conscience seriously and tells us not to violate it. It needs to be educated in order to become "strong," but while it remains "weak" it must be respected. A strong conscience will give us freedom; but love limits liberty.

(g) The church's influence on culture

We deplore the pessimism which leads some Christians to disapprove of active cultural engagement in the world, and the defeatism which persuades others that they could do no good there anyway and should therefore wait in inactivity for Christ to put things right when he comes. Many historical examples could be given, drawn from different ages and countries, of the powerful influence which—under God—the church has exerted on a prevailing culture, purging, claiming, and beautifying it for Christ. Though all such attempts have had defects, they do not prove the enterprise mistaken.

We prefer, however, to base the church's cultural responsibility on Scripture rather than on history. We have reminded ourselves that our fellow men and women are made in God's image, and that we are commanded to honour, love, and serve them in every sphere of life. To this argument from God's creation we add another from his kingdom which broke into the world through Jesus Christ. All authority belongs to Christ. He is lord of both universe and church. And he has sent us into the world to be its salt and light. As his new community, he expects us to permeate society.

Thus we are to challenge what is evil and affirm what is good; to welcome and seek to promote all that is wholesome and enriching in art, science, technology, agriculture, industry, education, community development and social welfare; to denounce injustice and support the powerless and the oppressed; to spread the good news of Jesus Christ, which is the most liberating and humanizing force in the world; and actively to engage in good works of love. Although, in social and cultural activity as in evangelism, we must leave the results to God, we are confident that he will bless our endeavors and use them to develop in our community a new consciousness of what is "true, noble, right, pure, lovely, and honourable" (Phil. 4:8, TEV). Of course, the church cannot impose Christian standards on an unwilling society, but it can commend them by both argument and example. All this will bring glory to God and greater opportunities of humanness to our fellow human beings whom he made and loves. As the Lausanne Covenant put it, "churches must seek to transform and enrich culture, all for the glory of God" (para. 10).

Nevertheless, naive optimism is as foolish as dark pessimism. In place of both, we seek a sober Christian realism. On the one hand, Jesus Christ reigns. On the other, he has not yet destroyed the forces of evil; they still rampage. So in every culture Christians find themselves in a situation of conflict and often of suffering. We are called to fight against the "cosmic powers of this dark age" (Eph. 6:12, TEV). So we need each other. We must put on all God's armour, and especially the mighty weapon of believing prayer. We also remember the warnings of Christ and his apostles that before the end there will be an unprecedented outbreak of wickedness and violence. Some events and developments in our contemporary world indicate that the spirit of the coming Antichrist is already at work not only in the non-Christian world, but both in our own partially Christianized societies and even in the churches themselves. "We therefore reject as a proud, self-confident dream the notion that man can ever build a utopia on earth" (Lausanne Covenant, para. 15), and as a groundless fantasy that society is going to evolve into perfection.

Instead, while energetically labouring on earth, we look forward with joyful anticipation to the return of Christ, and to the new heavens and new earth in which righteousness will dwell. For then not only will culture be transformed, as the nations bring their glory into the New Jerusalem (Rev. 21:24-26) but the whole creation will be liberated from its present bondage of futility, decay and pain, so as to share the glorious freedom of God's children (Rom. 8:18-25, TEV). Then at last every knee will bow to Christ and every tongue openly proclaim that he is Lord, to the glory of God the Father (Phil. 2:9-11).

Questions for Discussion

1. Is your local church "free" to develop its own selfhood? If not, what forces are hindering it? See Section 8 a-d.
2. Section 8 d has some hard things to say about "power-structures." Do you agree? If so, can you do anything about it?
3. "Provincialism" (8 e) and "syncretism" (8 f) are both mistakes of a church which is trying to express its identity in local cultural forms. Is your church making either mistake? How can they be avoided without repudiating indigenous culture?
4. Should the church in your country be doing more to "transform and enrich" its national culture? If so, in what way?

9. Culture, Christian Ethics and Life Style

Having considered in Section 7 some of the cultural factors in Christian conversion, we come finally to the relations between culture and Christian ethical behaviour. For the new life Christ gives his people is bound to issue in a new life style.

(a) Christ-centredness and Christ-likeness

One of the themes running right through our Consultation has been the supreme Lordship of Jesus Christ. He is Lord of the universe and the church; he is Lord of the individual believer also. We find ourselves gripped by the love of Christ. It hems us in and leaves us no escape. Because we enjoy newness of life through his death for us, we have no alternative (and desire none) but to live for him who died for us and rose again (2 Cor. 5:14,15). Our first loyalty is to him, to seek to please him, to live a life worthy of him, and to obey him. This necessitates the renunciation of all lesser loyalties. So we are forbidden to conform ourselves to this world's standards, that is, to any prevailing culture which fails to honour God, and are commanded instead to be transformed in our conduct by renewed minds which perceive the will of God.

God's will was perfectly obeyed by Jesus. Therefore, "the most outstanding thing about a Christian should not be his culture, but his Christlikeness." As the mid-second century *Letter to Diognetus* put it: "Christians are not distinguished from the rest of mankind by country or by speech or by customs...they follow the customs of the land in clothing and food and other matters of daily life, yet the condition of citizenship which they exhibit is wonderful...In a word, what the soul is in the body, that Christians are in the world."

(b) Moral standards and cultural practices

Culture is never static. It varies both from place to place and from time to time. And throughout the long history of the church in different countries, Christianity has, in some measure, destroyed culture, preserved it, and in the end created a new culture in place of the old. So everywhere Christians need to think seriously about just how their new life in Christ should relate to contemporary culture.

In our Consultation's preliminary papers two rather similar models were set before us. One suggested that there are several categories of customs which need to be distinguished. The first includes those practices which the convert will be expected to renounce immediately as being wholly incompatible with the Christian gospel (e.g., idolatry, the possession of slaves, witchcraft and sorcery, head hunting, blood feuds, ritual prostitution, and all personal discriminations based on race, colour, class or caste). A second category might comprise institutionalized customs which could be tolerated for a while but would be expected to disappear gradually (e.g., systems of caste, slavery, and polygamy). A third category might relate to marriage traditions, especially questions of consanguinity, on which the churches are divided, while into a fourth category would be put the so-called *adiaphora* or "matters indifferent," which relate only to customs and not to morals, and therefore may be preserved without any compromise (e.g., eating and bathing customs, forms of public greeting to the opposite sex, hair and dress styles, etc.).

The second model we have considered distinguishes between "direct" and "indirect" encounters between Christ and culture, which correspond approximately to the first and second categories of the other model. Applied to 19th century Fiji in the case-study presented to us, it was assumed that there would be "direct encounter" with such inhuman practices as cannibalism, widow-strangling, infanticide, and patricide, and that converts would be expected to abandon these customs upon conversion. "Indirect" encounter would take place, however, either when the moral issue was not so clear-cut (e.g., some marriage customs, initiation rites, festivals and musical celebrations involving song, dance and instruments) or when it becomes apparent only after the convert has begun to work out his or her new faith in the applied Christian life. Some of these practices will not need to be discarded, but rather to be purged of unclean elements and invested with Christian meaning. Old customs can be given new symbolism, old dances can celebrate new blessings, and old crafts can serve new purposes. To borrow an expression from the Old Testament, swords can be hammered into ploughs and spears into pruning-knives.

The Lausanne Covenant said: "The Gospel does not presuppose the superiority of any culture to another, but evaluates all cultures according to its own criteria of truth and righteousness, and insists on moral absolutes in every culture" (para. 10). We wish to endorse this, and to emphasize that even in this present age of relativity moral absolutes remain. Indeed, churches which study the Scriptures should not find it difficult to discern what belongs to the first or "direct encounter" category. Scriptural principles under the guidance of the Holy Spirit will also guide them regarding the category of "indirect encounter." An additional test proposed is to ask whether a practice enhances or diminishes human life.

It will be seen that our studies have focussed mainly on situations where younger churches have to take up a moral stance against certain evils. But we have been reminded that the church needs to confront evil in western culture too. In the 20th century West, often more sophisticated but no less horrible examples of the evils which were opposed in 19th century Fiji exist. Parallel to cannibalism is social injustice which "eats" the poor; to widow-strangling, the oppression of women; to infanticide, abortion; to patricide, a criminal neglect of senior citizens; to tribal wars, World Wars I and II; and to ritual prostitution, sexual promiscuity. In considering this parallelism, it is necessary to remember both the added guilt adhering to the nominally Christian nations, and also the courageous Christian protest against such evils, and the immense (though incomplete) successes which have been won in mitigating these evils. Evil takes many forms, but it is universal, and wherever it appears Christians must confront and repudiate it.

(c) The process of cultural change

It is not enough for converts to make a personal renunciation of the evils in their culture; the whole church needs to work for their elimination. Hence, the importance of asking how cultures change under the influence of the gospel. Of course, the evil and the demonic are deeply entrenched in most cultures, and yet Scripture calls for national repentance and reform, and history records numerous cases of cultural change for the better. In fact, in some cases culture is not as resistant to necessary change as it may appear. Great care is needed, however, when seeking to initiate it.

First, "people change as and when they want to." This seems to be axiomatic. Further, they want to change only when they perceive the positive benefits which change will bring them. These will need to be carefully argued and patiently demonstrated, whether Christians are advocating in a developing country the benefits of literacy or the value of clean water, or in a western country the importance of stable marriage and family life.

Secondly, cross-cultural witnesses in the Third World need to have great respect for the in-built mechanisms of social change in general, and for the "correct procedures of innovation" in each particular culture.

Thirdly, it is important to remember that virtually all customs perform important functions within the culture, and that even socially undesirable practices may perform "constructive" functions. That being so, a custom should never be abolished without first discerning its function and then substituting another custom which performs the same function. For example, it may be right to wish to see abolished some of the initiatory rites associated with the circumcision of adolescents and some of the forms of sex education which accompany it. This is not to deny that there is much of value in the processes of initiation; great care must be taken to see that adequate substitutes are provided for the rites and forms of initiation which the Christian conscience would desire to see abolished.

Fourthly, it is essential to recognize that some cultural practices have a theological undergirding. When this is so, the culture will change only when the theology changes. Thus, if widows are killed in order that their husbands may not enter the next world unattended, or if older people are killed before senility overtakes them, in order that in the next world they may be strong enough to fight and hunt, then such killings, because founded on a false eschatology, will be abandoned only when a better alternative, the Christian hope, is accepted in its place.

Questions for Discussion

1. Can "Christ-likeness" be recognized in every culture? What are its ingredients?
2. In your own culture, what would you expect a new convert to renounce immediately?
3. Take some "institutionalized custom" in your country which Christians hope will "disappear gradually" (e.g., polygamy, the caste system, easy divorce, or some form of oppression). What active steps should Christians be taking to work for change?

Conclusion

Our Consultation has left us in no doubt of the pervasive importance of culture. The writing and the reading of the Bible, the presentation of the gospel, conversion, church and conduct---all these are influenced by culture. It is essential, therefore, that all churches contextualize the gospel in order to share it effectively in their own culture. For this task of evangelization, we all know our urgent need of the ministry of the Holy Spirit. He is the Spirit of truth who can teach each church how to relate to the culture which envelops it. He is also the Spirit of love, and love is "the language-- which is understood in every culture of man." So may God fill us with his Spirit! Then, speaking the truth in love, we shall grow up into Christ who is the head of the body, to the everlasting glory of God (Eph. 4:15).

NOTE: Unattributed quotations in this report have been drawn from various papers presented at this Consultation.

In Attendance

PARTICIPANTS (Signatories of the Lausanne Covenant and/or committed to its framework and understanding of mission)

Dr. Saphir Athyal, Principal (President) of Union Biblical Seminary Yavatmal, India

Dr. Kwame Bediako, Lecturer in Biblical Studies and Theology, Christian Service College, Kumasi, Ghana

Prof. Dr. Peter P. J. Beyerhaus, Professor of Missiology and Ecumenics, Tubingen University, West Germany

Prof. Robinson Cavalcanti, Professor of Political Science at Recife Federal and Rural Universities of Pernambuco, Brazil

Dr. Chongnahm Cho, President and Professor, Seoul Theological Seminary, Bucheon City, Korea

Dr. Harvie M. Conn, Associate Professor of Missions and Apologetics, Westminster Theological Seminary, Chestnut Hill, Philadelphia, Pennsylvania

Rev. Dr. Orlando E. Costas, Director, Latin American Evangelical Centre for Pastoral Studies (CELEP), San Jose, Costa Rica

Mr. Edward R. Dayton, Director, MARC, Monrovia, California

Cand. theol. Tormod Engelsviken, Teacher of Theology, Fjellhaug School of Missions, Oslo, Norway

Dr. John A. Gration, Associate Professor of Missions, Wheaton Graduate School, Wheaton, Illinois

Dr. Donald R. Jacobs, Director, Mennonite Christian Leadership Foundation

Dr. F.S. Khair-Ullah, Director, Creative Writing Project of M.I.K. Pakistan

Dr. Charles H. Kraft, Professor of Anthropology and African Studies, School of World Mission, Fuller Theological Seminary, Pasadena, California

Rev. Dr. S. Ananda Kumar, Professor of Biblical Studies, Karnataka Theological College, Karnataka State, South India

Dr. Jacob A. Loewen, Translations Consultant for East Central Africa with the United Bible Societies

Dr. I. Howard Marshall, Reader in New Testament Exegesis, University of Aberdeen, Scotland

Dr. I. Wayan Mastra, Chairman of the "Gereja Kristen Protestan di Bali," Indonesia

Mr. Bruce J. Nicholls, Executive Secretary, Theological Commission, World Evangelical Fellowship

Rev. Gottfried Osei-Mensah, Executive Secretary, Lausanne Committee for World Evangelization

Rev. Dr. James I. Packer, Associate Principal, Trinity College, Bristol, England

Dr. C. René Padilla, Director of Ediciones Cereteza, International Fellowship of Evangelical Students

Dr. William E. Pannell, Assistant Professor of Evangelism, Fuller Theological Seminary, Pasadena, California

Rev. Pedro Savage, (Consultation Coordinator), Coordinator, Latin American Theological Fraternity, staff member of Partnership in Mission and of Latin American IFES

Rev. John Stott, (Consultation Chairman), Rector Emeritus, All Soul's Church, Langham Place, London

Dr. Charles R. Taber, Director, Institute of World Studies/Church Growth, Milligan College, Tennessee

Rev. Tite Tienou, Director of Bible School Bobo Dioulasso, Upper Volta, and Executive Secretary of A.E.A.M. Theological Commission

Dr. Alan R. Tippett, Hon. Research Fellow, St. Mark's Library, Canberra, A.C.T. Australia

Rev. Canon James Wong, Anglican Pastor and Coordinator of Asian Leadership Conference on Evangelism, Singapore

CONSULTANTS (in general sympathy with the Lausanne Covenant)

Bishop Kenneth Cragg, Reader in Religious Studies, University of Sussex, and Assistant Bishop of Chichester, England

Rev. Alfred C. Krass, Co-Editor of *The Other Side* magazine

67001

St8d **Canon Prof. John Mbiti,** Director of the Ecumenical Institute, Bossey, of the World Council of Churches, Geneva, Switzerland

Bishop Stephen Neill, Resident Scholar, Wycliffe Hall, Oxford, England

VISITOR (contributing to a Consultation committed to the Lausanne Covenant)

Rev. Louis J. Luzbetak, President, Divine Word College, Epworth, Iowa